# THE
# Maya
# Shamans

# THE
# Maya
# Shamans
## Travellers in Time

## Alloa Patricia Mercier

vega

ISBN 1-84333-596-4

A catalogue record for this book is available
from the British Library

First published in 2002 by
Vega
64 Brewery Road
London, N7 9NT

A member of **Chrysalis** Books plc

Visit our website at www.chrysalisbooks.co.uk

Printed in Great Britain
by CPD, Wales

Editor: James Harpur
Jacket design: Jerry Goldie Graphic Design
Index: Indexing Specialists

# Contents

This book is dedicated to
The cosmic and ancestral Maya
And those of the present who
Walk the path of the sun.

# Preface

I would like to thank Hunbatz Men, Daykeeper Itza-Maya tradition, Mexico, who fired the imagination of myself and many others when he said: 'To be Maya is not the colour of your skin – it is your consciousness, for the Maya created a cosmic consciousness.' His teachings and encouragement have been vital while writing this book. I would also like to thank Wandering Wolf, Guatemala, without whom none of my journeys on the threads of time would have been possible; Alberto Ruz, Rainbow Warrior; José and Lloydine Argüelles, USA, who are dedicated to ending mechanistic time concepts by introducing a natural 28-day moon calendar before AD2012; and John Major Jenkins, USA, and Carl Calleman, Sweden, whose debates on Maya calendars have fascinated me. I am also grateful to many others, including: Miguel Angel Vergara Calleros, Mexico; Miguel Angel, El Salvador; Mary Lightning Locke, Mexico; Ariel Spillsbury, Hawaii; Sandra and Dan Dayton, Mexico; Aluna Joy Yaxk'in and Star Moser, USA; Olympia, Tenerife; and all those supporters of the Sun and Serpent Maya Mysteries School, UK, who magically touched Maya cosmovision, especially at the Maya Dreamtime Festivals held in Glastonbury, England. And heart-felt thanks must go to Mikhail my husband, fellow traveller, constant source of inspiration and delight, who checked and rechecked the manuscript. Finally, I am grateful to all those Maya whose names I will never know and who, through their eyes and hearts, took me on my quest as a traveller in time.

I should like to point out that each chapter is numbered with the dot-and-bar sacred Maya numbering system, which represents a flow of energy that takes us through time. This energy can be used to unlock hidden shamanic knowledge, which is highlighted in special texts that occur throughout the chapters and begin with a 🐵 symbol. Each chapter concludes with a practical summary of ways in which you, the reader, may apply the teachings to your own life. I have also included diary extracts from actual journeys, undertaken during the years 1979 to 1999, by my husband and myself. Out of necessity some accepted Western shamanic terminology has been used in order to explain certain aspects of the dreamlike world of the Maya, although the Maya shamans themselves teach through experience and do not use such words for what is essentially a living tradition.

Throughout this book the spelling of places, names and the like, honours the Maya way when possible, rather than a European version. This means that in many words the letter 'K' is substituted for 'C' or 'Qu' because 'K', in Maya pronunciation, accurately connects with Maya 'serpent wisdom' (at the heart of their teachings). An 'X' in a word is pronounced like a soft 'esh' or 'sh'. For example, 'shaman' is more correctly spelled 'Xaman' (pronounced 'shaman'), while Uxmal is pronounced 'ooshmal'. The letter 'b' at the end of Maya words sometimes indicates plurals, for example 'Maya' becomes 'Mayab', and 'way', 'wayob'. Other letters in Maya languages are pronounced in a way similar to Spanish, rather than English. Intonation is important, for the Maya 'read' great meaning into sounds. They also read words backwards as well as forwards or for different or additional meanings.

Alloa Patricia Mercier, 2002

# Foreword

By Elder Hunbatz Men, Maya-Itza tradition, founder of the worldwide Maya Mysteries Schools.

The Maya prophecies are being fulfilled. Some are being fulfilled even now. Some will be fulfilled on the morrow. The Maya prophecies exist because the Maya knew the cosmic time. They knew that in certain times it would be necessary to keep this cosmic wisdom secret. This was the purpose of the prophecy so that they might be able to communicate their secrets to the initiates of the future. It is prophesied that initiates shall return to the sacred land of the Maya to continue the work of Great Spirit. Here in the lands of the Mayab, in the cycle of light, there surged a great wisdom, which would illuminate humanity for many millennia. This wisdom was given to the Maya-Atlantis Itzaes.

Now the reincarnated masters return to these lands of the Maya to communicate with the great spirits of the Itzaes so that together they may understand what shall be the new initiation which will be put into practice; so that humanity, the reincarnated masters and the great spirits of the Itzaes may fuse into one. Then they will be able to travel like the wind, descend like the rain, give warmth like fire and teach like Mother Earth.

These masters will come from many places. They will be of many colours. Some will speak of things difficult to understand. Others will be aged; some less so. Some will dance while others will remain silent as rocks. Their eyes will communicate the initiatic message, which is to continue through the cycles of this millennium.

It is also prophesied that this initiation of cosmic wisdom is for future initiates. They will be young and old, men and women, who will have the understanding that this modern civilization is not meeting its educational responsibilities. It is well known that this so-called modern civilization has caused a regressive effect in spiritual development.

The Maya ceremonial centres are beginning to emanate the light of the new millennium, which is much needed today. Many Maya cosmic ceremonial centres beckon, with their solar reflection, the numerous initiates who will come to continue the work of Great Spirit. In many of these centres, solar priests will begin to walk among the multitude of tourists. They will be touched by the solar priests to be initiated with the cosmic wisdom. It will be then that the initiates of the second level shall commence work among the new initiates.

The Maya masters will begin to manifest in the trees, in the sun, in the moon and in the stars. They will appear also in homes to inform families that the new time to begin initiatic cosmic work has commenced. Many people will not understand because this will happen when they are sleepy or when they have lost the notion of time, if only for a few seconds. Everything shall be moved to the new time, including human genetics which will be moved by the sacred energy of Father Sun and the seven cosmic brothers who will help elevate human consciousness.

When the sacred energy of the masters and students is begun at the ceremonial centres of the sacred Maya of Ek Balam, Oxkintok, Mayapan and Chichén Itzá, then shall the gods who are in the stars look upon us and bless the sons and daughters who have returned once again to continue the cosmic spiritual work for the new millennium. These gods of the stars will announce to the four cardinal points, the good news of the new beginnings of the human race. These gods of the stars will call the lords of the day, and of the night, and of the inner world and also of the exterior world and they will say to them to look again upon humanity and to assist them to awaken into the solar light. The gods will also look into the bodies of the humans and they will ask the heart to beat newly in rhythm to the universe; to the stomach they will ask to accept only natural foods. In this way will they speak to many parts of the inner body. To the head it will ask that it should not let itself be deceived by the false modern society. Then when the masters and the students are in one accord the manifestations of the spirits will come. The eagle will teach us what it knows about our ancestors. The serpent and the jaguar will do the same. Then the sacred tree will illumine us with its wisdom. They will all then begin to see us in the same manner as the ancient Maya. This will be the moment to begin the grand ritual of the cosmic conjugation within every living being.

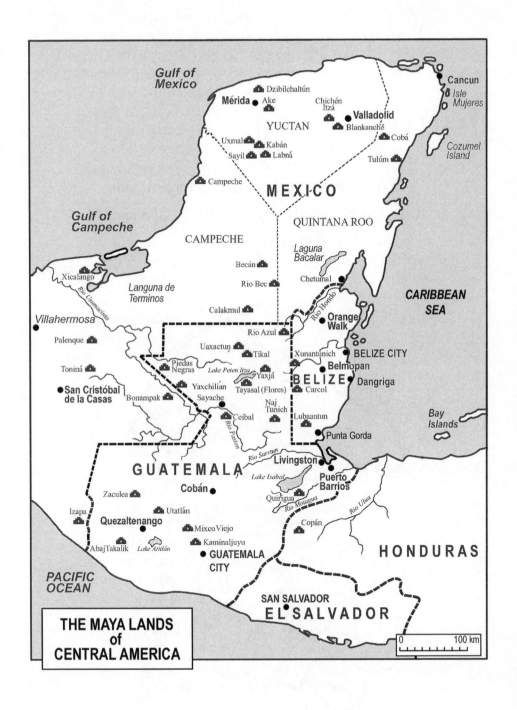

Gulf of
Mexico

Cancun
Isle
Mujeres

Dzibilchaltún
Mérida   Ake          Chichén
                      Itzá        Valladolid

YUCTAN          Blankanché

                              Cobá        Cozumel
Uxmal   Kabán                              Island
Sayil   Labná

Campeche              M E X I C O          Tulúm

Gulf of
Campeche           QUINTANA ROO

            CAMPECHE

                    Laguna
                    Bacalar

Becán
                Chetumal          CARIBBEAN
Rio Bec                            SEA

Xicalango
                Calakmul
Languna de
Terminos                    Orange
                            Walk

Villahermosa          Rio Azul

Palenque          Uaxactún
                          Tikal     Xunantúnich   BELIZE CITY
Toniná        Piedas                    Belmopan
            Negras   Lake Peten Itza   Yaxjá   B E L I Z E
San Cristóbal        Yaxchilián                Dangriga
de la Casas   Bonampak   Sayache   Tayasal (Flores)   Carcol
                    Ceibal           Naj
                              Tunich
                                   Lubaantun   Bay
                                              Islands
                    Rio Sarstun   Punta Gorda
                              Livingston
GUATEMALA        Lake Isabal   Puerto
            Cobán           Barrios
        Zaculea        Quirigua
Izapa              Rio Motagua        Rio Ulua
        Utatlán
Quezaltenango        Mixco Viejo        Copán        HONDURAS
AbajTakalik   Lake Atitlán        Kaminaljuyu
                    GUATEMALA
PACIFIC              CITY
OCEAN

            SAN SALVADOR
            EL SALVADOR

THE MAYA LANDS
of
CENTRAL AMERICA                    0        100 km

# Introduction

To be Maya is not the colour of your skin,
it is your consciousness – for the Maya created
a cosmic consciousness.

**Elder Hunbatz Men**

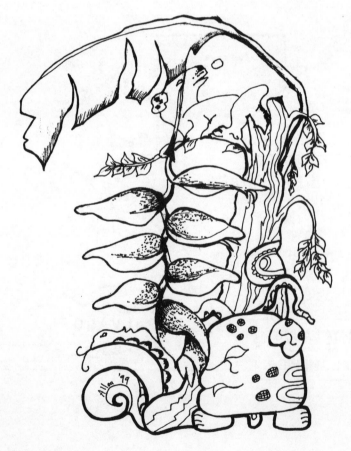

*The Shaman's Earth*

My quest in Mexico and Central America has taken me on a journey around and within the Maya medicine wheel and through hidden mysterious doorways guided by the people and creatures of their lands. It has revealed the present-day shamans' and wisdom teachers' deep concerns for the environmental sustainability of our planet.

There has been placed before me a new approach to understanding that I wish to share with those already on the threshold of a new understanding about our purpose here on Earth. Time as a reality offers to take us on a journey into realms quite separate from calendars and clocks as we know them; it waits to take us into timelessness.

Elusive Maya teachings are preserved in stone carvings within curiously shaped temples high above flat-topped pyramids – as well as within barely readable hieroglyphs recorded in precious books. They were inscribed at a time when medieval Europe was in the grip of a feudal system and research was exclusive to religious orders of monks. Incredibly, the Maya developed advanced scientific and mathematical concepts even by today's standards. Within their splendid, colourful cities lived priest-kings/queens, royal scribes, astronomers, astrological daykeepers, architects, artists, weavers and farmers. For over 3,000 years everything, from the affairs of state to the planting of maize, was magically directed by shamans, who undertook different specialized paths to ensure their people were guided by both their ancestors and by a kind of extraterrestrial intervention – by those I refer to as the 'cosmic Maya'. The Maya's hieroglyphic writing recorded everyday events as well as records of succession of rulership; but, more importantly, inspired through trance states, the 'glyphs' show keys to worlds beyond time.

So what better way to explore time and the Maya mysteries than through the way of the shamans? This is an adventure into their worlds and their closely held secrets, an adventure within inhospitable tropical rainforests that create an air of mystery and intrigue. But as the story unfolds, you may be left with many doubts, many questions. These questions are like seeds left to germinate within you, the reader; for this book is about rediscovering a mental vision that will appear to be beyond the 'normal' realm of our modern sophisticated world. This vision is the 'inner seeing' of the shamans. Like them I have used what they call the 'threads of time' to look with clear eyes, unclouded by materialism, at the historical past and an awesome future that awaits us.

The Maya made careful observations of the stars and what they

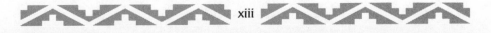

discovered they used in their immediate daily lives. They also applied this knowledge in a way that enabled them to be in tune with natural rhythms, thus placing them in a position to reflect upon both the wisdom of the stars and the wisdom of the Earth. Their calendars were, and still remain, one of their most outstanding achievements; yet, even so, why the Maya appeared to be obsessed with time poses many questions.

Theirs is a puzzle that has been created by cataclysmic events of earthquake, volcano and war. But fortunately they have left us some clues. To avoid persecution through the ages, their shamans and priests have preserved and kept hidden knowledge handed down to them through their families from a time when humanity was given keys to understanding its destiny. The Spanish systematically burnt most of the Maya books, or codices, which contained vital information, in a wave of brutal destruction that followed in the wake of the Spanish conquistadors in the early 16th century. Indeed, there is a temptation to feel that there is a pattern in history that whenever something outstanding is revealed to the human race, a dramatic counteraction to conceal the endeavour occurs.

If you journeyed to the lands of the Maya today, what you would see amid the damp, rainforest undergrowth of Guatemala and parched scrubland of the Yucatan are pyramids, temples and hieroglyphic writing on stelae, or giant, carved stone blocks, at thousands of distinctly different sites. Almost this entire, rich ancestral heritage remains embraced by flora and fauna in a climate of searing heat and, at times, torrential rain. While remarkable museum initiatives to protect this legacy have provided an assured future for some of the more outstanding archaeological sites, for others the jungle outpaces the meagre resources available to maintain them, and natural laws of 'recycling' prevail. Despite this, excavations during the last 50 years have uncovered some amazing finds.

There have also been breakthroughs in decipherment of the hieroglyphic writing. So the Maya 'story' is constantly being expanded in the light of these revelations. The ancient Maya are dancing their way into the 21st century, called by their cue to be the star players on our world's stage by 2012 – the end date of a 5,125-year, 'Long Count' cycle of time whose beginning coincided with the building of Stonehenge and Silbury Hill in Britain and the Carnac stone alignments in France. Their descendants, the shamans, elders, wise grandmothers, grandfathers and 'daykeepers', who even to this day keep the calendar counts, are beginning to share their knowledge

about the significant, cosmic, star-born heritage of our human race.

To learn that about 1,600 years ago the indigenous Maya in a hot, steamy Central American rainforest brought concepts of time to a pinnacle of perfection that NASA cannot fault today is a fundamental challenge to what has been traditionally taught at school. In addition to their astronomical achievements, the Maya used 20 traditional calendars, which in themselves would form a lengthy study. Whether with knowledge still available from an earlier, highly evolved society or through intervention from their extraterrestrial 'star' brothers and sisters, the Maya scribes and stonemasons left clues about time past, time present and time future. These clues are of great significance if we, the present-day inhabitants of the Earth, are concerned with what is to befall us.

The journey through this book will reveal ways in which you can take your own fantastic inner journey as we travel into the dreamtime of the shamans. However, as a starting point it is important to honour what archaeologists and historians have uncovered about the Maya.

## Development of Maya culture

The Maya were masters of illusion. Through paradigms of illusion they became the serpent-worshipping Naga Maya of India, who, according to Valmiki, the sage and author of the epic *Ramayana*, brought their culture to India in 2700BC They were the peoples known as the Cara Maya of ancient Greece and the Mayax of ancient Egypt. Manetho, an Egyptian high priest of Heliopolis in about 300BC, said that Maya teachings spread to Asia and Africa. Some of the old Maya shaman seers had the ability to transcend time reality as we know it.

The present-day Mayalands, comprising 20 indigenous nations, extend from the northern tip of the Yucatan to the coast of Honduras and El Salvador. Much is still conjectured about the early peoples of Central America. For example, recent excavations in the Copan Valley, Honduras, show habitation from 1100BC. Copan lay on the jade trade route to Belize used by an earlier race, the Olmecs, and eventually developed into a large city complex. But who were the Olmecs and from where did they come? Maya sources indicate only that they were 13 tribes that 'came from the east before the Maya'. On the coast of Tabasco State, Mexico, can be seen the giant, stone-carved heads of the Olmecs. More interesting – if we bear in mind Maya memories of Atlantis – are the pottery figurines found

in an Olmec grave that portray giants and people with strange, enlarged skulls.

The real origins of the highly developed Maya culture still elude us. It is as if it arrived from nowhere. There is little evidence to show how the rapid progression of knowledge and skills came about; yet for a relatively short time in history, the royal lineages flourished and cities were built that were vast and stunningly decorated and featured grand, colourful, elaborate sculptures. As part of this rapid cultural ascendancy the Maya showed an advanced understanding of life, death, resurrection and immortality. Indeed in terms of the collective soul of humanity, we, through the doorway of time, are witnesses to their resurrection by our present-day fascination for the enigmatic chapter they have left the human race.

## The pinnacle of civilization: the classical era

During the classical period of the Maya (AD300 to 843), intricate and highly complex hieroglyphic writing developed along with stylized art, much of which would not look out of place in a modern art gallery. Well-planned cities reflected a cosmic mythic order. They covered vast areas, and the adjacent, seemingly inhospitable land was farmed in an early 'permaculture' system of forest management. Archaeologists claim the Maya did not use metal tools and had not invented the wheel. Yet they moved millions of tons of stone and constructed towering stepped pyramids, temples, star observatories, palaces, ballcourts and ceremonial plazas – all decorated with colourfully ornate carvings and built with incredible precision.

Looking back through time to Maya cities like Tikal in Guatemala, we would see a vibrant panorama: from a vantage point on a mountainside we breathe in the sparkling life energy of a vast sealike expanse of deep emerald-green trees. Towering above this rainforest canopy are the tops of three stepped pyramids, more than 40 metres/130 feet high. Around them, stretching out for a number of kilometres, beneath the shade of the diverse rainforest trees are small dwellings and residential palaces for as many as 70,000 people. Focusing more closely, we would see a great hive of activity as a new pyramid is constructed, stonemasons carefully directing the covering of the most sacred carvings on the sides of an earlier pyramid. Where the building is complete, a scaffold, roped together with vines, supports a group of artists applying coloured pigments to the freshly moulded plaster scenes around the doorway of the temple at the summit. Sounds of gentle flute music merge with the raucous calls of

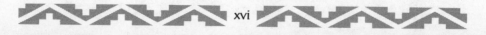

brilliant scarlet macaws as they skim the trees. Around the steps of another pyramid, crowds of dark-skinned people gather. Most are clothed in white, with the exception of the ruler who proudly wears an elaborate head-dress studded with long, quetzal bird feathers and, despite the heat, a jaguar skin, part of his insignia of office. Around him the shamans, masked as power animals and ancestral gods, are preparing a sacred fire ceremony.

*Serpent on Venus Platform, Chichén Itzá*

Returning to the present, we can learn through books of the many achievements of the classical Maya, who were expert in many areas – notably as artists, stonemasons, potters, scribes, farmers, but, above all, as shamans and astronomers. They made detailed and accurate calculations, including measurements of objects far beyond our solar system, that surpassed those made in contemporary European.

## Classical Maya social structure

The ruling elite of hereditary priest-kings/queens (most often shamans in their own right) laid claim to evocative names based on the day of the Maya calendar on which they were born, sometimes with the title 'Serpent Lord' or 'Serpent Lady' added. These rulers presided over

both the sacred and mundane organization of their lands, very much in the way of the Egyptian pharaohs. The social structure enabled the rulers, shamans, healers, artists and masons to be supported through a well-organized infrastructure that produced and distributed food, although it has been surmised that at certain times of the year the focus for nearly everyone was on ceremonial building construction. Recent advances in the decipherment of carved and written historical data are shedding new light on their lives, and now they are walking into the present day as people from whom we have much to learn.

One of the great puzzles of history is why the Maya suddenly stopped building in all their great cities within about 60 years of AD795 while seemingly at the peak of their power. The demise of many cities in this great civilization that stretched across what is present-day Guatemala and parts of Chiapas and Quintana Roo, Mexico, has caused much speculation. Recording of dates on buildings and temples ceased by the end of the ninth century. Whole cities were quickly overrun by voracious jungle vegetation, and any remaining people, or evidence of their highly skilled work, mostly vanished. They took with them a vast treasure of the human spirit that is still waiting to be understood. The physical collapse of Maya culture, just like its rise to prominence, was without identifiable development periods. Various theories have been put forward as to what happened and why, but none of them provides satisfactory answers to all the questions, especially given the enormous region covered by the great Maya cities. The somewhat inconclusive speculations of archaeologists have ranged from drought and war to disease and hunger.

## Travellers in time

Take a look back in time. The spiritual traditions of indigenous peoples the world over enable us to understand our own evolving spirituality. As each culture has developed, study of the celestial bodies and extraterrestrial phenomena has played a leading part in our understanding; and we have gained insights into the source of human existence, the meaning of life, and how time and space were central to creating order out of the apparent chaos. While intellectual thought and, eventually, science have opened our awareness to dimensions beyond time, it is to the Maya, one of the more accessible indigenous peoples of the present day, that we need to turn in order to gain a real insight into time.

The Maya who lived both before and up to the end of the classical period consistently recorded evidence in stone and clay to show that their archetypal mythology was firmly based upon momentous occurrences in the cosmos. So the question is: was their obsession to track time with calendars an elaborate and ingenious method to plot and anticipate much larger cycles of galactic influence – including a time yet to come? And were they introducing us to a cosmic picture of other intelligent life? Did they use hidden knowledge to travel in time and space? Were they, like the Hopi of North America, able to discover what will befall the human race centuries in the future? Did the Maya receive some secret insight and open doorways to another world as part of a greater unfolding plan?

This book is like a multilayered cloth, spinning the present-day Maya into a web-like pattern on a 'mat of time'. In the process of unravelling the Maya enigma, it is possible to learn the arts of the shamans and of dimensions beyond space and time. Some of their shamans and wisdom teachers have taken me on solar initiations and a quest that I share to re-empower your spiritual core, your own indigenous calling from nature. The Maya have provided the backcloth of times past and present upon which we may reawaken our hearts to the responsibility we carry – to set the pattern for the coming cycle of time predicted by the Maya so long ago.

I have connected the new astromythology of the Maya – myths of the stars and the Earth – in an entirely different way, showing how they have accurately pinpointed celestial happenings, including events still to take place. Astromythology opens doors of perception to human consciousness as the star-seeded matter of creation on this planet. The atoms of our bodies have come from the stars and to the stars one day they will return. Each atom is vibrating like a miniature solar system containing within itself a minute part of the electromagnetic spectrum – part of the seed of creation.

Walking the Maya 'path of the sun' has changed and enriched my life journey. It has detached me from the grip of materialism and through my experiences I have found unusual, mind-expanding levels of understanding. You, like me, may apply the Maya teachings to your everyday life. People around the world are awakening to an identical message from many indigenous peoples. The present moment on Earth is a crucial turning point, and within our lifetimes many may witness the end of life as we know it. Those beings of light, the cosmic Maya who guide the living Maya wisdom teachers, say that our galactic time has almost run its course. It is literally a few seconds to midnight – midnight being the moment of choice as to

whether or not the planet is able to continue as a sustainable home for the human race.

Maya shamanic wisdom teachings, with their wide 'cosmovision', lead us to look closely at global problems facing humanity and development of the human race in relation to a greater cycle of time than is taught through school history ('his-story') books. Physicists say that in the universe, time moves in waves of expansion, contraction and acceleration. Mystics refer to life, death and rebirth, or seeding, growth and decay. The Maya shamans and daykeepers are acutely aware that the point at which we now live forms a major event horizon. The Maya say that there have been three previous attempts to create humans on Earth before what they refer to as the present Fourth Creation. As we approach the culmination of this Fourth Creation, opportunity exists to give the human race the courage to engage with its true soul purpose – to learn how to care for the planet.

The ancient Maya also identified an area in deep space that coincides with recently discovered scientific evidence of a generative ray of light energy affecting our DNA. They left many clues and oblique references to this special light vibration, energy of renewal, for a time when it would be needed by the human race. *That time has come.*

# CHAPTER ONE

# The Door of Intention

The cities of the Mayab are like a string of precious stones.
In them live the children of the Gods and their servants;
Their temples are large and large also are their houses,
All these surrounding the plazas,
All made of carved stone.

The city reflects Divine Order;
The houses of the Lords and the temples are its heart;
And about them are the houses and the palaces of those who
spread their word,
Those who carry out their designs.

From the museum at Chetumal, Mexico

Prepare yourself carefully, for you are about to begin a journey through time into the enchanted lands of the most enigmatic people on Earth. You will enter a picture painted by words, symbols, hieroglyphs, colour and images that will transport you on your own special path to the Rainbow Feathered Serpent revered by the indigenous Maya. On this journey to the lands of the Maya Indians you will encounter giant trees with twisted roots like snakes; beautiful orchids hanging from branches; the dawn chorus of brightly plumed quetzal birds and scarlet macaws; miniature humming birds weaving

their paths around exotic perfumed flowers; and troupes of howler and spider monkeys leaping from branch to branch above. And you will hear the night-time calls of animals, sounding uncannily like jaguars, merging with sounds of the soft darkness; hundreds of bats sweeping by; snakes slithering in the undergrowth; and ten thousand soldier ants rustling through dried leaves on the forest floor. By day, in the dry season, the sun is an ever-present, potent symbol of life for the many who live by the ways of their ancestors. That same sun begins to burn questions into your mind as you explore the mysteries of the Maya people, whose physical, mental, emotional and spiritual lives are so imbued with its uncompromising rays.

The Mayalands of Central America, covering some 324,000 square kilometres/123,000 square miles, are found in the present-day states of Yucatan, Campeche, Quintana Roo, parts of Chiapas and Tabasco in Mexico; all of Guatemala and Belize and parts of El Salvador and Honduras. The Maya, along with other indigenous peoples in the Americas, prefer to call their continent the 'Land of the Sun'. Spread throughout the Mayalands today, some six million people of Maya origin live in a state that would generally be called poverty. Atrocities against village people by the army and militia occurred as recently as 1985; they were well documented by international non-government organizations. The shadow of death still stalks those who challenge corruption or take up human rights issues. Even a bishop, Juan Gerardi Conedera, and some environmentalists have become targets. Yet by and large the children are healthy, bright and happy, and the adults maintain a lifestyle close to the fruitful earth, little changed in 3,000 years. In the Mexican Yucatan, Maya village settlements situated away from cities are strung along the edges of main roads, wherever there is water nearby. Pigs and dogs lie on melting-hot road tarmac and children rush excitedly out of palm thatched 'palapa' dwellings to wave at passing travellers. Turkeys scratch in the yards and women sit beneath any available shade making the daily mound of corn tortillas (a kind of flat bread), ready for the men to eat when they come back from their work. In the mountainous volcanic areas of Guatemala the rhythm of time is little changed. Guatemala's road system is much less developed than its Mexican counterpart and this has allowed the Maya traditions to remain much more pure and untarnished by commercial tourism. In villages situated along a dusty track, perhaps up to 80 kilometres/50 miles from the nearest paved road, the ancient traditions are very much alive. Village councils, a mixture of both men and women, honour the elders in community decision making. Healer shamans and *curanderos*, who mostly use the rich variety of traditional herbal remedies, along with massage and steam baths, are still consulted when illness occurs. Incredibly, these beautiful, placid people have inherited one of the most mysterious cultural traditions on Earth.

This is a land where '*mañana*' ('tomorrow') is a way of life and the siesta rules. Although the natural flow cannot be hurried, people are hardworking, often starting their day as early as four o'clock in the morning. Road travel can sometimes be disrupted for hours owing to accident or landslide, but drivers and passengers accept this as an inevitability.

To sit in a roadside café out of the hot sun anywhere in southern Mexico or Guatemala is to immerse yourself in a place where the gentle rhythms of life are accepted as natural. At first this leads to a sense that time is beginning to play tricks, as heat shimmers on the dusty road at noon. The seemingly endless straight roads of Mexico appear to make time stand still or stretch to unbelievable lengths, like a mirage at the end of a long tunnel. Yet looking at time in a different way, we can also see that a rich weave of threads is pushing through the warps and wefts of traditional village life to produce a multi-layered pattern. The intricate and highly colourful hand-woven and embroidered clothing from many of the villages is a living example of their inhabitants' connection with time past, time present and time future. Traditional *huipils* (blouses) and other garments worn today give in their patterns a personal record of village events and history. But also, at another less obvious level set within the landscape of the Maya, there is a 'time fabric', where the warps are the long spans of time running from prehistory to the future and the wefts are shorter cross weaves of present-day encounters with ancient sacred city sites, living Maya people, strange animals, birds and trees.

Also woven into the pattern are blends of many races of people who have settled in these lands, arrayed like the exotic fruits found in their market places and moving the traveller's thoughts through timescales that are awe-inspiring. If you visit the Mayalands, these entwined, colourful threads will enchant you and take you in quite unplanned directions on your quest as you become a 'traveller in the time of the Maya', whose land it was before the Spanish arrived and to whom it really belongs. This is a place where vivid and memorable experiences are the 'everyday', not the exception.

In the Yucatan peninsula, in south-eastern Mexico, and the adjoining country of Guatemala, there are around 21,000 remaining Maya ceremonial cities or centres of which comparatively few, possibly

no more than five per cent, have been excavated, catalogued or restored. This book is based on a mixture of personal experiences and very real shamanic journeys undertaken with my husband to some of these places. During a succession of visits I have been privileged to meet special Maya elders, shamans, grandmothers and wisdom teachers who entrusted us with a responsibility to use what we have learnt for the benefit of the many people who are unable to undertake such a journey for themselves. Where appropriate, I have also drawn on archaeological and historical data. Perhaps the most stunning of all revelations is the realization that over the last 3,000 years the Maya have left numerous important clues that actually appear to have been timed to have present-day global relevance. They were indeed 'travellers in time' – a time that is now enshrined in Earth history, and yet a time, as I was to discover later, that is not of this Earth or even this solar system.

The Yucatan peninsula points out into the Gulf of Mexico with an extraordinary flat and arid landscape of dry scrub on bedrock limestone. The region has no rivers flowing across it. Small wonder that rain was vitally important to the many Maya settlements and ceremonial centres built there in the past. But all is not what it seems, for under the surface of the limestone rock, often only a few metres down, lies the region's main fresh water supply. A complex, natural underground network was known and used by the Maya three or more millennia ago. Large natural holes in the ground known as 'cenotes' – made as if by some giant's outsize drill and often measuring up to 40 metres/130 feet – are found throughout the area. They give access, if you are daring enough, to the cool, fresh, crystal-clear water beneath. Descent is precarious to say the least. Perhaps it was the Maya who, generations ago, were the forerunners of abseiling – for even today hanging vines and tangled roots, sometimes made into rough rope ladders, provide the only way down.

In other places cave systems give easier access to water and in some of the more secret caves, Maya elders and shamans collect 'sacred water'. This is water that has percolated through the rock and dripped into stone collection bowls, to be used for special ceremonies. Water means life. It did in ancient times; it does today for all who rely on the land for a living. It is hardly surprising to find that the Maya deified the bringer of this life-giving substance as Chak, the god of rain.

The path this book takes you on is a quest that may be quite different to your usual way of looking at things. As the story unfolds, so too will you unfold as you realize the Maya are not a dead ancient race to be read about only in history books. On the contrary, they are a living nation in the 21st century, and some of them carry vital clues to an extraordinary mystery that links all of us to star beings, Atlantis and to the mystery of why we are on this planet. Have you ever allowed yourself, perhaps in childhood, to look quietly into a pool of water? Do you remember how it was that you became aware of detail under the water, with perhaps layer upon layer appearing to alter as a puff of wind rippled the surface? This was the sort of experience I had – only mine was scaled up – when, having descended precariously some six metres/20 feet on a frayed rope ladder, I peered into the dark, clear water of a cenote and began to realize deep down that there lay a fuller picture behind the Maya people embedded in a matrix of time. Theirs is an astonishing story. But as with every book, the scene has to be set, the backdrop painted and the key players introduced. So I begin by revealing the foundations upon which an understanding of who the Maya truly are and what they have presented to the world may be built.

The Maya have been carriers of teachings spanning aeons of time – far beyond the realm of history books. Their daykeepers and shamans were, and still are, capable of accessing levels of wisdom, consciousness, perception and other realities that have considerable consequences for the whole human race if interpreted appropriately. The knowledge they acquired, particularly in respect to time (in shamanic terms referred to as 'serpent wisdom'), is hidden like pieces of a jigsaw puzzle. Piecing them together has generated an interest in the Maya, which is now worldwide.

*Images of serpents are ever-present in the Mayalands.*

## The teachings begin

Just one night beside the soft, sandy beach on the Caribbean coast is enough to make anyone realize why the Maya made connections to the sky above. Every planet, every star, even blurred masses of distant galaxies in the universe, shimmer against the deep velvet darkness of

night. Here, fortunately for the stargazer, the atmosphere is unpolluted by smoke or artificial lighting from cities. Whether you are by the sea or inland atop a pyramid, you will see the stars shine with a jewel-like brilliance from the moment they appear on the horizon to the moment they set. It is an indescribably awesome and unforgettable experience. The night sky, vibrant with energy, almost audibly playing its mysterious anthem of sheer vastness, is suddenly plucked with the blue-white light flash of a meteorite. Moonglow illuminates the green luminescence of millions of plankton on the surface of the water as hatchling turtles race for their lives to the water's edge. Centuries ago this nightly panoramic stage provided the Maya with the opportunity to take part in an interactive play with time and space beyond our planet; they could gaze upward and consider the mysteries of the cosmos and then down at the wonder of the rainforest fireflies or the sea shore. That other world of the stars was simply brought right down to earth, where giant twisting roots of trees became huge snakes and howler monkeys echoed the calls of the jaguar.

So, the first thing that becomes clear to a questor is the connection the Maya have with the cosmos. They have a saying, '*Bey t'kan, Bey t'luum*' meaning 'As in the Earth, so in the sky', which is almost identical to a phrase that is more familiar to Westerners: 'As above, so below'.

Maya cosmology centres on a symbol frequently seen as decoration in many of the temples: the cosmic 'G' shape. The symbol embodies the divine creative being whom the Maya know as Hunab K'u, who is 'the One Giver of Movement and Measure', or 'that from which all comes'. It is also a representation of the spiral movement of our own galaxy and the movement of all galaxies around a central core. And it shows us that light in nature is an essential part of the formation and maintenance of Earth.

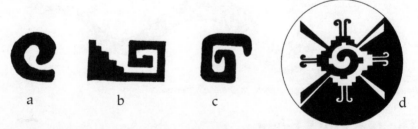

a.b.c. *The cosmic 'G' symbol appears with a number of variations in the Mayalands. It represents the spiral movement of our Milky Way galaxy and the god Hunab K'u, called the 'One Giver of Movement and Measure'. d. The Hunab K'u symbol shows two G spirals, one of a green colour (of Earth) that interlocks with one of white light – rather like the more familiar Yin-Yang symbol.*

## Riding the serpent: the Maya count of 13

Recording time with calendars was vital to the ancient Maya, and their way of keeping a calendar was quite different to the way we keep ours (which is known as the 'Gregorian' after Pope Gregory XIII). Like the early Celts, the Maya chose to honour the 13 moons that occur in a year.

The principle behind the foremost Maya calendar – known as the T'zolk'in – is based on a 13-day period. This 13-day count flows 20 times to complete a 260-day cycle (13 x 20 = 260 days); it then begins again. Thirteen is also a natural rhythm of a spiral or serpentine nature – 12 may be the number of equal segments of a circle, but 13 takes the initiate in an upward spiral of consciousness. Later in the book, in Chapter 4, we will look deeper, learning how the calendar keepers and shamans took this serpentine movement of 13 and built a structure upon which aspects of solar energy and the number 20 can work.

Thirteen-day periods can be applied to any life-enhancing project, to work with naturally occurring rhythms of 13. They may also be applied to any part of your personal life: a creative artistic/musical cycle, a business venture, a relationship pattern, a meditation plan, a health issue, or the like. When do you start? Right now! Take notice of your own cycles or your own 'calendars' and note particularly how instead of the cycle coming to an end, as one cycle concludes, it becomes a 'building block' for the next cycle to begin. At some stage you may wish to learn about more of the traditional Maya calendar counts and begin to integrate them in your life.

## Keeping a 13-day diary

Maya temples contain many examples of stone carvings that show zigzag patterns, snakes and images depicting serpents seen in visions. The Maya decorated artefacts and carvings to encode symbolic meanings, which we can draw on purely as an art form or take into ourselves at a deeper level to alter consciousness within. This simple act of looking for an hour or so at Maya art and glyphs reproduced in books will begin this process. You are also encouraged to 'ride the serpent' through its cycle of 13 teachings, which correspond to the periods of time in Maya calendars mentioned above. Begin in a simple way by plotting your 'journey of life' experiences through consecutive 13-day periods or pulses of time, noting how each day has a different quality of energy. Write your thoughts down each day so that you can reflect on the results more readily. Try to understand the energy of the days as a spiral movement – when you reach the 13th day, prepare to rise to the next turn of the spiral so that you need never start again at the same place, or with the same energy. You may commence your diary on any day that is significant in so far that it is a 'beginning' of something – for example a new project, a new way of seeing or doing things, or a creative surge of energy. Do not worry about when to begin – just start and see what happens to you.

Below are traditional influences, translated into modern terminology, that guide Maya people toward what they do and when they do it. After a while you will start to see the very same qualities for each day.

Day 1:    Receive intention of the 'work' you need to do.

Day 2:    Stabilize the energy qualities of this work within your consciousness.

Day 3:    Activate your vision of this task.

Day 4:    Define the vision clearly. Focus on what you need to do/achieve/understand.

Day 5:    Ask how you may receive empowerment from the natural world to achieve your vision.

Day 6:    Flow with the energy of empowerment.

Day 7:    The day when everything is in balance, the mid-point. If you merge with the transmission of energy that will surge in from Day 7, it will enable you to complete your vision or work, or this part of it, by the end of Day 13.

Day 8:    Harmonize your vision, or work with the creative pulse that comes from the heart of the galactic centre.

Day 9:    Allow the energy of the galactic creative pulse to work with you in a way that enhances everything you do.

Day 10:   Manifest your vision, your dreams of the work you need to do.

Day 11:   Integrate the wisdom you have received during this process. Note that wisdom is different from knowledge.

Day 12:   Acknowledge understandings you have received from undertaking this 13-day quest and the sources from which they came.

Day 13:   Be ready to return to the source of your understandings in order to commence the next spiral in the count of 13.

# THE MAYA COSMOS
## The Point of Balance

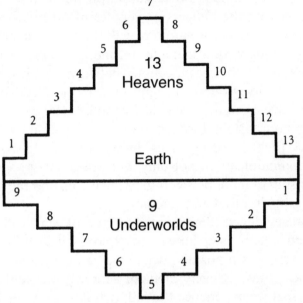

*The Maya cosmos: 13 heavens mirror 9 underworlds. The calendar shamans work on the favourable days of 6, 7 and 8.*

## The warrior: feet on the Earth, heart in the stars

*A Maya lord from the palace at Nah Chan (Palenque), Mexico, wearing an Ahau ('sun') belt.*

Representatives of the Maya people of today maintain close contact with other indigenous Indian nations of the Americas, who identify themselves as 'star nations'. It is not surprising to discover that the Maya, together with the indigenous peoples of Australasia, as well as others who choose to live in harmony with the land, can achieve levels of insight seemingly unattainable in more materialistic societies because they retain their connections between visible and invisible worlds. Their world is one of insight; ours is the world of 'outsight', because we have become seduced, hypnotized by the material. We need to regain our insight if we are to re-enchant our lives. The natural simplicity of these peoples' lives brings them into constant and immediate communication, not only with essential spirit essences in the guardianship of land, but with their ancestors and the mysteries of time by engaging in ritual and ceremony.

Much of the evidence coming to light in recent years calls for history to be rewritten. One big step forward in exploring the world of the Maya is to put ourselves in a position where we can experience time in the *now*. This means tasting every moment as if it is our very first, or our very last, so that we experience the full, rich flavour of the present.

When we start our walk into shamanic warriorship we begin to walk our talk .

The 'way of the warrior' enables us to live a kind of myth – that we are invincible, enchanted beings, living in the midst of everyday life. To do this we turn our highest aspirations into realities. The essence of the warrior is to bring magic into the mundane. So even while struggling against personal weaknesses, the warrior opposes the forces that would make him or her less than truly human. The loss of a sense of magic in the world is the main reason why some young people resort to recreational or illegal drugs. They feel a need to escape the materialist society and in their disillusionment seek an answer; but sadly that only leads eventually to a dulling of the senses rather than a sharpening of them.

This is not the way of those aspiring to the inner discipline of the modern warrior shaman. The warrior persists in always choosing the most life-enhancing action in any circumstances ('impeccability of action'). He or she achieves a symbiosis with living elements of Earth, water, fire, wind and spirit and uses them as keys to project into the world of nature. Through such a close interdependence with nature, today's warrior shamans and wisdom teachers have the ability to use elemental alchemy for travel to other dimensions. This follows the ways and traditions in which the ancient seers, prophets, shamans, healers and others, in cultures the world over, used substances produced from plants. During ritual and ceremony, through the guidance of the plant 'spirits', they shift into other dimensions, maintaining a specific focus of intent.

John Major Jenkins, in his book *Maya Cosmogenesis 2012*, says that 'The point of their [the Maya's] endeavour was to travel to the outer limits of the cosmos and return with an understanding of the "big picture". Like a Hindu yogi, Shamans could project their consciousness wherever they wished – into other realities, other planes of being, other planets and dimensions. They could journey back to the dawn of time, to the centre and source of all life and being, and return with power and wisdom. The Galactic Centre was the goal of their journey, for there the portal to infinity – the Grand Central Station of all beings and times – was located.'

There is an inherent guardianship of the pathway to other worlds and dimensions that is in place to prevent the unprepared from entering fully into these experiences. Such guardianship is identified with teachings that predate the Maya. It is the guardianship called 'serpent wisdom'. The present-day keepers of serpent wisdom have shown me four main entry points, beyond which are the keys to travel in time. They are:

- Immersion into life and nature.
- Maya time and calendars.
- Self-sacrifice. To show a 'sacred face' of oneself. To live truly with a deep respect for the sacred in the everyday. (For the Maya, this meant giving their own blood to the earth. In powerful shamanic ceremonies, drips of blood were burnt on pieces of bark paper placed in a fire, and visions induced took participants into worlds beyond.)
- Medicine wheel teachings and a journey to the four directions to seek the wisdom to be found at the centre, both of the wheel and of oneself.

The chapters that follow will enable you either to have an understanding that forms the basis of the vast Maya cosmovision, or, if you follow the path of the shamans, to undergo deep personal transformation as you search for higher knowledge.

The elders say we are just beginning to emerge from the dark ages of

history. Many of them are prepared to help us reinterpret 'messages' about their knowledge of time and the creative impulse of the universe left for the human race as tantalizing clues, or jigsaw pieces waiting to be fitted together. In everyday life you may often demand that certain information be given to you; but in the worlds of the shamans everything moves in a different way. Small hints and suggestions will be offered to you, the questor, in the way that they have been given to me, the author, to provide an authentic way to proceed. It is not until the close of each chapter that these are summarized in a practical way.

## Visions of the cosmos

The Maya vision of the cosmos is immense, stretching through light years of time to the Pleiades, Orion, the Big Dipper, Sagittarius and Scorpio constellations. The Maya kept detailed astrological and astronomical records of these constellations centuries ago. Today, they occasionally talk of their extraterrestrial connections and communications with star brothers and sisters named the 'Mishule'. They assert that our own sun is the eighth main star in the Pleiades group and that these eight stars, including our sun, are a source of teaching about the 'great powers'.

Since around 1979, ceremonies to heighten human consciousness have been taking place at the ancient Maya ceremonial cities, referred to as 'cosmic universities' by the elders. Some of the Maya priests from the 440-strong Maya Council of Elders are prepared to open esoteric communication to would-be initiates worldwide. In 1989 they asked for six ceremonial centres in Mexico (Nah Chan – Palenque, Loltun, Chichén Itzá, Kabah, Uxmal and Edzna) to be reopened for cosmovision teachings. Sixty thousand people from all over the world went to Chichén Itzá for the spring equinox, when the opening ceremonies took place. By doing this, the Maya were making a statement of their empowerment.

Despite restrictive laws in Mexico and civil war in Guatemala, indigenous Maya, together with hundreds of people from countries worldwide, have continued to join the Maya at solstices and equinoxes each year. Many who call themselves 'rainbow eco-warriors' – activists for environmental awareness – now support them. On an unprecedented level, representatives of many indigenous nations are regularly meeting together to re-establish their common bond and purpose, sharing their deep concerns for the viable future of our Mother Earth. Some of these people are ready and willing to speak to interested foreigners, for they realize that this is one way that their own voices can be heard across the planet. It is as if the three symbolic national birds of the Land of the Sun (the Americas) are joining together: the Eagle of the North is meeting the Condor of the South, and the Quetzal bird of the Maya at the centre holds them in balance. (The use of animals and birds as guides will be discussed in Chapter Ten.)

## The stones speak again

Special teachers have emerged for me while I have been following my quest for the shamanic meaning of time, and I have been prepared to listen to a quiet inner voice that talks to me when I am in nature. I recall one such occasion when I was sitting within a ruined temple contemplating the achievements of the forgotten ancestors of this extraordinary Maya race. Around me twisted roots and hanging vines had split temple walls and roofs apart and decorative plaster stucco images crumbled away in the searing heat. Ravaged by time and tropical storms, once brightly-painted colours had faded into grey shadows.

Formerly resplendent palaces and temples are now steeped in beautiful dereliction as nature embraces them with rich jungle foliage. Out of such scenes another sense talked inside me, and the ancient stones seemed to speak, telling of time and traditions long past from which I could draw meaning. A story began to emerge that told of the Maya creation. I retell it here for you.

## Maya creation story

Storytelling plays an important part in every indigenous culture. Read this story, which is based upon the traditional Maya book the *Popul Vuh*, preferably aloud to yourself or to others, and if you have a drum, drum quietly at the same time. (Remember that the letter 'x' is pronounced as a 'sh').

Our story begins as all good stories should – a long, long time ago ... In the House of Heaven – house of Xpiyakok, First Mother, and Xmukane, First Father – the star people gathered. They had come from distant galaxies, travelling through time and space to the House of Heaven in order to make a momentous decision.

They called together all the lesser gods, the ancestors and those yet to be born, asking them to look into their hearts for the way to interpret the desire of Hunab K'u, the One God, and Giver of Movement and Measure. After great deliberation they decided to sow seeds in the Earth's soil, ready for human life, and to sow the sun, moon and stars around her.

For the gods and star people, the idea of creating human beings was as old as the Earth herself, but three times they tried and three times they failed.

The first humans they made were unable to honour the gods: all they could do was to squawk, chatter and howl. So the gods decided to make their flesh into lowly animals. They then destroyed them but allowed their service to the gods to be that their flesh might be eaten, even to this day.

Next they tried to make humans from mud and clay. But these creatures were unable to walk and certainly not able to honour the gods. So in the end a great flood poured down on the earth and destroyed them too.

The third attempt involved making humans from wood, and although they could walk and talk they were so stupid they forgot to make prayers to the gods. This outraged the god Hurricane so much that he brought a tremendous storm and flood upon them. Even their own dogs, turkeys, tools and cooking pots rose up against them and smashed their faces in so that they were destroyed. Their descendants are the monkeys with squashed faces seen in the forests today.

The fourth effort to make humans was successful, for it began with a prayer:

> **Maker-modeller – Name-bearer – Begetter.**
> **Hunanpu Possum, Hunahpu Coyote, Great White Peccary, Tapir,**
> **Sovereign Plumed Serpent.**
> **Heart of the Lake, Heart of the Sea,**
> **Maker of the Blue-green Plate,**
> **Maker of the Blue-green Bowl.**
> **Three times the midwife, three times the matchmaker,**
> **Xpiyakok and Xmukane, help us now.**

And this is what happened ... Some used to say that the shell of a sea turtle split apart and the maize god emerged. Others said that from the part of the sky near the constellation of the Great Turtle, three stars shone brightly that were called the Hearthstones of Creation. These stars had miraculously entered the sky, forming a new constellation just at the moment that the previous human creation had been destroyed.

From these stars a brilliant ray of light was sent out that caused the Sovereign Plumed Serpent, the Great Feathered Serpent God, to rise up in the heavens. He pulled maize plants from the earth, ground up the kernels and mixed his own blood with them. Then the Maker, the

Modeller, used this dough to form humans. This was the Fourth Creation of our own ancestors on Earth.

The gods rejoiced, for this was a successful creation. The first four humans were made exactly in the likeness of the gods and called mother-fathers because they were androgynous. They had perfect vision and knowledge and great power to 'see' as far as the gods. But by worshipping the gods, they irritated the jealous lesser gods so much that the latter caused a misty veil to blind the eyes of the humans that has lasted to the present-day (and which we can now choose to remove).

It is also told in the ancient books of the Land of the Sun, that these four true humans were known as the four Balaams. They were the first intergalactic travellers to come to our planet from the light of the Pleiades stars. They were the ancestors of the wise ones of Atlantis. And on starry nights, around the three hearthstones of the cooking fire, it is told that the people of Atlantis were the ancestors of the Maya.

Here the story ends… with an ancient prophecy that this creation, too, will end in AD2012.

> **Oh Hunab K'u!**
> **We, your cornseeds,**
> **have been ripened by you, Hunab K'u,**
> **and Great Father Sun,**
> **in preparation for the awesome cosmic time ahead,**
> **when First Father prepares to meet First Mother**
> **in the dark rift of the Milky Way at the end of the year 2012.**
> **Allow the misty veil to clear from our eyes.**

**Channelled by Mikhail Baker, Solar Initiate, Sovereign Solar Order of Chichén Itzá, Co-Director of the Sun and Serpent Maya Mysteries School for the 1998 Maya Dreamtime Festival, Glastonbury, UK**

## Practical summary of the key to the door of intention

The present-day Maya have 'their feet firmly rooted to the earth and their heads and hearts in the stars'. How you can interpret this is to find practical ways to connect with the earth – grow plants, especially food plants; walk in natural surroundings; open your eyes to the beauty of the sky (even if you live in a city).

1. Learn about star constellations. Meditate outside if possible, especially at dawn and sunset.

2. Keep a 13-day diary.
3. Use your intention in the way a warrior would aim an arrow – with clarity, one-pointedness of intent, focused. If the intention is weighed down with conditionality, it is not focused. Be aware that should your arrow of intention be unbalanced in any way, it will not reach its target.

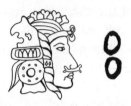

# CHAPTER 2

# Vision Quest Mountain

Today my beloved brothers is for determining
the spirit of our liberty.
I, Ah Canek, Maya prophet, have walked through
all the province
Looking at the sun and able to interrogate the stars.
I have formed insoluble pacts with the spirits of the water,
With the dew of the sky, with the venerable
Feathered Serpent.

**Maya Priest Ah Jacinto Canek (barbarically put to death by being drawn and
quartered in Mérida, Mexico, by Spanish colonists in 1761)**

## What is a shaman?

Present-day writers on shamanism tend to describe all shamans by
the same word. 'Shaman' comes from languages of the Siberian
region; but the Maya use a very similar word – that of 'xaman' (with the
letter 'x', of course, pronounced as 'sh'). The name 'shamanka' has
been popularized to refer to a female practitioner of shamanism.
However, I am using 'shaman' as the Maya do – to mean a male or
female. The roots of shamanism are diverse, stretching worldwide, from
Siberia to the Americas, from Africa to northern Europe. They
encompass early Bon shamanism in Tibet and the very ancient ways of
Australasian aborigines.

Anthropologists and historians can find evidence of shamanism as
far back as into the Palaeolithic period, for example by studying cave
paintings. It seems early people in the Stone Age, some forty to fifty

thousand years ago, forged deep links between their collective consciousness and that of the creatures and plants of the Earth. The meaning of 'shaman' and related words is said to be 'one who sees' or 'one who knows ecstasy'. Strangely, the English words 'witch' and 'wizard' come from an Indo-European origin and also mean to 'see', or to 'know'. Authorities of the Christian Church sought to discredit most of the old knowledge by labelling witchcraft and Wicca evil and 'weird' (from the Anglo-Saxon word 'wyrd' – 'that which happens'), but actually in essence the sources of witchcraft were shamanic too.

The shaman has a foot in two worlds – the world of matter that we see around us and the world of spirit, or perception of inner realities connecting us with the cosmos. Perceiving the interdependence between the outer world of nature and the inner world of spirit is the essential starting point for those wishing to understand shamanism. A person may then feel his or her desire grow to experience these worlds more fully, to 'communicate' within them and perform 'work' while journeying through them.

A shaman works with life-force energy. He or she travels on strands of the 'web of life', seeking a spiritual path. These strands, or 'luminous fibres', will be explained more fully later on (page 40). However they can be described as connecting us by 'coordinates of resonant frequencies' to the interlocking matrix of time and space' (the Native American 'web of life'). The goal of a shaman is to engage fully with life by living with awareness in a universe that he or she perceives as multidimensional. Not surprisingly, a shaman's path is mainly independent of organized religion, although I have heard Maya shaman-priests add a few 'Hail Marys' for good measure when reciting long prayers during ceremonies in one of the many Maya languages. Most present-day shamans live apparently ordinary lives, only using shamanic abilities, their power, when appropriate.

A shaman has usually realized his or her abilities through a combination of inherited position and traumatic events or illness. Within the Central American tradition, it is likely that potential shamans will be recognized from birth, by being born on an auspicious day, or through their displaying unusual abilities from an early age. These abilities often run in families, sometimes skipping one generation and emerging in grandchildren, nieces or nephews. The potential shaman, the 'one who sees', then undertakes a long period of apprenticeship to an older shaman.

## Shamanism and healing

The way traditional Maya society copes with illness is by first letting the mothers and grandmothers treat the ailment by boiling up healing herbs and potions according to family recipes that have been in use for generations; or they may use steamy herbal baths in a specially constructed shed. If the person does not recover, the local *curandero*, a very experienced herbal healer, who may also use massage techniques, is called upon. Only if these remedies fail is the village shaman asked to perform a healing ceremony for the patient's spirit in order to heal the body. In Belize and parts of Mexico, such a shaman would be called a 'H'men'.

*A shaman stands smoking a sacred pipe. From the entrance to the inner temple in the Temple of the Cross, Nah Chan (Palenque).*

Shamans say that the main cause of illness is 'separation' from nature, a person's community and oneness with spirit. Their role within traditional societies is to keep people in unity with spirit, so that they know their path. Sometimes when a person appears sick or lost, the shamans will undertake methods to retrieve his or her soul and bring it back into full resonance with the powers of the universe, so that the soul may sing its song of freedom. Travel into the worlds of lost souls is fraught with danger for even accomplished shamans, and soul retrieval requires the shaman's entire range of warrior skills.

To the North American Indian, 'medical treatment' involves more than substances to make the body well again. It is about living in balance with the material and spiritual worlds, and also with the life force within the 'web of life' and Great Spirit.

One typical characteristic of shamans is their ability to heal themselves, through being able to go to the point of death and return. Most likely they have done this more than once and have perhaps even invited it many times over. Research into near-death experiences has established that people who have them are into living with a far greater wisdom and perception of the world. Shamans also regularly enter peak experiences through trance – experiences that are usually considered paranormal events, such as dreaming states (both asleep and awake), meetings with ghosts and spirits of ancestors, communication with extraterrestrials, as well as periods of apparent insanity.

Traditionally, the calling to become a shaman may not be 'formally' recognized until the elder village shaman is on the point of death, when he instructs a younger person through a series of initiations. These take many forms, varying even between regions in the Maya world. Some Mayanists (Maya students and scholars) call the shaman's knowledge 'costumbre', but this word also means 'folklore'. Shamans have told me personally that it is correct to think of their knowledge in terms of 'walking the path of the sun' or 'walking the path of the days', both of which are very important pointers to the essence of Maya teachings.

It is spirit that decides whether and when one takes the shamanic path.

If you are a modern-day seeker on the shamanic path it is likely that you will experience initiations that will guide you towards your own power as you seek the keys to healing and personal liberation. Paramount in this process is self-knowledge. It is at this point that you can safely begin to experience shifts in consciousness in order to instigate heightened states of awareness and ecstasy. Spirit cannot begin to work unless it has a fertile, unpolluted mind in which to operate – our bodies being rather like earth that needs to be nurtured with water, sun and compost in order to produce a strong plant and eventually flower and seed. One way to explore consciousness is to undertake a vision quest (pages 49–51).

## The hunter shaman and 'attention'

There is a hunter in each one of us, waiting to be released from the slow death of First World consumerism. The shamanic way was ever-present when men were hunter gatherers and women the home-makers and bearers of children. Now hunting is limited and controlled in our lives and fails to satisfy the sharper edge of hunger – sadly, perhaps, for some men now channel their aggression through violence, war or acts of terrorism, which is a distorted and sickening degradation of life's purpose. However, the ability to return easily to the basics of life is ever-present in the lands of the Maya.

A short time ago I discovered that I, too, am a hunter – not (being a vegetarian) with a spear or gun, but on a practical level. I have been given guardianship of a small piece of land in Mexico. Surrounded by typical Yucatan scrub forest, this is a hot, inhospitable-seeming place, the soil parched ochre, the vegetation thorny or invasively vinelike as it hangs from tall chacah trees. These common trees have a peeling, reddish brown, paper-like bark, and the Maya compare them to 'gringos' (white men) who have spent too long in the sun!

Into this arid, timeless landscape I was dropped off with little more than a hammock and the knowledge that there was a well nearby. So I became a hunter, asking that my needs be met. Pushing my way through the undergrowth I found many plants that I knew the Maya used. Tamarindo trees, whose pods are boiled to make a sticky drink; chaya bushes, the leaves of which are cooked like spinach; the roots of sabin, the 'snake-bite tree' that has a double thorn two inches long and yields a juice that slows down snake venom in the body long enough for a person to travel to get the antidote. I saw tancaché, the 'headache tree'; ramon the 'hunting tree'; lemongrass (*zacate de limon*); mint (*herbabuena*); cedar, the 'haemorrhoid tree'; and in very dry, rocky places, the large, prickly, flat pads of the Nopal cactus – used in many traditional dishes – that also bears delicious, sweet seedy fruits.

Of course, in such a location the first thing to do is find a way to make a shelter. Among the forest trees grow many guano palms. They have strong leaves that are woven into a type of thatched roof for Maya *palapa* huts that are, for country-dwelling Maya, their homes.

Gathering some of the food plants in my hands and looking out for edible fruits, I decided to walk on, away from the thickest undergrowth. Eventually I found a long, straight, white road. Following it I came to a small *palapa* and was greeted by an old woman, who asked me in. After I explained to her that I had nowhere to sleep that night she immediately said that I could string my hammock under her veranda. So, on my first night in the Yucatan, listening to the unusual night-time sounds, I slept safely away from prowling jaguars, insects and creatures of the dark.

## The technique of 'second attention'

The hunter lives life fully. On a shamanic level he or she is always ready to step forward, poised, 'stalking' his intention, in tune with nature and all the natural elements.

> One of the shaman s goals is to be totally immersed in everyday reality, from the distant cry of a child to the alarm call of a bird; from the splatter of rain on a tin roof to the rustle of a jaguar in the undergrowth.

A statement such as this may sound strange upon first reading; but take a moment to put this book aside. Look around your environment as if with fresh eyes and allow them to alight on one natural object, for example a tree just outside the window. Observe the whole tree, its shape, texture and movement. Focus on one branch, one leaf and enter into the life of that leaf. How does it feel to be the leaf? Imagine the heat of the sun or cooling rain. How is the leaf nurtured by the tree? And, are *you* observing the tree or is the tree observing you? Are you hunting and stalking the tree so that you understand everything it can tell you about its world? Perhaps you found that as you looked at the tree, time appeared to change. Did your breathing, or your body, seem different?

What you have just done is to use a shamanic technique called 'second attention'. This is best described as the 'reality within the everyday'. 'First attention' is what most people know. It is how they order their lives and work without looking at what is inside the doors that open onto second attention. But with second attention a whole new world of magic opens up. I recall the occasion I started to paint part of a coastline in Mexico. My eyes saw for the first time subtle differences in the colours of the sea and the luminosity of the sky as blue faded towards the horizon. I have always looked at nature with second attention since that revelation. Usually the two attentions do not come into direct contact, for 'parallel lines' within the web of life separate them. However, we, like shamans, have the potential to use second attention gently; or we can rush into it and, as it were, jump off a cliff into an unknown and sometimes terrifying vastness. Perhaps it is best simply to look at any ordinary thing in an extraordinary way, resisting the temptation of the hungry brain to alight on the next image in order to consume it.

> Concentration is important. Time perception changes. This practice is one of the keys to time that the sorcerer shamans of old knew well.

(Within the Central American shamanic tradition such as that described by Don Juan in the books of Carlos Castañeda, a sorcerer shaman was one of the most powerful types of shaman, able to journey through the dimensions and change form at will into, for example, animals or even inorganic beings. Many ages ago, when the old sorcerers were alive, there was greater duality in human consciousness than there is in the present day. The sorcerers developed the tension within the duality as special powers, which we would now call magical, for either 'good' or 'evil' purposes.)

To summarize, the hunter's task could be divided into the following stages:
1. To stalk one's prey.
2. The 'kill'.
3. The consuming.
4. The digestion (absorbing).

In the modern world of materialism, our abilities to stalk and hunt in the shamanic sense are limited. Because our minds are constantly consuming coarse foods we are becoming more and more tired as we try to digest what we have consumed. We are not hungry for life. Can we still feel this real hunger any longer?

## House of Stones, House of Snakes: Nah Chan (Palenque), Chiapas, Mexico

Nah Chan has a magnetic quality all of its own, for it pulls unsuspecting travellers and those interested in shamanism inextricably into a love affair with the rainforest. The Maya call it House of Stones,

House of Snakes. There are records of people living at Nah Chan that date back to 967BC, when Ahau Kin Chan, Lord Sun Snake, came to rule over the original inhabitants called Halach Uinik ('Real People'). It is shown on the map as Palenque, which is the Spanish name given to the town that has grown up just a couple of kilometres away. Covering an area of about six square kilometres/two square miles, it is a jewel of a city, standing between the Underworld and the heavens, set down among giant trees on the edge of the Chiapas highlands. Nah Chan shifts into many different moods, for it is a place where you can be enraptured by swirling pink mists during a summer dawn, or caught in the vivid purple lightning of a tropical thunderstorm, or enchanted by the soft darkness of the night sky, illuminated by ten thousand fireflies. But its greatest claim to fame in modern times was the excavation in 1952 of the first elaborate ceremonial burial and entombment in a pyramid, to be found anywhere in the Mayalands.

### Diary extract: the ruined temples of Nah Chan

On this occasion, my husband Mikhail and I had driven overnight from Mérida, 590 kilometres/365 miles to the north, following the infrequent road signs. Cartography is not one of Mexico's strong points; maps, such as they are, give little other than basic information of road networks and infrastructure away from the tourist playgrounds. Maya names of towns and villages appear on signboards, frequently rusted and pitted with the same bullet holes seen 20 or so years before.

In the first light of morning we reach a familiar Pemex gas station. Drivers rest here after the long, super-straight roads of the Yucatan, their huge lorries parked against a backdrop of beautiful, soft rose and green light, as sun filters through the horizon mists.

The 20-kilometre/12 mile sign to Palenque (Nah Chan) gives us a surge of adrenaline to take us down the home straight to this small town, which has a tourist industry that has flourished since the famous tomb discovery in 1952. We head for our usual simple accommodation, check in and immerse ourselves in the cosmopolitan atmosphere of world travellers.

Next morning, we rise before first light, intent on hearing the incredible dawn chorus of the intense, raucous activity of birds, howler monkeys and insects about 10 metres/33 feet above in the lower forest canopy. It has become a tradition for us to stand at the gateway entrance to the ruined temples of Nah Chan and hear this song of nature. The walk there takes ten minutes, now that a straight stretch of road has been cut through the last few miles of the National Park, and our early arrival causes little groups of coatimundis (raccoon-like creatures) to rush around, with their long, striped, comical tails waving excitedly. We pass a large, starkly designed, ultra-modern concrete building – a museum awaiting its daily round of tourist life. In contrast, the ancient stone buildings of the kings of this forest appear to hover in splendour, barely manifesting through the dawn mists beneath the pyramid-shaped mountains, as if the mountains themselves are other, still unearthed, edifices. Temple upon temple sit atop viridian, sculpted hills and emphasize behind them one particularly magical-looking, pyramid-shaped mountain, often laden with blue mist. The shape of this pyramid gives a timeless, overpowering feeling of protection, as it rises behind the Temple of the Foliated Cross as a guardian. The Maya call it Yemal K'uk, saying it is a *witz* or 'doorway' into other dimensions. What secrets can we access here? The mysteries are profound, encapsulated in stones and in yet-to-be discovered royal tombs.

## The Lacondon of Nah Chan – guardians of the tombs

Rusty chains bar the entrance to the small car park at Nah Chan. In two hours time it will completely change. Birds and monkeys become silent as they retreat deep into the forest trees, escaping droves of tourists disgorging from air-conditioned, monster coaches. Although rarely seen, jaguars still roam by night, taking unsuspecting prey, like the Lords of the Underworld they appear to be to other forest creatures.

At the main entrance are thatched *palapas*, in which can be some fifteen or so Lacondon Indians – who are there outwardly as visible reminders of their tradition and inwardly as guardians of the place. The name 'Lacondon' originally meant 'builders of stone idols' or 'worshippers of stone idols'. Possibly it also signified 'builders of temples', but it was used in a pejorative sense by early Christians to mean 'pagans' or 'savages' – their perception of the Indians who retreated deep into the forest before the onslaught of the conquistadors. Present-day Lacondons still live by hunting and gathering and, above all, by growing maize and yucca in their *milpa*, an ancient term meaning a plot of land cleared in the forest. They are part of an ethnic group that live in an area richly studded with Maya ruins, from the Yucatan peninsula to the frontier of the Río Usumacinta and Guatemala, and their physical features are noticeably different from those of other Maya. These beautiful, dark-skinned, proud people now number no more than about two hundred of which only about twenty are of pure descent. Calling themselves Halach Uinik ('Real People') like their ancestors, they are the last survivors of this group, taking a special pride in claiming ancestry from the great Maya civilization that thrived there for centuries.

The Lacondon at the entrance to Nah Chan seem to glide effortlessly around or sit calmly in the shade with the wares they have brought to sell. I go in search of copal incense that I know they gather from trees deep in the forest by cutting a criss-cross pattern in the bark to extract the sap, rather like rubber tapping. On this occasion they have none available, but in broken Spanish (neither their language nor mine!), I manage to agree to meet them again in two days time when, they assure me, a kilo of copal will be brought from their village for me to purchase.

I explain to them that I will use it for ceremonies in England to honour the Maya. I wonder if they really understand. If they do, can they appreciate my respect for the Maya, or do they consider I am just stealing their traditions and ways as the conquistadors did? As ever, they stand and smile, eyes reflecting pinpoints of light as if they are doorways to worlds beyond.

I pause for a few moments, breathing in the intense sweet smell of burning copal as it wafts between the wooden trusses of the palm-thatched roof, countering the offensive diesel smell of the first of the tourist coaches now idling nearby. The Lacondon stand waiting, their long dark hair falling from their handsome heads, ready to sell obsidian-tipped arrows to tourists. Feathers collected from brightly plumed birds adorn the arrows, but they are now made to fit suitcases that will take them to the jungles of New York, Frankfurt and London. What questions could I have asked these Lacondon Maya and what answers could they have given? What practical skills and inner knowledge could such people share if only one could speak their own language and above all gain their trust?

I felt helpless, swinging on a trapeze between the culture back home and that of these peaceful people, living so simply. Once again, questions and more questions hung in my mind. Never answered.

One of the last direct Lacondon descendants of the great dynasties of kings who ruled Palenque, Yaxchilan and Bonampak seven centuries before the arrival of the conquistadors was Chan K'in (Snake Sun), a great elder and shaman. Until ten years ago he still lived in a village three days' walk from Nah Chan. It is his relations who sell arrows and seed necklaces to the gringos. Now the numbers of tourists are increasing dramatically, threatening to destroy a paradise of natural beauty in the very sites they come to see. Where once pure stream water was drunk there is now a Coca-Cola and ice-cream stand. Where there were fireflies are now electric lights. Can the ancient cosmic Maya still linger in the sound of the wind? Can their spirit touch the burning hot stones and run dancing and bright in the almost dried-up waters of the River Otolum, which crosses their sacred plaza? Like the howler monkeys and jaguars their spirit retreats farther into the rainforest.

Chan K'in, at the grand old age of 102, said on one occasion: 'The quetzal bird no longer flies, men cut down the forests and no longer respect nature. Where the forest disappears there is no place for the Lacondons. The sons of my sons sell arrows to tourists and the god Mensabak no longer speaks to me.' In a tiny hut he crouched down on his heels, sipping *balché*, a sacred alcoholic drink, and turning to a bemused researcher muttered barely comprehensible words. As if to exorcize his anguish at the huge changes he had experienced he softly moaned in broken Spanish: *'Veinte anos, no más, el mundo se acaba'* ('Twenty years at the most and the world will end').

Present-day Maya wisdom teachers call their ancient cities sacred sites , in sharp contrast to the official state-sanctioned name: Zona Archaeologica. The Maya teach that the way to enter the sites is by pausing respectfully at the original entrances in order to ask permission of the forest guardians. Sometimes it is important to sit down and meditate, to make a little offering of flowers or just listen to inner guidance to know when it is appropriate to walk on. You may use this approach when going into any sacred site in your own country.

## The Temple of the Four Winds

Once inside the sacred city of Nah Chan, the first view is a large, grassy plaza with numerous temples on small, green hills that speak to the initiated of wonders still to be discovered or prompt hardened tourists to reach for their camcorders. How different this must have looked even in the mid-1800s when Americanized Frenchman Claude Charnay first came here on the back of a mule along hot, steamy jungle trails. Later at the end of the 19th century, the Englishman Alfred Maudslay made seven expeditions to Central America, recording for posterity with camera and plaster casts the remaining vital information that had escaped the winter rains and burning sun. It is not until you have experienced the energy-sapping, sultry heat that you can really understand the commitment those early explorers had. What difficulties they must have encountered on mule back, hacking their way through dense vegetation for months at a time, placing their trust in the guiding skills of a local chicle tapper (chicle, the sap from the chicle zapote tree, was once the main ingredient of chewing gum). Now the encroaching trees, their roots twisting and turning around the stones, have mostly been cut away, the grass neatly trimmed and the steps made safe for visitors.

Through my journeys from one ancient city to another, I began to be aware of a typical Maya urban pattern. The tall, square Tower of the Four Winds at Nah Chan, however, stands out for its uniqueness. It dominates the skyline and the mind of the serious questor, for surrounding it are dramatically sculpted 'T' shapes, which seem to form a processional route around the tower's base. The significance of the 'T' shape lies in its numerous meanings throughout history in many traditions from all over the globe. It is a symbol that is widely used in Eastern philosophies, and it also has a place in Christianity in the Greek Orthodox and Coptic traditions as the 'Tau' (Greek for 'T') cross. There are minor variations of the shape, but essentially a 'T' is used. As a Maya carving or glyph it represents 'breath', 'wind' and 'spirit'. Climbing in and around the narrow courtyards and passageways littered with symbolic and sacred shapes, I found it easy to understand why Elder Hunbatz Men says that here in this 'cosmic university' are to be found many aspects of world religions.

In 1696, Father Francisco Ximanez said that in the tower some books were found (they have since been lost) that had characters resembling Hebrew and Chinese script. In the mid-20th-century, Guadaloupe Pech, chief excavator for Alberto Ruz Lhuillier, the eminent archaeologist of Nah Chan, revived the idea of cultural diffusionism, believing that cultures such as that of the Maya at Nah Chan evolved to a high degree of sophistication because of their interaction with other, widely separated cultures.

So what can we make of the Tower of the Four Winds? The first amazing discovery is that its overall measurements exactly mirror the King's Chamber inside the Great Pyramid of Giza, Egypt. The second discovery, which involves Sirius, will be revealed at the winter solstice of AD2012. As for the four winds, or breaths, this tower was the scene of an initiatory process similar to those of ancient Greece and elsewhere in which initiates sought to create light from breath. (This approach is mirrored today in modern societies with 'initiates' who use breath in the therapeutic art of Reiki.)

The tower also plays a significant part in the mythological aspects of the site. One evening each year, at the December solstice, the sun sets directly behind the Temple of the Inscriptions. Viewers from the tower would see the sun appearing to enter the mythic Underworld through this temple, where deep within was found the stone burial chamber of shaman-priest-king Pakal Votan. Like other members of the ruling elite, he was also called Ahau (plural Ahob) or Solar Lord. His life and death are something of an enigma, with more than one mystery about him still unsolved – despite the glyphic decoding that has been achieved and enabled scholars to read his name as Ahau Shield Snake ('Pak' means both 'shield' and 'look through the dimensions', while Votan means 'snake').

## Jaguar shaman

As I walked the pathways and the interminable steps upward into the temples, I wondered exactly what could be gleaned from yet-to-be discovered royal tombs. How could I journey farther into Maya cosmovision and a shamanic quest for the meaning of time?

I was to find that the answers were all around me. Almost all of the temples and many of the largest trees, standing stones and mountains around a sacred site such as Nah Chan were so powerful they were regarded as *witz* – doorways between the worlds to the Maya who originally lived there.

The shamans of today perform a ceremony at the powerful Temple of the Cross, a building to the north of the site called Wakah Chan, which contains a stunning stone carving visible from the doorway. The most instantly recognizable image on the stone is a shaman dressed in a jaguar skin, smoking a ceremonial cigar. As if indicating that the door of the temple is a way into other dimensions, he stands right at the entrance to the interior shrine or *pibna*, the Maya word for 'underworld house'. I had found the shaman there as a guardian of the otherworld, waiting to reveal the message on an adjacent carved panel. On this, the main motif is a tree – in fact it is the World Tree at the centre of the world that also holds up the heavens and arises from the mask of the Great Earth Monster, who is the raw, terrifying primal energy of Earth. The twin branches of the tree make a cross and support the double-headed serpent bar symbol, one of the primary motifs of kingship, with a bird known as the 'Celestial Bird' perched on top.

## A place of power for a vision quest

For a moment, transport yourself back in time to an age when the great Maya cities were first built. The stones, fashioned to lock together without the need for any cement, were covered in stucco or stone reliefs and adorned with natural pigments of red, green, yellow, black and blue. These dazzling colours vibrated in harmony with the brilliant hues of tropical animals, birds, flowers and butterflies by day and

dancing shadows of lamps, fires and moon by night. Maya cities would once have been seen from a distance as rainbows arising from the dense greenness of lush rainforest. But time and nature have once again taken their toll. Now devoid of paint, the grey, weathered stone ruins succumb to irresistible forces – only the descendants of forest creatures, nature's guardians – live on to tell their story to those who listen and care to communicate with them. Standing magnificently behind is the mountain, the *witz* entrance, beckoning to seekers with lush, green slopes tantalizingly shrouded in mist.

If you were drawn to undertaking a vision quest, then what I have just described would be a special location in which to begin a search for a *place of power*. However, you do not have to travel thousands of miles to find your own place of power. It could just as easily be in your back garden, a local park, or a remote seashore; but it must be a natural environment. Wherever it is, try to choose somewhere you will not be disturbed for a considerable time.

Once you have sensed a suitable location, sit quietly practising second attention, as explained earlier (page 42). When you know your place of power really well you can consider spending much longer there in order to follow a vision quest. The more you use your place of power, the more it will become a portal or doorway to the other dimensions.

You may choose a particular focus for your quest that in itself marks an aspect of your search. It becomes a *rite de passage* that takes you to a further stage on your path of self-knowledge through shamanism.

There are a number of important points to note when undertaking a vision quest. Here are eight to bear in mind:

1.  Establish your place of power (see above).
2.  Clarify your intention and what you are seeking.
3.  Use a stone or crystal to meditate with, as the Maya shamans do, to link you to the world of crystals – the human race's 'oldest relatives'.
4.  Take ritual objects with you that you have made yourself. Traditionally these would be a drum, rattle, arrows, beaded bag for incense or herbs, and they would be wrapped up in a sacred bundle.
5.  Ask permission of the natural world to merge with its life force.
6.  Use dance, drumming or singing to create the sacred space in a circle around you. A steady, almost monotonous drumbeat at 200 to 280 beats per minute changes brainwave patterns and helps to still the mind. The Maya shamans have a particular way to open

the doors to second attention. They use words and the toning of sacred sounds. During solar initiations and ceremonies they intone the word '*K'in*' (meaning 'we are all little pieces of the sun'), which brings them into resonance with the energies of the sun.

7.  Seek the guidance of the ancestors and the beings of light (among whom are the cosmic Maya) who guide humanity, and ask for empowerment to continue your quest.

8.  Ask what conditions existed here in your chosen place one hundred, one thousand and one million years ago or more. Ask what will happen here in the future.

Only when you have taken care with all of the above does your vision quest really begin. Maybe you have decided to stay out alone overnight (or more traditionally for three to four days and nights). You will probably not need food; but take plenty of water to drink and let a friend or relative know where you are and that you do not wish to be disturbed. *Do not take drugs or alcohol.* Further instructions for a vision quest are unnecessary as you will know intuitively what to do as you pray for a vision to open to creation and Great Spirit.

When you finally come to the end of your vision quest, close it by showing appropriate appreciation for what you have learned and asking that you may return safely. In these ways you build a relationship with your place of power.

## Practical summary of the vision quest mountain

1.  Practise second attention.

2.  Talk to the trees, rocks, plants and animals – make them your friends not your challenges – for they too are part of the great web of life. Ask them when it is appropriate for you to undertake your own vision quest.

3.  The Maya explain in their teachings that time, and the greater cycles of time are as threads within the 'mat of time'. A very clear way to show a thread of time, that is more a vibration of energy, is not by a straight line, but by a zig-zag. And a zig-zag is exactly what is shown on a snake's skin. Can you begin to sense a much deeper meaning behind the snake symbolism that abounds in the enigmatic lands of the Maya and which we will explore in the following chapters?

CHAPTER 3

# Travellers on Ancestral Time Threads

*That place is not a tomb, it is a temple. It is a temple where they deposited somebody to work forever – the messenger for ever – the messenger in the future in this new Light Age. That message can transmit to all the people. The spirit of Pakal Votan is waiting for us, a message is there.*

**Spoken by Elder Hunbatz Men during a ceremony at the foot of the Temple of the Inscriptions, 1995**

## The Temple of the Inscriptions

Present-day visitors to Nah Chan barely give a second glance to the modern tomb on the grass below the Temple of the Inscriptions. There the remains of the archaeologist Alberto Ruz Lhuillier were placed as an act of respect by the president of Mexico to honour his achievements, especially his discovery of a royal personage within the temple (which is called the Temple of the Laws by the Maya). What was subsequently believed to be the remains of Pakal Votan heralded the most significant era for the Maya in modern times. The opening of the lid of Pakal's mysterious tomb in 1952 was a turning point in Maya archaeological studies and subsequently revealed hitherto unknown astromythological connections. Evidence in the inner temple tied Pakal's ancestral lineage to an ancient god of a previous creation 1,246,826 years and 270 days in the distant past. Starting from the day of his birth, Pakal also seems to have projected a date into the future – equal to 80 'calendar rounds' – that falls on 23 October AD4772.

However, these incredible dates had not yet been decoded when in 1947 Alberto Ruz Lhuillier noticed strangely plugged holes in the stone floor of the temple. Investigating further, he found that he could remove a slab and that beneath it was what seemed to be a stone staircase filled with rubble. It took another five years working in high temperatures and humidity to clear the stairway. In June 1952, his archaeological team finally moved aside the last barrier, a huge triangular stone, to reveal what looked like a crystal chamber. Water seepage over the centuries had caused long stalagmites to form from the curved walls, creating a shimmering effect in the beam of the flashlight as it illumined the dank space for the first time in over a thousand years. This chamber, lying some 23 metres/75 feet beneath the floor of the upper temple where the excavations began, is situated below the level of the plaza outside. The chamber was filled by a huge sarcophagus, carved from a single block of stone estimated to weigh 15 tons. The elaborately decorated stone lid, weighing more than five tons, was carefully prized open with car jacks and levers to reveal the most dramatic find since modern archaeology began in the Mayalands during the latter years of the 19th century. The information and artefacts it yielded were as momentous in their own way as those of Tutankhamun's tomb in Egypt. Understanding the significance of the tomb proved to be one of the most enigmatic and mysterious quests that I would undertake in my search for the meaning of time.

The body of a tall man had been reverently laid to rest in the fish-shaped, red-cinnabar-painted coffin. The extent to which he was revered as a ruler could be perceived from his body remains, which were laden with treasure. There was jade in abundance: a jade mask with shell and obsidian eyes; carved T-shaped jade between the teeth of his mask (the T symbol in this instance was representative of breath and the World Tree); a pearl in his mouth (suggesting that he spoke 'pearls of wisdom'); and carved jade in each hand, one piece shaped as a sphere (representing movement) and one a cube (representing measure). There were mother-of-pearl disks that had been used as ear spools, and jade rings adorned his fingers. All had remained hidden and undisturbed for 1,300 years.

***Diary extract: recollections of 1995 spring equinox at Nah Chan***
Mikhail and I joined with several hundred people from many countries who had been honoured by the Maya as solar initiates. We waited in ceremonial ranks, 20 abreast, to ascend the steps of the Temple of Inscriptions. We had knelt for many hours in the midday sun as the shamans, lamas from Tibet

*Young Pakal Votan. Older Pakal Votan.*

and elders performed appropriate ceremonies in preparation for everyone to go up. Finally, in groups of five, we went slowly forward snake-fashion, first stepping sideways seven steps to the right, then seven to the left, up the narrow steps. The shamans, calling on the power of Father Sun, drew us up the steep ascent as if by an invisible cord. We paused in silence, gazing out across the hazy landscape – just as the Maya would have done hundreds of years before. A slight breeze contrasted with the sultry air of the plaza beneath. Filling our lungs with a few deep breaths, and moistening our lips with 'Agua Purificado', we got ready for our journey to the symbolic Underworld. Silently, and in single file, we went down, stopping in the lower chamber to attune ourselves with the contrasting cool, dank darkness and to offer prayers.

I stood and sounded an ancient mantra with a friend and an unknown visitor. The three of us were wrapped in a vibration of universal kinship until we could intone no more – the stones had worked their magic upon us and our eyes had become accustomed to the darkness. We began the final descent – ready to honour what was to greet us there – and stepped down a further number of very steep stone steps to reach the iron-barred entrance to Pakal Votan's chamber. We gazed into this Underworld like voyeurs of time, trying to make meaningful connections from the clues that had been left. In a state of wonder, we looked around for the clay speaking tube (or 'Telektonon' as it is now known) that snakes up to the top temple. I sat quietly and understood through my meditations that this tube enabled Pakal Votan to communicate with his priests in the temple above and with other dimensions beyond death.

A sudden realization! I had discovered an oracle mystery centre equivalent to the ancient Greek sites of Delphi, Samothrace and Ephesus. Places of oracular power were located on a deep well of Earth energy that empowered the oracle (in non-Maya cultures usually a female priestess) with Earth wisdom and cosmic truths. Was this the purpose of the Telektonon tube – that it allowed the discarnate Pakal Votan, shaman-priest-king, revered as the embodiment of a snake god, to speak to his people after he had departed from this world? I was left, as always, with many questions.

I gazed again and again into the dimly lit chamber to glimpse the wall carvings. It felt important to redress the imbalance caused by archaeologists' descriptions of them as the 'Nine Lords of Darkness'. When they are given their correct title of the 'Nine Lords of Time', they take their proper place as weavers between the worlds and manipulators of time dimensions. As the lords of darkness they had held a covert plan to keep open the 'gateway' of death, so that those who passed through it as they took their last breath did so with fearful apprehension of a horrendous, dark underworld. Yet mastery of darkness has been central to many deeply profound initiations, from the Eleusinian mysteries in classical Greek times to Druidic rites in the Celtic lands. When the dark ages of oppression into which the Maya were plunged, beginning with the Spanish conquest, had ended, the maligned lords were redressed by present-day shamanic ceremonial reactivations of the temple sites that began in 1989 through to 1995. They returned as the Lords of Time. Darkness and the Underworld were vanquished.

Reluctantly we left the chamber with its welcome coolness and began the return to Father Sun. Standing under shady trees after my careful climb down the steep external steps of the pyramid, I paused to watch as a black, crocheted fringe of cumulus cloud decanted rainwater heavily into the cups of waiting bromeliads hanging in the forest canopy. Echoes of thunder reverberated around the mountains towering above Nah Chan and from a moist leaf an open-mouthed, emerald-green frog looked intently at me before it took a dive into a pool forming beneath his tree. A column of large soldier ants maintained its invincible formation as the first heavy drops of rain reached ground level and were sucked into the thirsty earth. High above, a

troupe of spider monkeys abandoned a feast of small orange fruits from the nancy trees and swung down, sheltering under favourite branches. A deep-throated chord of thunder vibrated through the earth beneath my feet like creation's organ playing its deepest notes in the cathedral aisle of ceiba trees. Soft mist rolled through the branches and a vivid violet flash illuminated the sky as the great rain god Chak washed all beneath. Sheltering below the mossy stones of a crumbling temple I contemplated the experiences and thoughts I had had within the tomb.

## *Panche Be* ('seeking the root of truth'): the ancestral time thread of Ahau Pakal Votan, Serpent Lord

Pakal Votan, who is said to be the occupant of the tomb in the Temple of Inscriptions, was the most enigmatic of all the shaman-priest-kings/queens of Nah Chan. Today's Maya say that he was a Votan, an oracle, a serpent lord, a lord of time, born with his leg and foot looking like a snake. I went to study stone carvings that do indeed show his leg resembling a snake, with his foot like a snake's head. His son is also shown having six fingers and six toes. These images are a riddle, for Maya stonemasons were not prone to making such glaring inaccuracies.

The length of Pakal's life has also become the centre of intrigue. Inscriptions record that he was born in AD603 and that he ascended to the throne of the city in 615 at the age of 12 after the rule of his mother, Lady Zac Kuk, White Resplendent Quetzal Bird. He is thought to have ruled until his death in 683. If so, this would have made him 80 years old when he died. But Pakal Votan's sarcophagus contained bones that appeared to be about 40 years younger than they should have been.

It seems that every mention of Pakal Votan is cloaked with some mysterious aspect or happening. The Votan dynasty is known to have been synonymous with serpent wisdom of time from ages past. Even Count Wardeck, an Austrian explorer who lived in the ruins of Nah Chan from 1832 to 1835, thought the city had been built by survivors from Atlantis. Serpent wisdom, originating in Atlantis, appears in myth and the context of the healing arts time and again within cultures stretching from India and Australia to North and South America. The serpent is even carried into the present-day with the caduceus symbol (two snakes entwined around a staff), used as a logo by the British Medical Association. Images of snakes or the Feathered Serpent are shown repeatedly at the Maya sacred sites.

So we have a curious mixture of clues and circumstances surrounding Pakal Votan, or Snake King, for example:

- The dating of his bones fails to confirm the hieroglyphic inscriptions in his temple that give his age as 80 years.
- The unique speaking tube connecting the so-called burial chamber with the outside world.
- Objects that would certainly be regarded as highly symbolic by any present-day freemason surrounded the burial remains contained within the sarcophagus.
- An example of yet another child in history becoming revered as a god king – in Pakal's case at the age of 12 (the same age as Tutankhamun in ancient Egypt).

Embarking on a shamanic spiritual quest of a high order would undoubtedly have meant Pakal, the shaman-priest-king, challenging the Underworld through experiences that were only possible in the sealed chamber deep within the Temple of Inscriptions. But what were the ancient Maya actually doing? I felt the need to investigate further and rationalize my wild thoughts. What if there had been no body of Pakal to bury? What could have happened?

Incarceration of a living initiate in a tomb was a common way for ancient Egyptians to experience a *rite de passage*. A shaman's path and practices were considered appropriate and natural states for warrior kings in the lands of the Maya. I wondered whether the whole burial event was an initiation for Pakal Votan in order to prepare him for a life without a fear of death? Shamanism worldwide encourages release of death fears, for death is the ultimate shapeshift. Instead of engendering fear, death becomes an ally. By taking a person across the divide between life and death, such near-death initiations kindle personal consciousness of being a human emissary of light – as embodied within a true warrior of spirit.

There is yet another still stranger possibility: was Pakal Votan really the embodiment of the Ahau sun god king, carrying serpent wisdom about time, who, like others in history, became so developed spiritually as to be able to ascend to other dimensions. In some instances this has been ascension *with* the physical body. The Maya expected to descend to the dwelling place of the dead, the Underworld of Xibalba; but did Pakal Votan, with the assistance of the Nine Lords of Time who dwelt in the Underworld (what we today might call the darkness of space) 'enter the road' by transcending death and return a traveller in time to Hunab K'u, the source?

Pakal Votan left us a message about Xibalba. Along with many other Maya words it has a double meaning. It is known as the underworld place of the dead, but it is also the name for the dark rift in our Milky Way. It is prophesied that our physical sun will appear to arise at dawn through the rift on 21 December 2012.

## The ancestral time of Atlantis – known as Atlantiha or Kak Uleu ('red earth')

Perhaps one way to understand some of the questions about Pakal Votan is to put time into a context that does not accord with accepted academic theories of world civilizations. For this we may look back to the era of Atlantis in order to discover answers to time itself.

It is not appropriate here to argue points about the location or dating of Atlantis. Instead I shall concentrate on information that can be accessed in the collective human consciousness, which really does contain a strong memory of these other times. This can be opened up during shamanic journeying, meditation or channelling. Gradually these clues will piece together a deeper understanding about Atlantis. While writing this book I have been guided by what I refer to as the cosmic Maya, who are actually the spirit, rather than the biologically related, ancestors of the present-day Maya peoples. The cosmic Maya carry information of profound importance to humanity as we journey through the last 13-year-cycle of two special Maya calendars up to 2012. The current burgeoning interest in Atlantis may be because its apparent destruction could so easily chime with the sense of foreboding that many spiritually aware people are experiencing concerning the fate of our own civilization at this present time. By far the most powerful memories carried through time about Atlantis concern its catastrophic destruction.

Returning to Central America, we find enlightening information in the *Popul Vuh*, the most complete extant Maya codex or book. The origins of this folded manuscript can be traced back to 100 BC. In the 1550s, a version of it was written that now only exists as a copy made in the early years of the twentieth century. It records that the forebears of the Kiché Maya of the present nation state of Guatemala arrived from a distant country situated to the east in the ocean at a very remote epoch. These people were among those who had escaped from the lost continent of Atlantis before its destruction.

One way that the Atlanteans left their island just before its cataclysmic end was through underground tunnels that extended for very long distances under oceans and continents. A Guatemalan shaman has recently confirmed to me that his ancestors did indeed leave Atlantis this way. He told me that in those distant times it was the practice for the Atlanteans to review at a large meeting the state of Atlantis every 52 years in relation to the rest of the planet. On one of these occasions it became evident to a number of influential people that imminent changes to the Earth, caused by the misuse of power, would destroy the island completely. Some enlightened Atlanteans managed to escape secretly through the tunnels to what is now the Mexican Caribbean coast. The place where the tunnels ended was to become the location of the Maya city of Tulum (some 20 kilometres/12 miles south of Cancun). These survivors managed to stay underground until the intense climatic and geological effects of the sinking of Atlantis abated. They then began to rebuild a life for themselves, starting to construct the stone temples of Tulum, which they strategically placed over a network of caves giving entrance to the tunnels.

Atlantean survivors had travelled by sea and land both to the east (first towards Europe and then through to Egypt, India, Cambodia and Thailand); and to the west (towards the Americas, in particular the Gulf of Mexico). In many of these lands they became founders of new civilizations.

The Maya are not the only people in the Land of the Sun to believe that their ancestors came from the east: the Toltecs and Aztecs speak of their former country being called Aztlan; a white-skinned tribe living in Venezuela inhabited a village called Atlan; and there is a large lake in Guatemala called Lake Atitlan. Also, all of the following god-men or wise founders of civilizations came from the east at unknown dates to these countries and areas.

- Peru: Manco Capac, Viracocha and Pachacamac.
- Columbia: Bochica.
- The Yucatan region of present-day Mexico: Itzamna or Zamna and Kul-kuul-kaan.
- Northern Mexico: Quetzalcoatl.
- Guatemala: Gugumatz.
- Brazil and Paraguay: Zume, Tamu, Caboy or Camu.
- Peru: Viracocha.

Whatever the truth may be of the actual location of Atlantis, there does seem to be substantial evidence that a large landmass once existed in the middle of the Atlantic. As you will see in the following chapters, there are shamanic ways beyond the strictly scientific that enable us to

connect with different time periods and dimensions. The human mind has the ability to access a huge untapped pool of information.

## Time doorway to the ancestors

One way that the shamans prepare to meet the time threads that weave their way between Earth and cosmos is to maintain awareness and dialogue with their ancestors. I have repeatedly seen shamans honouring ancestors at sacred sites in Mexico, Guatemala and Honduras. Upon arrival at the central focus of a city, such as Tikal in Guatemala, these shamans will immediately walk to the most actively potent, round stone altar, situated directly in front of the carved stone stelae (called *te-tun* or 'tree stones') and towering stepped pyramids. There they make small offerings of tobacco or herbs, invoking their ancestors for protection with prayers and meditations.

At Copan in Honduras, the extraordinary stelae in the plaza seem to many Westerners to be just elaborately carved stones showing human figures wearing multiple head-dresses or masks. But to the Maya they are *their ancestors actually living in the stone in a different life form*.

Every mark carved upon the stelae has a story to tell, maybe a date, a record of a dynasty or part of the creation myth. Every ruler – 'king' or 'queen' for want of a better English word, but in Maya he or she was called Ahau (plural Ahob) – was also a shaman priest or priestess and the head-dresses are actually their shamanic guides manifesting.

Connections to the ancestors are still apparent in Mexico today. The majority of village people honour the Day of the Dead on 1 November as well as the evening before, when all-night vigils take place in cemeteries and people make offerings of cakes and sweets to their departed loved ones. In adjacent lands, many people with indigenous roots have a tradition of being able to recite their family lineages, with names of parents and grandparents going back eight generations or more. How many of us could do that?

The ancestors were represented on the sides of many pyramids in great style. Huge, ancestral face masks, some three metres/ten feet high, have recently been discovered – they were excavated in the last five years on pyramids near the vast plaza at Tikal, Guatemala, and at Kohunlich in Mexico. All of these masks had been carefully covered with rubble infill before construction had begun on the pyramid's next layer. When the Maya friends I was with saw these masks they became tearful with emotion, saying they were their ancestors and that they had something to tell them. They read the glyphs carved in the eye sockets and treated the facemask as if it were alive. From the Maya symbol that means 'breath coming from the nose' they knew the face of the ancestor was not dead but contained important information.

*Part of a large, carved stucco frieze showing the four creations. Notice the bands of feathers and the head of Quetzalcoatl/Kul-kuul-kaan descending. From Toniná, Mexico.*

I had the opportunity to speak to the young Mexican woman leading the archaeological team at Kohunlich. Every day for months she had been painstakingly brushing away the soil and rocky infill to reveal more of the mask. 'This,' she said, pointing to the mask, 'has totally changed my life. I'm having vivid strange dreams. I'm being shown many things about the ancient Maya that I wasn't told in my archaeology degree studies. My life purpose is now clear, I have great respect for what is here – I am listening to the Maya shamans and all the visitors who come here with the new consciousness of the cosmic Maya, like yourself. This amazing giant mask has become a doorway for me into other consciousness and other dimensions. I cannot tell you how much it has affected me.'

## Summoning the invisible council

In spring 2000, I had left Mexico and was travelling with a translator, a

driver, and one of the most respected Maya shamans from the 440-strong Maya nations' Council of Elders. Out of respect for his real identity I refer to him by the other name he uses, Wandering Wolf.

### Diary extract: spring 2000 – a 13-day spiritual journey

We are somewhere on the long, bumpy roads of 'Guatemaya', having driven for endless hours through repetitive landscapes of gargantuan rocks and dry riverbeds, interspersed with small, hard-fought-for strips of earth, painstakingly cut out of the dusty slopes where the soil deepens, supporting yellowing maize. My mentor and friend Wandering Wolf suddenly stops singing sweet mournful songs of love long lost and begins a teaching. I stir from sticky half slumber, opening my eyes to the ever-present, searing sun, and arrange myself upright between luggage caked with red earth as fine as talc and bags of fruit becoming squashier by the minute. Taking a sip of lukewarm, plastic-tasting water I'm now better able to listen and comprehend. I concentrate on what he says, which is translated for me, hanging on each word like the pouch containing a crystal mascot that swings crazily from the rear-view mirror when we crunch into yet another pothole in the *camino* ('road').

'There are many things we Maya know but do not talk about, except in the villages; the authorities do not listen to us so we do not tell them any more.' My eyes opened wider, mirroring his as they began to sparkle with excitement for the story. 'You know we have a council of 440 elders that come from the villages and towns of the Mayalands. We will shortly be stopping to find Oxtok, an elder from the Mam village of Ixatan. I was with him when we performed a special ceremony to ask the Hidden Council to advise us.' He chuckled, a gold-capped tooth glinting. 'Not many know of the Hidden Council – it is a very well-kept secret. But its members can be sought if you prepare yourself and use *all* your senses. A small group of us sit still in a darkened room and suddenly there is a "whoosh" in the corner, a large noise, and a strong wind rushes through. A powerful energy has come into the room. You have to remain very quiet and focused. Those who have prepared themselves with ceremony can then ask questions as the Hidden Council "appear" to them, one by one. Those who have not done the ceremony, who do not walk on the path of the sun, cannot see them.'

Who are the Hidden Council I ponder as I write? If they are ancestors, Wandering Wolf would have said so. They must be none other than the cosmic Maya, spirit ancestors, beings of light, who are 'seen' (as by tuning in to second attention) and who communicate between the dimensions when the threads of time are opened by ceremony. I am amazed and honoured by this sudden revelation, but nothing will induce Wandering Wolf to say more. He meets every question with a nod of his head, but he remains silent as he absorbs the reactions of his audience and decides whether or not to speak of another mystery. He drops his head forward, seeming to sleep, yet we travellers know he is just slipping into another world from which he will emerge once again to share thoughts that will guide each of us in the next steps of our 13-day quest.

Later we stopped at a roadside café, a timber shack with plastic tables and the inevitable Coca-Cola slogans on the chairs, where we asked for cacao. Some 30 minutes later old chipped cups arrived containing luscious, thick, dark brown, whole fat cocoa, the surface swimming with hot oil. Savouring this reviving traditional drink that was sacred to the Maya elite, I asked Wandering Wolf: 'By the way, who decided to call this country Guate*maya*?'

'Of course it was me,' he replied with a wide grin splitting his leather-brown face, 'for it *is* our land.'

## Practical summary of the ancestral time threads

In this chapter I have brought together many aspects of the ancestors that open doors and 'portals' of time, which sit as layers upon the mat of time. Portals will be explained more fully in the next chapter.

In summary, the main points of the ancestral time threads are: Atlantean ancestors, perhaps from a previous world creation; the mystery of Pakal Votan; ancestors and other spirit ancestors who guide us from the other worlds, such as the Hidden Council of Elders and the cosmic Maya.

1. Contemplate the details of Pakal Votan's 'tomb'. Be open to a world history that is different to what is written in school books. Allow for the possibility of civilizations such as Atlantis and other creations that the Maya speak of and left clues to in their temples.
2. Contact your own ancestors. These are both the people you are directly genetically descended from and the 'overlighting' ancestral mythic dimensions of your own land that can be accessed in shamanic vision quests and dreams.
3. Deepen your connections with your own 'tribe', those non-family friends with whom you share common bonds at soul level.
4. Study serpent wisdom from many different cultures throughout history. Examine your findings as if you have entered a great living

library belonging to the minds and consciousness of all human beings that have lived, are living and will come to live. Be aware there are pages you cannot yet open.

# CHAPTER 4

# Chichén Itzá:
# A Place of Power

*Three salutations when my word falls there in Chichen for the four Great Gods of Rain, for the Four Great Jaguars.*

**From the *Chilam Balam of Chumayel***

The grandeur of Nah Chan still hung around my aura like a green velvet robe as I journeyed north-east. Much had been revealed in Nah Chan through my contemplations of Pakal Votan and how serpent wisdom could turn the keys of time. Now the shamans had told me that I must go to Chichén Itzá (pronounced 'Chi Cheen Itza') in the Yucatan to really comprehend what lies within time, because the huge pyramid there is actually a calendar – in stone.

I found that when I arrived there I was presented with a completely different, although still Maya, culture – compared with what I had experienced in Nah Chan and Guatemala for so long. To understand Chichén Itzá from a tourist's day trip is impossible, so I sought a Maya who would take time to guide me through the hidden dimensions of this large ancient city. Before going any further, however, it is necessary to explain something of the portals that were revealed to me, for they are central to this story.

## Portals: openings in time and space

Those with inner knowledge call Chichén Itzá 'the city of the seven golden doors' because it has seven places that still enable journeying between the worlds. The names of the places are:

1. The Great Pyramid and Outer Temple of Ku-kuul-kaan
2. Interior Temple of Ku-kuul-kaan (The Red Jaguar)
3. Temple of the Warriors
4. Temple of Venus – Nohoch-Ek (The Great Star)
5. Temple of the Eagles and Jaguars (Innermost and Divine Spirit)
6. The Court of the Sun (Ballcourt)
7. Temple of the Liquids (Annexe of the 'Nunnery')

Throughout the Mayalands are potent energy places that have been sanctified through centuries of ceremony by the Maya Ahob (rulers), elders and shamans. These places are known as portals or doorways out of and beyond the third dimension and may be found within the natural physical world as caves, mountains, special trees and waterfalls. Of course the ones that spiritually awakened visitors may be drawn to are within the ancient cities constructed by ancestors of the present-day Maya. The portals of temples, pyramids and carved statues are the earthly, third-dimension access points to other realities.

The purpose of portals may be described as openings in time and space that present human beings with opportunities to communicate with gods or ancestors and/or travel through dimensions beyond time. They are also used as two-way openings where gods and ancestors can pass through into *this* world in order to have communication with humans. Portals hold an increased vibrational rate that sometimes correlates to the interaction between crossing Earth energy lines (known to many people as ley lines) and places where the web of life's luminous fibres have been gathered together and intensified or focused by human intent. The Maya used ritual practices, hallucinogenic plants and personal bloodletting to control and limit the powerful forces brought through portals during ceremonies. The potency of portals in sacred temples that housed these forces built up over the years to become 'energy accumulators', which may be accessed by today's shamans at will. In modern times, during the mid-20th century, the concept of energy accumulators was investigated by American inventor Wilhelm Reich, who used them as healing chambers.

## The spiral of time
The Maya understood that our galaxy spirals through space. They have mastered an incredible vision of time as a continuing spiral or helix of movement. In this manner they see it relating to everything in the world

of nature. But understanding how the Maya measure time can appear daunting, especially when you discover that they used 20 calendars! As far as we know, the Maya did not develop any type of clock or watch as we understand them. Their whole pace of life was fundamentally different to ours. They lived by the rhythms of nature – by the sun, moon, stars rising and setting, by the sowing and ripening of crops, and by habits of bats, bees and jaguars; and it is reasonable to conclude they did not suffer from a stressful way of living.

Perhaps this is why so many people in the West are attracted to Maya calendars. In the back of their minds they nurture a desire to return to natural cycles of time, to give meaning to their everyday lives. For we have natural rhythms and cycles at the very core of our three-dimensional existence, such as those of our heartbeat and menstruation.

Making discoveries about Maya calendars could be compared to a snake peeling off its old skin. At first it comes away easily – just a few different titles and names like T'zolk'in, which means 'little pieces of the sun'. However as the skin over the whole length of the body is shed, the snake writhes and twists, and it becomes apparent that there are many convolutions to Maya calendars. Of the 20 calendars known today, some relate to natural rhythms, such as human gestation and menstruation. The Maya say that a person's 20 fingers and toes each have invisible threads – those of our fingers connect us to the stars and those of our toes connect us with the Earth. In addition, 13 points of power within the body correspond to the Maya 13-day cycle. By following their calendars ritually, the Maya have traditionally connected human beings with dimensions of Earth and sky, as well as with the more obvious dimension of time, which is not confined just to the Earth's rotation around the sun.

Close observation has shown that throughout history there has been a 'blueprint' of creation that is the pattern that we, the human race, are currently following. The Maya foretell that this blueprint is to culminate at the end of the present world age, generally agreed to be 2012. That date is in the lifetime of the majority of you who are reading this book! This is the decisive point in this book. Do you just read on, externalizing yourself from what unfolds in the coming pages, or have you received the equivalent to an electric shock – for the Maya have given clear indications that each and every one of us is able to contribute to, or hinder, the outcome of our world.

To access this blueprint we can take a route, prepared by present-day shamans with ceremony, in places that are portals. This opens a crack between the worlds that we can follow slithering and sliding like snakes, sometimes fully aware, at other times retreating into our dark caverns of misinterpretation.

This is not a logical or rationally scientific route, and those who allow themselves to become trapped within calendar interpretation become prisoners of the logical left side of their brain, instead of freeing their consciousness to use whole-brain capabilities. Only by expanding consciousness to encompass the cosmovision of the Maya can we see how many of their calendars interlock, weaving a pattern through time and space that bring together 'everyday secular life', the 'spiritual or religious', the 'divinatory', as well as cycles of crops, Venus and the Pleiades star system (see Appendix II, page 211).

The Maya keepers of the days did not compartmentalize time by allocating a fixed day each week for religious purposes. The sacred was considered to be part of the everyday, as it was with the majority of early peoples. When the Maya elders and 'wise ones' developed calendars to measure time, they entered into relationship with the blueprint of the cosmic plan in order to discover universal truths. Deep within the underlying order of all things, both within the sky above and in the Earth beneath, they realized spiralling movement was a key to understanding the measurement of time. It was a cyclical movement that could be found through the study of ants in ant hills, or from comets to a snake shedding its skin, from hurricanes to bees in a hive. They could see there was a greater plan; and that everyday life confirmed that everything in the natural world around them demonstrated the spiral phenomenon. They used the spiral as a decorative pattern, depicted carved representations of snakes and zig-zags on numerous temples throughout the Mayalands, and they recorded the spiral in their folded bark paper books or codices.

## The portal to the heart of heaven

The ancient Maya were masters at identifying fundamental truths and drawing hidden meanings from them in the manner of second attention. Apart from looking at temple decorations and artefacts, a way we can still connect with the ancient Maya is through their predictions. One such prediction is now occupying the minds of many people, namely the one mentioned before that states that the end of this world creation is precisely timed to occur on the solstice of 21 December 2012. This date was calculated by the Maya counting back to the start of the Fourth Creation on 11 August 3114BC (13 x 144,000 days prior to 2012). Two of their major calendar counts culminate on 21 December 2012. They are the ending of the significant

13th Baktun cycle of the Long Count and 7,200 rounds of the T'zolk'in calendar. On this day, solstice skywatchers will see a central dark cleft in the Milky Way called the 'dark rift'. The Milky Way itself will lie all around the horizon at dawn.

The Maya predict this is the time when the heart of heaven is opened.

## The Haab and the T'zolk'in calendars

A comfortable beginning for the would-be initiate into Maya calendars is the Haab, a secular calendar based on a 365-day cycle. It consists of 18 'months' of 20 days, after which comes a five-day celebration cycle called the Vayab. This is both the most well-known, as well as being an exact, measurement of time. The calendar keepers had a concept of zero and a binary system of calculation centuries before the Western world adopted the present-day Gregorian calendar. According to NASA space age measurements, the Haab has a 0.00000001 degree of accuracy to the atomic clock, requiring a one-day adjustment in every 180,000 years. Most people would agree this is pretty phenomenal given the limited resources that archaeologists claim the Maya had.

Elder Hunbatz Men frequently began his teachings by reminding me 'that we are all little pieces of the sun'. I found it more than a coincidence when astrophysicists discovered that the surface of our sun rotates on a north-south axis as well as an east-west axis and that a different little piece of the sun faces the Earth every 260 days. The T'zolk'in calendar (also called Chol q'ij) has a repeating rhythm of 13 x 20 (=260) of these sun faces. Note also that the development of the human foetus takes place over 260 days.

This is a 260-day sacred calendar and runs complementary to the Haab secular calendar of 365 days; when used together they are known as the 'calendar round'. The Maya say that the traditional classical T'zolk'in count is actually the hub of all the other calendars. As far as is known, this count (not the Dreamspell, which is a modern count devised by José Argüelles) has been in existence for around 2,500 years. The two calendars interlock to perform the ultimate 'dance of time' by relating to the movement of the Earth and the Pleiades. At the moment a person is born, the Pleiades mark a certain position in the sky. And it is a period of exactly 52 years before the Pleiades again mark the same position in the sky. Fifty-two years have to elapse before the same named T'zolk'in and Haab days again coincide. During these years, a person has potentially lived through a complete 'round' of conscious wisdom.

The T'zolk'in's 13-day period is likened by the daykeepers to the steps of a pyramid: for the first five days we climb with much effort; on days six, seven and eight we enter the temple that stands on the top to do our work, to absorb what we need to understand; and in the last five days we descend in preparation 'for a giving out' of our experience.

If you have been keeping a 13-day diary as suggested in Chapter One you will begin to understand some of the different qualities in the days that occur in the repeating cycle of 13. In Central America, the shamans generally choose to work on days six, seven and eight, the most potent points of the 13-day cycle. There are interesting interpretations of the days, particularly originating in the Guatemalan Highlands, that reflect traditional village life. In this region the shaman daykeepers are totally immersed in both the mythical as well as the practical aspects of days. They look at the whole 13-day cycle and base their advice and predictions on their understandings that days one to seven are an aspect of the *tonal*, and days eight to 13 are an aspect of the *nagual*. The *tonal* is a shamanic term that refers to, among other things, the everyday world; the *nagual* refers to other worlds and the hidden or subconscious aspects of a person or his or her soul. The *nagual* may also be spirit allies – teachers who have passed on to spirit, or to animal and bird 'familiars' such as a jaguar, dog, eagle or macaw.

## THE MAYA COSMOS
### The Point of Balance

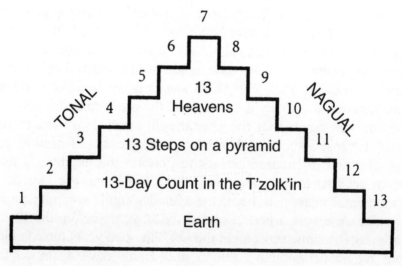

*Diagram of a stepped pyramid.*

# Time portals and the T'zolk'in

| Day | | | | | | | | | | | | | |
|---|---|---|---|---|---|---|---|---|---|---|---|---|---|
| Iq' (ik). | 2 | 22 | 42 | 62 | 82 | 102 | 122 | 142 | 162 | 182 | 202 | 222 | 242 |
| Aq'ab'al (akbal). | 3 | 23 | 43 | 63 | 83 | 103 | 123 | 143 | 163 | 183 | 203 | 223 | 243 |
| K'at (kan). | 4 | 24 | 44 | 64 | 84 | 104 | 124 | 144 | 164 | 184 | 204 | 224 | 244 |
| Kan (chicchan). | 5 | 25 | 45 | 65 | 85 | 105 | 125 | 145 | 165 | 185 | 205 | 225 | 245 |
| Kame (cimi). | 6 | 26 | 46 | 66 | 86 | 106 | 126 | 146 | 166 | 186 | 206 | 226 | 246 |
| Kej (manik). | 7 | 27 | 47 | 67 | 87 | 107 | 127 | 147 | 167 | 187 | 207 | 227 | 247 |
| Q'anil (lamat). | 8 | 28 | 48 | 68 | 88 | 108 | 128 | 148 | 168 | 188 | 208 | 228 | 248 |
| Toj (muluc). | 9 | 29 | 49 | 69 | 89 | 109 | 129 | 149 | 169 | 189 | 209 | 229 | 249 |
| Tzi (oc). | 10 | 30 | 50 | 70 | 90 | 110 | 130 | 150 | 170 | 190 | 210 | 230 | 250 |
| B'atz' (Chuen). | 11 | 31 | 51 | 71 | 91 | 111 | 131 | 151 | 171 | 191 | 211 | 231 | 251 |
| E (eb). | 12 | 32 | 52 | 72 | 92 | 112 | 132 | 152 | 172 | 192 | 212 | 232 | 252 |
| Aj (ben). | 13 | 33 | 53 | 73 | 93 | 113 | 133 | 153 | 173 | 193 | 213 | 233 | 253 |
| I'x (ix). | 14 | 34 | 54 | 74 | 94 | 114 | 134 | 154 | 174 | 194 | 214 | 234 | 254 |
| Tz'ikin (men). | 15 | 35 | 55 | 75 | 95 | 115 | 135 | 155 | 175 | 195 | 215 | 235 | 255 |
| Ajmaq (cib). | 16 | 36 | 56 | 76 | 96 | 116 | 136 | 156 | 176 | 196 | 216 | 236 | 256 |
| No'j (caban). | 17 | 37 | 57 | 77 | 97 | 117 | 137 | 157 | 177 | 197 | 217 | 237 | 257 |
| Tijax (etznab). | 18 | 38 | 58 | 78 | 98 | 118 | 138 | 158 | 178 | 198 | 218 | 238 | 258 |
| Kawoq (cauac). | 19 | 39 | 59 | 79 | 99 | 119 | 139 | 159 | 179 | 199 | 219 | 239 | 259 |
| Ajpu (ahau) | 20 | 40 | 60 | 80 | 100 | 120 | 140 | 160 | 180 | 200 | 220 | 240 | 260 |

*The T'zolk'in calendar. Each square represents a day. Days follow in a descending order from the top left-hand corner of the first column. The 21st day starts at the top of column two, and so on.*

The Traditional T'zolk'in calendar, originating from classical Maya times and still used today by the Guatemala Highland Maya, synchronizes us with the galactic pulse of time. It is a real spiritual calendar around which we can, if we wish, surf the 'web of creation'.

Fifty-two days in this sacred calendar are portals or doorways (shown in black on the chart above), because they increase energy – somewhat in the manner described for portals in temples at the beginning of this chapter. The base energy of a portal day is the integration of two cycles merging together to create a more accelerated and defined pattern. These two merging cycles consist of that of the group of stars known as the 'Pleiadian cycle' (upon which the T'zolk'in is based) and moon cycles known as 'Tun Ux'.

The pattern of the portal days of the T'zolk'in also resembles the twists and turns of a person's DNA double helix. The T'zolk'in chart can be read in a number of ways: on the left side of the chart, the portal days transduce energy or information coming from Hunab K'u, the supreme Maya creator, into the physical world. This side of the chart is also our 'history'. If you are working each day with the T'zolk'in, this is when all the information that has been received begins to make sense. Conversely, the pattern made by the portal days on the right side of the T'zolk'in represent energy and information returning to Hunab K'u. This is the time in the calendar count when we may expand our horizons, absorbing new information and frequencies of Great Spirit.

In the centre, where the two patterns merge together, a diamond pattern is created, made up from the two intersecting pyramids. The central 'spine' of the T'zolk'in running down the very middle is the place of unity between Earth and Hunab K'u in the cosmos. It integrates past and future, synthesizing energy and information into an understandable form that individuals working with the calendar can grasp. These central days situated in the seventh column are sometimes called 'core days' and they are 20 in number.

In this Fourth Creation, in which we are living at the present, there are 7,200 T'zolk'in rounds. At some point in the years of the powerful shaman-priest-kings, the Maya daykeepers decided to fix the first day of the creation. They did this in order that calendars throughout the regions could be synchronized and regularly checked by themselves, astrologers and priest-kings. It also gave them the basis on which to connect with their mythological origins. However, as already stated, many people today anticipate that this count of days will end shortly. In order for this cycle to end on the date that most say will be 21 December 2012, the period would have begun on the Maya date equivalent to 11 August 3114 BC. This is called the GMT (Goodman-Martinez-Thompson) or Thompson Correlation and is accepted by the majority of Maya researchers. It is named after two major contributors to Maya scholarship along with Sir Eric Thompson, who dominated studies of Maya religion and iconography for most of the 20th century. Throughout the Mayalands today, many still follow an unbroken count of days in repeating cycles of the T'zolk'in calendar, following a count used by their ancestors during the classical era.

## Explorations of Chichén Itzá: City of Seven Golden Doors

In the ancient city site of Chichén Itzá, one giant pyramid, which stands 30-metres/98-feet-high, dominates all else. This magnificent structure overwhelms visitors, many of whom are transfixed upon first encountering it. Its real name is the Great Pyramid of Ku-kuul-kaan, sometimes mistakenly called 'El Castillo' by Spanish-speaking Mexicans (the Maya did not have a word meaning 'castle'!).

Mikhail and I were fortunate to be accompanied in our exploration of Chichén Itzá by a shaman called Jorgé, who in everyday life acted as a guide to the site. Like most of the hundreds of pyramids in the Mayalands, the Great Pyramid of Ku-kuul-kaan is built in stages that rise like huge steps to the flat apex. The building has flights of narrow, steep steps ascending each of its four faces. This pyramid has many unique features. Jorgé began by explaining that 'Ku' is the Maya name for pyramid. He also told us that this pyramid has a fascinating link to ancient Egyptian times, for it has been discovered that the Great Pyramid of Cheops was actually called Ku Fu – just one example of the points of connection between the Egyptians and Maya. The size of the pyramid is exactly four times smaller than Ku Fu, but still covers some 3,000 square metres/32,000 square feet. As seen by present-day visitors, the Great Pyramid of Ku-kuul-kaan has undergone partial restoration, enabling them to climb to the top temple by way of one of the steep stone stairways. Down the north face, two giant, serpent-body balustrades edge the steps, culminating in two huge, carved serpent heads.

Tourist information books and guides readily inform the inquirer about the numerology of the pyramid – for example the 91 stairs on each of the 4 faces and how they relate to the number of days between solstices and equinoxes – as well as the unique phenomenon of light and shadow that occurs there. The four original flights of steps added together, plus the one final step to the temple atop, make 365, the number of days in the Haab calendar (page 69). Each year since the pyramid has been restored, thousands of people make special journeys from Mexico and across the world to witness an unusual light and shadow effect caused by the sun. It is most spectacular at the spring and autumn equinoxes.

In the Gregorian calendar the spring equinox usually occurs on the 21 March, but it is known by the Maya to have a different quality each year in their sacred calendar. The Maya, in common with people in other ancient traditions around the world, used to consider (and some still do) the spring equinox as the start of their new year. So, as the first day of the new year in many Maya calendar counts, it carries a 'year bearer' name, and it is believed that whatever occurs on that day sets the tone for the whole year.

Today, like their ancestors, the shamans understand that the entire pyramid of Kul-kuul-kaan is full of vibrational light encodements. Experiencing the light and shadow phenomena down the giant north staircase for the first time is an awesome event. Time itself seems to be frozen in sunlight and shadow as the crowd of onlookers anticipates the coming of a serpent of light. Seven triangles of light alternate with six triangles of shadow, forming an effect like a snake's body with diamond-shaped skin patterns. At around 4.30 p.m. on 21 March each year the carved stone balustrades down the sides of the steps and huge carved serpent heads at the base become illuminated with full sunlight and an impressive shadow is cast. A zig-zag of light and shadow plays along the precisely aligned stone work, cleverly and deliberately shaped as the body of the great mythic serpent Ku-kuul-kaan. At that moment each stone of the pyramid is charged with the unworldly quality of Father Sun's rays. 'Sun-potentized' consciousness for the whole year ahead flows down into the serpent's head. Through its open mouth it is delivered into surrounding Earth energy lines (ley lines). Like veins and arteries of Mother Earth herself, the lines distribute the solar energy to renew the people and the Land of the Sun.

This union of sun and carefully constructed pyramidal shape demonstrates the great skill of the Maya astronomers and architect priests. One can only marvel at the feat of undertaking such a construction. In its original splendour, the four parapets atop the square temple at the summit of the great pyramid were adorned with images of the five solar lords of each of the four directions. These 20 lords are central to the sacred work of the T'zolk'in calendar, for here they are literally 'little pieces of the sun' (see Appendix I). The pyramid rises at the correct angle and is set four-square on its foundations so that the serpent of light occurs at certain other times of the year too, with sometimes six, sometimes eight and sometimes nine triangles making the zig-zag of the serpent's body.

Take a moment to imagine the organization required to move all the dressed stones into place in exhausting tropical conditions. Not only is its angle on the ground planned precisely at 18° in respect of the astronomical pole to permit the sun/shadow phenomenon to occur, but also the vertical angle of each sloping side, from top to bottom of the pyramid, requires similar precision for the light/shadow markers to appear down the stairway balustrade, with the effect being created from accurate positioning of the rising corner stones *several metres away*. While a similar effect could be achieved by a steeper or shallower angle of 'rise', only this particular angle produces this specific effect of seven triangles of light precisely on the day of the spring equinox. Seven is a number of significance to the Maya, for it represents the point of balance in the count of 13.

Our companion, Jorgé, told us: 'Most people who come to watch the effect of the serpent of light down the stair balustrade at the spring equinox only understand it in a very superficial way. To them it is nice, it is pretty, it is time to party! I tell you there is much more to it, but you have to go on a journey first, a journey of initiation.'

Jorgé explained that when the shamans gather at Chichén Itzá they begin in a ceremonial manner to lay out a medicine wheel to connect to the four directions or cardinal points – to honour the World Tree – and light a bowl of fragrant copal incense at the centre of their impromptu altar. Amid the trumpeting of conch shells and the beating of drums, a fine wooden flute takes up the words of the shamans as they chant greetings to the four directions and associated correspondences, including colours:

'Greetings to the east: Red – Lak'in – Chac – Xib – Chaak.
Greetings to the west: Blue/black – Chink'in – Ek – Xib – Chaak.
Greetings to the north: White – Shaman – Sak – Xib – Chaak.
Greetings to the south: Yellow – Nohol – K'an – Xib – Chaak.'

### Diary extract: Mikhail's account of Kul-kuul-kaan

Visiting any of the Maya ancient cities can be an exhausting experience. Heat and the sheer distances walked, often involving climbing over rough ground or ascending a towering pyramid, means needing to leave adequate time for rest stops and consumption of Agua Purificado. Three or four hours are about all I can comfortably take. It can be mentally quite taxing to undertake the kind of in-depth study to which we are accustomed, because there is just so much to learn from being here. Probably the best way is to make recurring trips to see temples at various times of the day or when the elements are in different moods.

On this occasion I sat cross-legged on the ground facing the north stairway of the Great Pyramid of Ku-kuul-kaan. It is my usual spot and about the sixth time I have been here. I was following my usual practice of meditation and prayer, mindful that it was the first day of the Maya month (elders refer to this as the 'seating day').

The sun was already high and the temperature soaring. There had been a period of drought for some time, so the grass was dry, the soil cracked and parched. The early morning wave of tourist buses was preparing to depart, and the massive edifice in front of me seemed almost to sigh with relief – a sigh that was actually a slight breeze through the stones. Even I, a sun

worshipper of the 1960s, began to feel an extra-special burning. I covered my balding head with a white cloth kept for the purpose and continued the meditation, vaguely aware there was nobody else to be seen. It was then that the most unexpected thing happened. The central flight of steps in front of me quivered as if it were a dancing heat mirage. Suddenly the 91 steps turned into a roller blind and slowly but surely rolled up to expose ... I remember my brain pulsating and fumbling for mental pictures to record. I experienced doubts, thoughts of sunstroke and delirium, and all manner of culturally reasonable pictures tried to block what was happening. My shamanic discipline enabled me to marginalize the cultural stuff and to remain sufficiently focused on what was happening. 'This vision is a privilege,' I thought to myself.

I maintained my focus on the face of the pyramid. The inner darkness, utter intense darkness, began to be softened by white swirling mists from which brilliant points of light were bursting like tiny balloons. I was aware of being drawn towards an entrance – whether I physically walked or not, I do not know. For a moment, I seemed to be in deep space, with stars and galaxies all around. Then, as if some giant movie picture had stopped because of a projector defect, it all vanished. The familiar long flight of steps rolled back down and the Kul-kuul-kaan pyramid was there, looking just as it ever did.

For a minute, maybe longer, I remained cross-legged alert and aware, checking my reality by moving my head from side to side, placing hands on the parched earth palms down. The surprise of what had happened gave way to an unusually high state of consciousness. Everything around me appeared in intense contrast: colours brilliant and billowing white cloud in cobalt blue sky.

I could see the familiar outline of Jorgé ambling towards me in the distance. As he approached, I stood up and, in an excited and somewhat confused voice, fumbled for words to explain what had taken place. He fixed me with a stare, silent for maybe 20 seconds, his dark brown eyes becoming transparent windows as he said, 'Well you might have been surprised, but that's the way things happen here. Our teachers working with the cosmic Maya, the Ascended Masters, the Great White Brotherhood, know when the time is right to open the portals to a person. You see, here at Chichén Itzá the initiation route is around the seven temples and where you were sitting is the starting point. What you experienced was real. Do not doubt it, for if you do, it will become more difficult to progress in the initiatic journey. You have been introduced to the portal of wisdom and esoteric knowledge that links Chichén Itzá with the star beings.'

Later Jorgé added: 'Here at Chichén Itzá there are the Seven Temples of the

Light and the House of Men of Giant Spirit. Each of these temples is a place of power that is entered, after ceremony and initiation, by passing through an interdimensional portal, like a doorway of golden light. Each of the temples will become active at particular times of the day and "light up" your chakras, the subtle energy centres of your body.'

*The Temple of the Liquids, also known as the Church, is a major teaching temple that aims to understand or heal the three precious liquids of our bodies: blood, lymph and bone marrow.*

I spoke to Mikhail and together we tried to summarize all our thoughts about the Great Pyramid of Ku-kuul-kaan. It can be understood as an almanac, aligned to astronomical events and calendars; but this almanac is not printed on paper. Its message has been preserved in stone, graphically presenting deep secrets to be directly imprinted within our minds, synchronizing human consciousness at the spring equinox every year. As the shamans say:

'May the sacred energy of
Nohoch-Yumtzil, Yumtzil, Mehen-Yumtzil [Father, Mother, Son]
Guide your footsteps to the Pyramid of the Sun Serpent.'

## Practical summary of the place of power

1. How does the spiral of time affect your life and how you understand the universe?
2. Question why the Maya of Chichén Itzá built such a powerful pyramid to make a point about calendars when they could have written all the information down instead.
3. Learn to meditate or to be silent and free yourself from everyday thoughts – to create space for Great Spirit (Hunab K'u) to work.

# CHAPTER 5

# The Road to the Sky

The more I learn of physics, the more I am drawn
to metaphysics.

Albert Einstein

## Resonant lenses and walking the 'road to the sky'

'*K'in... K'in... K'in...*' – the sound of the mantra echoed through the inner sanctum of the temple, a blue haze of smoke from copal incense suffused my body and I drifted between worlds as a prayer was said, first in Yucatec Mayan, then in English.

> May the heart of the universe be in my heart
> May my heart be in the heart of the Earth
> May the heart of the Earth be in my heart
> May my heart be in the heart of the universe.

The words ran again and again through my head until I had them firmly fixed in my everyday consciousness. I knew I needed not only to say this prayer, but actually live it. At this stage in my quest for the meaning of time, I had to balance both my spiritual and my academic study of the Maya. As if it were a song of creation I constantly repeated the words and in response heard a dull echo through the mists of time that said, 'Walk your talk, Patricia, walk your talk.' I had heard of the 'road to the sky' before, but now I thought it was time that I set about learning more about it.

Throughout the Yucatec region of the Mayalands are long, straight roads built, so archaeologists tell us, by Maya of the classic period. They are called '*sacbe*' (pronounced 'sackbay'), meaning 'white road', or 'road of light'. The roughly dressed rock and crushed limestone remains, sometimes as much as 10 metres/33 feet wide, can still be found cutting their way through jungle vegetation or providing raised paths, varying in height from one to two and a half metres/three to eight feet above the swampy ground. At Coba, Quintana Roo, Mexico, 45 *sacbeob* (plural of *sacbe*) have been found. The longest of them still stretches for about 100 kilometres/60 miles between Coba and Yaxuna – it possibly goes on farther to Xcaret on the Caribbean coast – and then branches south to Tulum.

In the last years of the 19th century, a local Maya man from Valladolid in the Yucatan told Alfred M. Tozzer, an explorer and author, that a cord suspended in the sky once linked Tulum and Coba with Chichén Itzá and Uxmal. Clearly this was not a *sacbe* on the ground. It is more likely that this was a popular folk memory of the 'Kuxan Suum', which literally means 'The road to the sky leading to the umbilical cord of the universe'. It is a word that defines the invisible, galactic life threads or fibres that connect ourselves and our planet through the sun to the central core of our galaxy. These threads or fibres are the same as the luminous threads extending from the solar plexus described by the shaman Don Juan in Carlos Castañeda's books.

These fibres act as a pathway for resonant vibrational frequencies, both within the known electromagnetic spectrum and, more importantly, those of a faster or higher vibration beyond x- and gamma rays, providing us here on Earth with a continuing information channel and cosmic lifeline, rather like a constant television news broadcast. As a television signal coming from a transmitter, so the Kuxan Suum comes from Hunab K'u, the One Giver of Movement and Measure, who 'sits' at the centre of the galaxy, the centre of creation. The 'signals' or emanations transmitted are powerful beyond description, but since human development has not as yet reached full potential, these emanations have to be stepped down into a form that can be absorbed and understood. To make this possible, inconceivably fast vibrations pass through what is best described as a series of vibrating resonant lenses. We learn at school that a concave lens made of glass magnifies and focuses light, and that a filter either reduces or changes the quality of light. The lenses I describe here operate above the vibrational speed of light. This ancient knowledge was passed to the shaman-priest-kings and is still able to be accessed; but before we proceed to the next stage, a further explanation is required so that this profoundly important process linking humans with the divine creator is better understood.

Beginning from the centre of creation, Hunab K'u, the first 'lens', directs the creator's 'intention' into the multitude of galaxies, focusing emanations from one star system to another, each of which also acts as a lens. The first lens, which is closest to Hunab K'u, is imprinted with the common pool of galactic centre information. In other cultures in the world, this pool is described as the web of life, the 'harmonic matrix' (as author José Argüelles has termed it), the collective consciousness and unconsciousness of all life, or the Akashic Record (a spiritual 'library' of all that is, ever has been and ever will be). The first lens creates a pathway that passes through lenses of the stars as well as lenses created by our sun, moon and planets, sending frequencies of radiation, light, sound, heat and immeasurable cosmic rays towards the Earth (which in turn is also a lens). Each lens acts to both focus and step down (or, in electrical terminology, 'transduce') the energies from source. If this did not occur we could not live here on Earth, for the intense energetic emanations would be too great for us to survive. We live at the electromagnetic spectrum's vibrational level of light, sometimes called the 49th octave.

Each human also has the equivalent to lenses in their body. They are the subtle energy centres within the electromagnetic field of our auras (called chakras in the Indian yogic tradition), linking our subtle anatomy to parts of our body and brain. Of prime importance in the filtering and lensing process are three chakras connected with the head known as the Crown, the Third Eye and the Alta Major. In a previous book of mine entitled *Chakras*, I wrote that 'The Crown or Thousand Petalled Lotus is the chakra that activates and opens us to higher consciousness. The two basic energies of duality, which we call masculine and feminine, unite, bond and transcend at this chakra, making possible (when fully active) a super-consciousness beyond time and space.' These three chakras associated with the head, brain and higher mind (super-consciousness) interact to channel 'life force' or bio-energy (called *prana* in Indian Ayurvedic and yogic traditions). This measurable energy is a 'cosmic food' that has been received through the higher chakra lenses and is carried throughout the body's central nervous system.

All of this is relevant if we are to understand the altered states of consciousness that shamans enter into. The cerebellum, the oldest part of the human brain, processes the actions of our lowest, most animalistic self and our primal survival instincts (physiologically concerned mainly with balance and muscle coordination). The considerably larger brain (cerebrum) connects us to the higher mind and therefore to our highest potential as humans, as well as to all the other physiological brain functions, such as hearing, speech, vision, sensation, behaviour, emotions and skilled movements. This part of the brain has evolved (but not in Darwinian terms) in response to resonant frequencies and electromagnetic energy fields that constantly bathe our planet. It also acts, like the chakras, to filter electromagnetic and other subtle energy frequencies lensed from the moon, planets, sun and stars so that they can be utilized at a human level. In order for the shamans to enter into altered states they go through a number of processes. One of these is to reduce the levels of everyday 'clutter' in their minds, thus opening the pathways between the shamanic worlds that can lead all the way back to the creative source, Hunab K'u.

We, too, learning the ways of the shamans can choose to go into altered states of consciousness. It is also our personal choice to use, every moment of every day, our higher consciousness, which urges us to act as the enlightened beings we really are. But this choice of whether or not to use our higher consciousness remains central to our individual destinies while we are incarnate. Because we are living in these end times of the Fourth Age, the pull of lower brain consciousness is present in the world in increasing density – a battle is taking place that is not of this world (but that is not for these pages!). However, this is another example of the dynamic duality from which a creative force emerges. It is part of the shamanic journey, and how we interpret and use this knowledge is important, for it takes us on the shaman's path back to the source.

Finally, when people's luminous threads – the shamanic equivalent of the *pranic* pathways and chakras – are intentionally opened and aligned, another lens activates or comes into focus. It is the consciousness of Father Sun, the realized Solar Mind called in Maya Kinich Ahau, that is able to communicate directly with human beings. At this point it is important to note that the Maya ruling Ahob normally prefixed their names with the title Kinich Ahau – Lord of the Sun.

## Flying on the road to the sky

In the previous paragraphs you have been introduced to some advanced concepts to which your logical mind may well react. That is to be expected, because this book is the result of personal experiences with people in a culture where glyphic images convey non-written concepts and a living inheritance that is not intellectualized. The Western mind is challenged to take quantum leaps into the unknown, but not the unknowable.

So, when we understand the idea of there being various lenses, they become for us portals or interdimensional doorways through which we may choose to travel by stepping up, quickening, and using our own vibrational frequencies together with the properties of the lenses. As humans we then perceive time, space, distance and separateness. From another perspective, that of the Galactic Mind of Hunab K'u, our understandings are minor and at a childlike level. Separation does not exist, for within the Galactic Mind there is no time, space or distance as we know it. All becomes coherence and unity in layer after layer of resonant matrix, within which information transmission is virtually instantaneous. This is not spiritual speculation but a reasoned understanding of the creative emanations that were 'seen' and known by the shamans. It is backed by up-to-the-minute research into astrophysics and, for example, the reconciliation of relativity and quantum theory into 'Super String Theory'. According to this theory, which closely parallels shamanic teaching, all matter is made up of tiny ten-dimensional strings. Although we appear to live in a universe with just four dimensions – three for space and one for time – the theory suggests that the other six dimensions are curled up upon themselves so tightly that we cannot detect them directly. In the words of Paul Steinhardt of Pennsylvania State University, USA: 'When you unwrap the extra dimensions, you don't know what they'll be like. It may be that you even have two timelike coordinates, or more.' The uncertainty principle that is central to quantum theory dictates that the smaller the scale you want to investigate, the higher the energy you need to use. Elevated energy is certainly something the shamans knew all about!

In our human bodies the spine and lateralized brain form our personal Kuxan Suum, the road to the sky . In the heavens, the Kuxan Suum is an energy pathway that passes through the interdimensional doorways of the planetary, moon and solar resonant lenses, all the way to the Galactic Mind of Hunab K u — and back.

The road to the sky is the shamanic flight path that has been used by shamans in all cultures. The Maya certainly know how to do this themselves and induce such states in others. To them it is the flight of the Rainbow Feathered Serpent, Ku-kuul-Kaan, or, to other peoples of the Americas, Quetzalcoatl, or the Eagle. The portals to the pathway are opened by inducing visionary states with ceremony, personal bloodletting, sound, light, dance, herbs and hallucinogenic substances. In a rather different way to modern cultures, the shaman seers (literally 'those who see') of old found their spiritual direction not with organized religions but through an intimate relationship with the life energies of plants and animals that occurred in the natural world all round them. Throughout the Mayalands the shamans used special fungi, forest plants, herbs and trees, as well as a toad whose skin secretes a hallucinogenic substance, to induce dreams and visions.

Imagine a time, not so long ago. Over a hundred people have been drawn from all corners of the world to be present for the reactivation of cosmic energies at a Maya temple at Aké, in the Mexican Yucatan. Here it was intended to re-open portals (that had been closed since just before the arrival of the conquistadors) with the assistance of interplanetary and solar lenses. For many years the astrologers had been watching the panorama of the star-studded night skies for an alignment of the planets to coincide with a particularly auspicious Maya calendar date. This date, the beginning of the Maya new year in the Itza count of the Yucatec daykeepers, spring equinox 1998, was also when day and night were of equal length.

Here at Aké all those present have already undergone ceremonies, through their Maya birth, or studies with the wisdom teachers, to become solar initiates. They are standing at the foot of the temple, clad in white, with the shamans in their colourful ceremonial regalia managing to move among them quietly, as inconspicuously as shy quetzal birds.

These initiates are being prepared to climb the huge stone blocks of the temple, fashioned, some say, by the hands of ancient giants at one of the oldest Maya sacred sites. Impressive stone columns stand like fingers pointing upwards, and the whole top ceremonial area is a large platform open to the sky. Three of the shamans are cleansing the initiates with *pom*, a special copal tree resin that is burnt as incense. Others, just as their ancestors did, stand at the foot of the time-worn steps opening the first portal in the form of a medicine wheel to the four cardinal directions and the centre of the World Tree. They carefully place offerings of herbs, alcohol, tobacco and special objects from their sacred bundles on the round stone altar. Among these revered objects is an ancient, human-sized, clear quartz-crystal skull that intermittently flashes light and colour.

As the shamans begin their low chants the clear air becomes charged with expectancy. The initiates form into a long line and one by one, following exactly in the footsteps of the person in front, begin a snake walk, alternately taking first a large zig-zag step to the right then left, until the whole line is weaving with a serpentine motion across the dry grass of the city plaza directly in front of the temple. They move as the body of a snake, their feet, brushing the grass stems, causing a swishing sound, just like that made by a fast-moving snake. They pause in front of one of the shamans, who is already deep in trance. He senses their presence and breaks away from his circle and begins to lead them, still in snake motion – but now with seven steps to each side – on a slow ascent of the temple steps. Suddenly there comes the resounding echo of large, natural conch seashells being blown like trumpets, heralding the opening of the portal.

*The shaman's conch shell.*

The initiates already know where they will stand on the large, rectangular platform of the Aké temple, for each has been prepared to work with the resonant lens of a particular planet – or the sun or the moon – that forms a serpent in the sky at noon (*see illustration below*). They spiral around the perimeter of the platform then take their places in smaller circles that reflect the positions of the heavenly bodies in the sky at the exact point of noon. The people of each circle direct their collective thoughts to focus on becoming a lens for their chosen planet, to strengthen their luminous fibres, and to connect to the Kuxan Suum, the road to the sky. To every one of them comes a sudden shift in consciousness as they align their intention – the intensity of their experiences directly relating to the extent of their personal power.

Some people, despite being held hand to hand in the circle, begin to sway, taking shamanic flight to the sky. One is describing how he has been transformed into a huge snake and has been picked up by an eagle and carried across the landscape, then on through the resonant lenses towards the planets. Others talk in tongues, channelling hidden messages from once-lost languages. Each person has his or her own experience and, maintaining the circle, communicates it through the whole group, which acts as another resonant lens, to the other initiates.

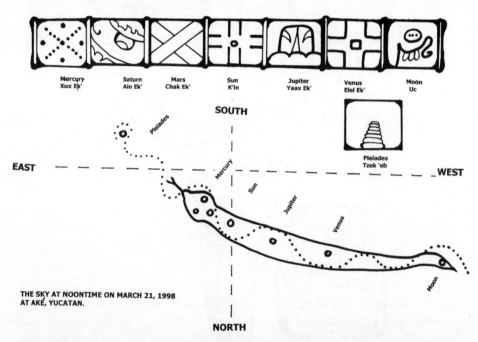

| Mercury | Saturn | Mars | Sun | Jupiter | Venus | Moon |
|---------|--------|------|-----|---------|-------|------|
| Xux Ek' | Ain Ek' | Chak Ek' | K'in | Yaax Ek' | Elel Ek' | Uc |

SOUTH

Pleiades

EAST

Pleiades
Tzek 'eb

WEST

Mercury

Sun

Jupiter

Venus

Moon

THE SKY AT NOONTIME ON MARCH 21, 1998
AT AKÉ, YUCATAN.

NORTH

*The serpent in the sky at noon on 21 March 1998, as perceived by the Maya astrologers for the ceremony at Aké, Yucatan, Mexico. The planetary glyphs are arranged in a similar manner to the skyband bench upon which the Ahob (rulers) sat.*

The shamans move around, assisting in the opening of the portals, and as the ceremony draws to a close the groups look up at the sky. Around the noonday sun a rainbow of iridescent light has turned into a bright circle. They look again, it is gone, but wisps of cloud form into winged serpents and the intensity of the sun increases. The shamans, realizing Father Sun's portal is too intense for many, call to the wind to come to cool the temple.

Within moments a cooling breeze springs up, the initiates begin a chant of 'K'in, K'in...' to honour Father Sun and begin a slow descent of the steep steps.

## Crystal mysteries

My work in the United Kingdom, in what now seems many lives ago, had taken me in diverse directions. One of these was to study crystals and undergo training as a healer with crystals. From this I learnt that crystals could link us through meditation techniques and shamanic journeying to past, present and future experiences. Although the genesis of crystals lies within our Earth as a result of fire, air, water and great pressure, we need to remind ourselves they are composed of the same chemical elements and colour vibrations as distant stars. This is shown by spectrographic analysis of both crystals and the light from stars. Incredibly, the human body is also composed of about 30 of these same elements, listed in the periodic table of elements, commonly learnt at school. Because of this connection, a special relationship, or a resonance, links us with crystals and the stars. Invisible to the naked eye, these physical elements within the human body correspond to similar elements in the animal, plant and mineral kingdoms. Although the physical creative processes that utilize them largely remain a mystery, scientists affirm that because of these physical elements, light penetrates and enlivens every cell of a living body. One example of this is shown in the work of the Japanese Hiroshi Motoyama, who, during research carried out from 1970 to 1990, was able to measure low light levels emanating from yoga practitioners.

Many people who have received Maya initiations have been entranced by the sheer beauty and mystery of the very ancient, human-sized skulls made from pure crystal that are held in great esteem by the Maya. The shamans say that the genuine Maya crystal skulls that are not held in the Mayalands at present need to be reunited in a sacred place, known only to themselves. When this occurs, appropriate ceremonial activation of the skulls will enable coherent energy fields of light to manifest. The latest work from Sweden and the USA has demonstrated the therapeutic properties of coherent polarized light emitted through an energy field generator. Time anomalies are also created when this generator is used. It may not be long before we, like the ancient yogis in their caves, can create light in the darkness or bioluminescence in order to travel within the light and to access other realities and worlds that the shamans describe.

The shamans often produce their *sastuns* or quartz-crystal stones of light from their sacred bundles. Rarely do they have guardianship of a genuine, ancient crystal skull. When they do, the power of the ceremonies is amplified many times over. Having participated in such rites, I have wondered whether these crystal skulls indicate that hidden within the structure of our own body cells and subtle energy chakra centres is a beauty and wisdom that is carried to us on a pulse of light lensed from some distant star. This question has driven me on to further in-depth studies of both crystals and the Maya. The answer is stranger and has more profound consequences for the human race than I could have ever envisioned at the start of my shamanic quest.

The Maya, like many other indigenous peoples, have preserved much information on traditional healing methods originating from very early times, such as the Atlantean period. Even today this information is not written down, but passed on orally from master to pupil. In healing ceremonies, the Maya, like other indigenous American Indians, show great care and respect for their environment, crystals and individuals with whom they work. For example, in order to obtain the best possible results they first cleanse the area of unwanted energies by burning incense, dried sage, cedar, sweet grass or fragrant copal tree resin. Next, they clear the auras of the people in the ceremony in a similar way. The smoke bonds with the positively charged ions in the air, leaving only negative ions that are beneficial to us. Using incense in this way is called 'smudging' by those who live in the Land of the Sun.

## Crystals, meditation and the 'assemblage point'

Maya traditional healers or *curanderos* are able to use a quartz *sastun* to move the luminous fibres, part of our energy body, that hold us within the web, or matrix, of life. I have already mentioned that the chakras are part of this energy body and the term 'chakra' is now quite well known in the Western world. But it took me by surprise to find the Maya have a similar word, '*chacla*', to describe the subtle energy centres of the body.

While journeying in the Mayalands, Hunbatz Men pointed out to me

numerous statues and carvings indicating the chakras as circles or marks on the body as well as the aura as rays coming from the body or head. He said there are seven powers connected with the *chaclas* as follows:

| Power | *Chacla* |
| --- | --- |
| 1. Sex | Coccyx |
| 2. Youth control | Spleen |
| 3. Solar energy | Navel |
| 4. Sensibility | Heart |
| 5. Speech | Throat |
| 6. Clairvoyance | Forehead |
| 7. Spirituality | Top of head |

Hunbatz Men said to me that 'all of the sacred Maya centres [i.e. ancient cities] have a specific function to awaken the seven powers contained within our bodies. Only by initiation can the sacred human race wake up and be the true sons and daughters of the cosmic light.'

In addition, the shamans of the Mayalands work with another critical part of the auric field known as the 'assemblage point'. It is where the personal bundles of luminous fibres meet the threads of time. It results in us usually being fixed in everyday consciousness on the web of life. In other words, it gives us a coordinate on a matrix or grid. While a person is in his or her physical body, the assemblage point normally hovers in a position around the solar plexus; but during an illness it drops lower until, at death, it is slowly released. The art of the shamans involves deliberately moving their consciousness and sometimes their bodies temporarily away from this coordinate in order to 'fly' in the other worlds. The manipulation of the assemblage point is a specific, advanced shamanic technique that requires great skill to achieve safely.

To begin with, it is better is to undergo training to work with crystals and their inherent, vibrational nature and healing properties, slowly attuning our bodies to the vastness, the greater whole of cosmic order. There we will first find revealed the inner worlds, the timeless places, the realms of the crystal beings, devas and *los aluxes* (nature spirits) of our Mother Earth. They have been there all the time – we just have not been able to see and understand them; but shamanic practice, healing techniques and meditation link our very similar energies to theirs. Harry Oldfield, a healer in the UK, has begun to develop very interesting crystal technologies that enhance the ability of the human

body to resist imbalances that can cause disease. During the course of his work, he has actually captured on film the life energy of crystal beings momentarily becoming visible as shapes of light.

Crystals are amplifiers and transformers of energy. This is why it is so important to make connections to them in a way that enhances positive energies. For example, if you are tired or angry, trying to work with crystals will only amplify that. But if you access your higher consciousness with clear intention by focusing on a certain spiritually open approach – which is not necessarily religious – results can be enhanced with crystal energies.

One of the best and safest ways to come into harmony with the inner hidden worlds of Mother Earth's life forms, including crystals, is to learn meditation. It allows the mind to relax and become inwardly focused. What happens can also be scientifically measured. Brainwave frequency patterns will drop from the usual active conscious level of Beta (13–30 cps, or cycles per second) to Alpha (8–12 cps), or even touching into Theta (4–7 cps). When the activity of the brain falls to these slower vibrations we pass through levels where rapid learning ESP (extrasensory perception), sleep or deep meditation occurs. At Delta (1–3 cps), one begins to approach the vibrational levels at which crystals resonate. It has been shown by medical research that as soon as a quartz crystal comes close to, or on, the body, there is an instantaneous flare of Delta frequency in the brain. This is the brainwave level that predominates during very deep relaxation and meditation. In this way the crystal reduces body stress, the precursor to many illnesses. You are a reflection of the crystal and, really, the very first crystal to get to know is yourself!

Apart from the *sastun* stones of light that the shamans usually possess, other crystals have traditionally had importance in the Mayalands, and are sometimes found as 'grave goods'. They are: jade, turquoise, amber, obsidian, blue haematite, cinnabar as well as pearls and gold.

### Diary extract: record of a divination ceremony from a previous journey in Guatemala

I arrive at the village scattered among precarious ridges of mountainside overlooking Lake Atitlan – a ripple of water far below, illuminated by sparkling points of light that belie the mysterious depths beneath. Volcanoes ring the lake and the cone of Pacha Mama is visibly smoking intermittently in the blue haze of the far distance. A small boy, barefoot, leads me through a maze of houses and yards, fragrant with the smell of turkey, pig and jasmine,

into a tiny palm-thatched, sparsely furnished *palapa*. In the centre of the house is the place of the fire. The usual three large stones representing the Three Hearthstones of Creation are set up to support a cooking pot. (These hearthstones are actually stars that are in the constellation known to us as Orion, but to the Maya as the Turtle.)

I stand entranced before a glittering altar, which is lit by many candles and adorned with brilliant tropical flowers around faded pictures of long-dead saints, remembering that this culture is a strange mixture of Christianity and shamanic tradition. The healer, or Ah Q'ij, motions for me to sit opposite him at a rough table, on which he has placed his magic stones of many different shapes and varieties. Tiny quartz crystals are piled together with greenish hued and blue stones. Next to them are numerous hard, bright, scarlet seeds, known as Tzite seeds. His head crowned with a colourful woven band, the man turns his dark, leathery, world-worn face towards me, his timeless eyes probing mine. Then suddenly nodding his head he asks my name and date of birth in the Maya count, repeats it out loud and begins mumbling a long, unintelligible prayer or perhaps an incantation. He gathers all the red seeds together into a pile and then sensing, rather than counting, moves some seeds into another group, all the while reciting the Kiché Maya names for the sacred days.

Next, he arranges his collection of stones together with the seeds into groups of four. He sits very still, occasionally looking down to his feet or hands, feeling the movement of energy or 'blood lightning' (*coyopa* in his language) course through his body. Then he noisily clears his throat and tells me an utterly precise divination and practical ways of achieving the next stage on my path. I must watch the serpent he tells me... his voice trails off as he piles up and selects seeds and stones twice more, each time adding further detail to the divination. It seems I have chosen, in this life, to play a part that will help right the wrongs against the Maya. He tells me I am a scribe and a weaver of energy able to reconnect the broken threads of time. I am amazed, but nothing will induce him to say more. A broad smile flashing incongruous gold-capped teeth indicates the end of the reading. Stunned, I thank him, press a banknote into his palm and emerge into blinding sunlight.

## The next steps

After listening to a number of shamans talking about the future, and recalling my own divination with the Ah Q'ij, I was determined to piece together more of the Maya mysteries. Clearly we are living in the 'end times'. The time when there will be no time. Two Maya calendars are culminating and unless we can preserve ancient traditions, the time keepers of the cosmos, the Maya daykeepers themselves, will be no

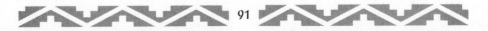

more. I suspected that this was the reason they were becoming more prepared to share their prophecies and had started to talk about their calendars. To summarize:

- The Maya shamans today have a global focus and cosmovision.
- They see into the other worlds, they commune with their *naguals* and consult their *sastuns*, for their vision, unlike that of the rest of humanity, has not been blinded by the gods of the *Popul Vuh* (the gods of consumerism, I wonder?).
- Their clarity of vision – some would say clairvoyance – enables them to offer their prayers, not for themselves, but for their communities and the environmental sustainability of Mother Earth.
- The crystal skulls have an unknown, but not unknowable, part to play in the ending of this, the Fourth Age.

## The Pleiades and other stars

The Pleiades star group recur again and again in the teachings of the present-day wisdom keepers. They travel a path in the cosmos that brings them to the same apparent place in the night sky every 52 years.

The Pleiades are given a number of names, including the 400 boys ; they are also described as a handful of seeds of maize planted by First Father, the maize god, who created human beings from the blood of the serpent mixed with maize flour. The seven main stars of the cluster are considered to be Tzek eb — the tail of a rattlesnake or, more precisely, the serpent in the sky . On a number of occasions I have taken part in ceremonies, like the one at Ak , when the shamans have identified the serpent in the sky by saying that the Rainbow Feathered Serpent lies in a particular alignment of planets, stars and the Earth. Hunbatz Men frequently refers to our sun as the eighth main star of the Pleiades group. (See the illustration of the serpent in the sky, page 86).

According to Carl Johan Calleman in *The Maya Calendar*, the Pleiades, together with a number of other stars that surround our own sun, are called Gould's Belt. Astronomers say this 'belt' was created 60–100 million years ago. The Maya believe the Pleiades serve, together with part of Orion, as a relay for a particular aspect of our consciousness, possibly as further resonant lenses. Is this the reason, I wonder, why many people feel a great affinity with this star group?

Other stars that figure prominently in Maya mythology are those of

Orion, which the Maya call the Turtle of Rebirth, and those of Gemini, which are depicted as copulating peccaries (a kind of wild pig) and were sometimes shown as the place of rebirth. However, most people who have studied the Maya codices, as well as the Maya astrologers themselves, now agree that it was the Orion Turtle that was the rebirth place, for on its back it carries the three stars known as the Hearthstones of Creation.

The Maya were not by any means the only ancient peoples to accord the significance of creation and resurrection to the heavens. The Egyptian pharaohs, for example, also prepared themselves for rebirth. Egyptologists Robert Bauval and Adrian Gilbert in their book *The Orion Mystery* suggest the pyramids at Giza were aligned on the ground near the River Nile to give an almost exact replica of the positions of the three stars in the belt of Orion in relation to the Milky Way. It was believed this would allow the pharaohs to be reborn as a star in another location in the sky that was called the '*duat*' by the Egyptians and 'Eight-Partition-Place' by the Maya. Curiously, the Egyptian symbol of rebirth was an eight-petalled lotus flower, depicted on wall paintings and carvings. But as I will reveal in the last chapter, the exact location that has great significance for the destiny of the human race in the years following 2012 lies elsewhere in the heavens.

Piece by piece a little more of my shamanic quest to understand the travellers of time was revealed. As a Westerner trying to unlock the mysteries of the Maya mind of more than 1,000 years ago, I knew I still had a long path to tread. I thought it would be wise to ask questions of present-day wisdom keepers and shamans from many of the Maya nations rather than embark on lengthy academic research. The Yucatec Maya have taught me a great deal in their lands but there was something missing, something elusive. The imprint of the conquistadors is still keenly felt, and administration of tourist centres and once-proud Maya cities, now called archaeological zones, is mainly by non-Maya people. Is it this that makes Chichén Itzá seem so cold to me whenever I am there, despite the searing heat? I wonder to what extent the weave of time was disarranged there by the impact of invading Spanish soldiers, priests and colonists some five hundred years ago? A karmic debt has been incurred that may be resolved before the end of this Fourth Age. However, an eye for an eye only makes the whole world blind. Since karma works not through retribution but by cause and effect, will today's Maya be the instruments through which their gods in the creation stories bestow humans with insight, removing the blindness from their eyes?

It seems that the essence of the ancient Maya – those I call the cosmic ones – is no longer in the hidden portals of Chichén Itzá and other places overrun by highly commercialized tourism. The spirit of the Maya shamans has retreated farther and farther into the green embracing arms of the rainforest. It is time to leave Mexico and take an aeroplane flight to return to Guatemaya.

## Practical summary of the road to the sky

1. Understand the subtle energy centres of the chakras and assemblage point within your auric field. They are 'entry points' for subtle energies into our physical bodies. They also serve as transmitters and transducers of energy to and from the cosmos via the luminous fibres of the web of life.
2. In your shamanic work use crystals, particularly clear-quartz ones.
3. Reflect upon the 'serpent in the sky' and the stars that are important to the Maya.
4. How do you understand resonant lenses?

# CHAPTER 6

# Lake of the Impeccable Warrior

The winds are your *nagual* ... You have the spirit of a comet.

**From the *Chilam Balam***

### Diary extract: Lake Atitlan, Guatemala

Volcanoes rise steeply, grey, smouldering, shuddering, in the 'ring of fire' around the centre of Guatemala. It is a powerful, primal landscape and I couldn't imagine anything more different to the flat, arid scrublands of the Mexican Yucatan. A long journey from the capital of Guatemala City took me first to Antigua, then early next morning, in an ageing rattling bus, to the shores of Lake Atitlan. It shimmers through the heavy morning mist, distant lights crystalizing momentarily on its surface. Ripples on the shore turn to wavelets as a small, heavily laden ferry boat arrives from a community some 15 kilometres/9 miles distant across the huge lake. As I sit awaiting sunrise, my eyes slightly close. The first rays of the sun light up the water and dancing before me are points of light, each shaped like the diamond pattern of a serpent's skin. A path of liquid gold stretches between me and the rising orb of the sun, pausing momentarily on the horizon – then the pattern takes on the likeness of a great snake writhing across the surface.

## The *tonal* and the *nagual*

Imagine living all your life on a small island on a lake. The lake is so vast, you cannot usually see the distant shore. Normally the still surface of the water is covered in a rising mist that totally obscures your vision from seeing beyond a few metres. Just occasionally a shaft of light breaks through the blanketing gloom and you glimpse a great vista beyond, which is there in a moment and in an instant gone. Yet you

thought you saw an amazing thing that appeared like nothing you had seen before and had only heard tell of in childhood stories: a mountain monster smoking and bellowing out showers of red glowing ash.

The *tonal* is your island, your only reality that you experience day after day. Outside of it is a place that is unthinkable, only imagined in dreams. You are blind to this other place; it is a mystery that cannot be spoken about. You can only witness and experience it if you break away from the island. Did you fly in your childhood dreams? Do you fly now? Are you trapped on the island or can you move from the everyday, called your right side or *tonal*, and fly to the totality of yourself, called your left side or *nagual*? Memories such as flying while in your body are part of what is stored in your 'left side', your other self, and are quite distinct from memories of ordinary consciousness. The *nagual* memories are so out of synchronization with what you have built up as your view of the world that you cannot reconcile them, and they are not recognized. Like the smoking volcano on the far shore of the lake.

The whole art of the shaman is directed towards breaking the spell of cultural hypnosis in order to perceive awareness of other forms of life, such as minerals, trees, animals – any of which can become, or be, part of our *nagual*. It is the part we merge with when we invoke our power animal, or ponder upon a crystal. The *nagual* is the totality, that which lies behind the little life and opens onto the possibility of a creation greater than ever imagined. For the shamanic questor, this is not likely to be a comfortable, sugary-sweet creation – but a wild place ready to trap the unwary in all the nightmares that could ever be dreamed, rather like the exploits of the Hero Twins in the *Popul Vuh*.

My arrival at the side of Lake Atitlan, in the region of Guatemala that is home to Maya of Cakchiquel and Tzutuhil descent, was like passing through a cultural portal into another world. Certainly a good place to release cultural hypnosis. The pulse of time seems strong here. Despite the three smouldering volcanoes of San Pedro, Toliman and Atitlan, the Earth is solid, ancient. Notwithstanding the ravages of recent civil war, the determination of the people is so completely enshrined and linked with their old customs that little seems to have changed. Everyone wears the colourful, hand-woven dress traditional to each village rather than cheap western clothes. The little children are mostly barefoot and play simple games in the yards along with the turkeys, dogs and pigs. As they reach the age of six or seven, the girls help their mothers, looking after younger siblings, and the boys work in the fields when extra hands are needed. From their homes wonderful cooking aromas spiral into the air along with the haze of blue smoke from the hearth. I wonder what the men do for employment these days and suspect that beyond the smiling, happy faces, existence is at subsistence level for many.

The Catholic Church has minimal influence here, and life carries on according to village customs barely changed in a thousand years. One of the few concessions made to Catholicism is Maximón, a thinly disguised Saint Simon, but actually a representation of the much earlier earth monster featured on many classic-period carved panels. People in the small villages around the lakeside live every day according to their calendars and their myths. The *Popul Vuh* stories are ingrained in the lives of the majority of the Highland Maya peoples, with elders, shamans and daykeepers using them in their teachings. Because the translations of the stories from the old *Popul Vuh* manuscripts had caught my imagination in many ways, and also because I refer to them in the creation story in Chapter One, I give a summary of them now.

## A short précis of the *Popul Vuh*

The story of the *Popul Vuh* ('Council Book') recounts the Kiché creation myths of the four creations by many gods who are aspects of the One God, the Heart of Heaven, Heart of the Earth. As outlined in Chapter One, the book relates that following the creation of the world, the gods decided to populate it with beings who would honour them. But the first three attempts to make humans failed. The next attempt, however, was successful, and four people were made from maize dough. But because their abilities rivalled those of the gods, the latter were jealous and partially blinded them. After their eyes were dimmed the humans were given four noble women as their wives and they became the ancestors of the Kiché nation in Guatemala.

The *Popul Vuh* then moves to a complex story of elemental forces and astronomical events that are given human form, and the action takes place both in this world and in the Underworld. Time is mixed up – it is non linear – and much of the story is so otherworldly that some commentators in their translations believe it symbolically expresses the movements in the sky of Venus and Mars rather than the exploits of people. There is a long and cunning battle between two generations of Hero Twins, Hunahpu and Xbalanque, and the death lords of the Underworld of Xibalba. The twins have to endure initiatory tests in underworld houses of darkness and are beset by hail, fire, ferocious jaguars, flesh-eating bats and slashing obsidian blades. Finally, having survived all these tests, they are challenged by the death lords to a ballgame in which they play valiantly in order not to be sacrificed. Not surprisingly, the Hero Twins eventually defeat the death lords in this last test. This causes them to rise heroically into the sky as the sun and full moon. From that time onwards the death lords maintain a pact with the Hero Twins. The lords can only receive offerings of 'tree blood' (resin) made into incense or smashed pottery, and they are only able to lure wicked and worthless people to premature death. The names of the lords of death have been colourfully translated as: One Death, Seven Death, House Corner, Blood Gatherer, Pus Master, Jaundice Master, Bone Sceptre, Skull Sceptre, Trash Master, Stab Master, Wing and Packstrap.

The ancestors of the Kiché people that endured the rigours of the creation worshipped their creator with this prayer:

> Heart of Heaven, Heart of Earth,
> give us our sign, our word,
> as long as there is day, as long as there is light.
> When it comes to the sowing, the dawning,
> Will it be a greening road, a greening path?
> Give us a steady light, a level place,
> A good light, a good place,
> A good life and beginning.

## Hero Twins

After reading the *Popul Vuh* translations I embarked upon research into Hero Twins. Some modern psychologists and writers such as Joseph Campbell believe that myths have a foundation within the collective unconscious and have a universal, archetypal quality. Stories of hero twins are found throughout recorded history and embedded deep in archetypal world myths. They represent the powers of darkness and light or the Yin and Yang (in Eastern terminology) that create the tension needed for life to manifest. In all of the myths the twins are portrayed as opposites to remind us of our own duality. (From another perspective we can say such twins are opposites – biologically they came from two different eggs. Otherwise they would have been identical twins from one egg or ovum).

The cult of the twin reached its peak in Didyma, in what is now Turkey, and was a way of preserving occult knowledge – for example the idea that Jesus had a twin brother who was called, appropriately, 'doubting Thomas'. Other twins in the Bible include Cain and Abel, who again represent opposites. To the Aztecs, Xolotl was Quetzalcoatl's dark twin, who was represented by Venus as the evening star descending into the underworlds of night. This is an example of the cosmic duality of twins.

Then there are the founding twins of Rome, Romulus and Remus, Sumerian Enki and Enlil, and Isis and Osiris of ancient Egypt. In this tradition, Osiris is tricked into his death and his body is dismembered and scattered throughout the known world.

Time is a human concept used primarily to measure our sojourn in the body or historical events. Look at this in another way: when we are alive in our body this is when we are physical humans. When we are in spirit, having returned to creation, we exist as another part of ourselves. And what is that other part of our self but the spiritual twin, the soul mate, often a 'fallen', 'dark' or shadowy counterpart, nevertheless earnestly sought by the ancients and encoded in their myths.

Certain incarnations of powerful people manifest with such intensity in the physical that another aspect of their spiritual twin becomes apparent, namely that of their shadow. Because of the intensity of their light, they have to face their twin shadow; and sometimes this shadow is actually born into physical existence. This was the root of the cult of the twin. Rudolph Steiner, founder of anthroposophy, said that before the fourth century AD human beings were fundamentally different and the spiritual atmosphere around our planet had great clarity. Today we have virtually no ability left to understand just how brightly the divine could shine into the physical. The veils between the worlds were thinner, with some evolved humans having a finer, less dense form that was susceptible to spirit. But as light attracts darkness, so the dark side was able to challenge an enlightened person, resulting in the manifestation of duality.

But to return to the Maya: even the Maya gods had a complement or a twin part of themselves. Itzamna's *nagual* or spirit is Itzam Yeh, the Celestial Bird, which is frequently illustrated, most notably on the lid of Pakal Votan's tomb at Nah Chan (see illustration, page 164). The Hero Twins of the *Popul Vuh* have numerous hidden meanings. I have already hinted that they are connected to two celestial bodies and postulated that these could be Venus and Mars, or the moon and sun. But what if instead they are representative of two stars or star groups? As you will see later in this book, there is strong evidence that Orion, and particularly the stars of the Three Hearthstones, are the source of our present creation. Perhaps they are also the origin of our DNA encodements and therefore our animal or physical body? And what if the Pleiades, of which we hear so much in Maya cosmology, represent the other part, our twin? It is said that the four great lords, the Balaams, came from the Pleiades; and they are the civilizing, spiritual influence in the Maya stories. So the Pleiades (also known as the '400 boys' or the 'Corn Seeds') were, then, the source of the refining of consciousness, star-seeded human consciousness.

The *tonal* is that part of ourselves which is concerned with the physical; it is the twin that is in his or her most vulnerable human body and links to origins in Orion. The *nagual* is this twin s complement, which is our spiritual life and our Pleiadian connections to super-consciousness.

## The impeccable warrior and Ix Piyacoc ('solar teachings')

I realized as I wrote these two profound sentences (above) that I was working as a 'monkey scribe' (Ah Tz'ib), who symbolized remnants of knowledge from the Third Creation and was frequently portrayed by the Maya in stone or paint. I have sat for hours sketching glyphs and carvings, endeavouring to bring the mysterious knowledge of the Maya into present-day relevance. While recording my feelings in pictures and words as my journey to understand time unfolds, I have drawn yet another profound message of truth into my consciousness – that I am working just as a monkey scribe would have worked: using a thread of time to connect me to how it once was way back in history. By writing down the knowledge in this book, I am recording the orally transmitted knowledge of the Fourth Creation in readiness for the Fifth Creation yet to come in 2012. My concern is to make the Maya and their myths relevant to the way we all wish to live our lives, to our own truth as the beings of light that we really are. What we seek when everything is lost, and what we find when love lays us bare, is the source. Shamanism, which underpinned the whole of Maya society from the shaman-priest-king down, takes us on paths that eventually lead to the galactic source.

The real message of the Maya shamans is both interpersonal and galactic. It is a message to care for our planet before time runs out. This is not just for personal satisfaction or development, but a wake-up call to open our hearts and eyes beyond this world into cosmovision. In this way we will see universal threads of time – singularly different to time as we experience it upon this planet – woven into the mat of creation. The quest for the clarity of this message takes strange twists and turns, and it helps to study some of the interpretations of shamanism.

When we say that warriors have 'impeccability', we are referring to their constant search for the best possible way to use all their positive skills – much in the same way that in myth the Hero Twins always find a way out of their terrible predicaments. They achieve this through right use of energy or personal power. Everything that living creatures and humans do is decided by their ability to utilize energy. The level of energy they can attain depends on three main considerations:

1. The amount of energy with which they were conceived.
2. The way in which they use energy at the moment.
3. The way in which they have used energy in their lives.

How you use your energy is up to you – but if you want to be fulfilled to your inner source, do not give it away: do not become a victim of cultural hypnosis and consumerism. In Chapter Two we already looked at the way the hunter stalks his intention and his prey. The warrior is a specialized type of hunter who has eliminated his self-importance, which creates cultural hypnosis. Self-importance is a huge drain on energy. Can you observe for yourself what drains your energy the most and causes you damage? Notice what increases your energy and make an effort to increase it, so that instead of feeling weak and worn out you are feeling good and happy.

Throughout the world the sun has been revered as the source of life energy, and capturing the energy of the sun is central to the Maya. Recall the word 'K'in' that was part of the meditation at the end of Chapter Four. Hunbatz Men teaches that when we make the sound 'K'in' we are converting the breath we receive through our nose into wind. This wind is the breath of Father Sun and it activates our spirit, purifies our blood and gives us perfect health. He also says that the word 'K'in' can convey the following meanings and associations: when read backwards for enhanced understanding (a common peculiarity of many Maya words), 'Nik' means 'pendular'. (Note that the sun, when observed from the Earth, has a pendular movement across the sky.) 'Ki' means 'blood'. 'In' means 'I' (me). 'Ni' means 'nose' and 'Ik' means 'wind'. Solar knowledge-keepers are to this day called 'Hau k'in' priests.

## The Rainbow Feathered Serpent: Ku-kuul-kaan/ Quetzalcoatl

In this section we enter into a collective dream, that of Ku-kuul-kaan/Quetzalcoatl, the god-aspect of ourselves that can fly along the

Kuxan Suum, the road to the sky, to the stars.

Quetzalcoatl, the Rainbow Feathered Serpent, or plumed serpent, has been dominating the spiritual focus of Central American civilizations for at least two thousand years. Later legends that date from the classical period of the Maya (AD200 to 900) and possibly earlier say that 'he' was a divine incarnation. Stories told to the Spanish conquerors say that he manifested as a human god-king of Tula, capital of the Toltecs in northern Mexico, around the year 950. Nevertheless, it was mainly the Aztecs who worshipped the divine manifestation known as Quetzalcoatl. The name itself is derived from 'quetzal', a shy, forest-inhabiting bird that sports a long green tail and has been adopted, in modern times, as the national bird of Guatemala; and 'coatl', which means both 'serpent' and 'twin' – in fact the word also means 'precious twin'. But why would the divine god principle of Quetzalcoatl be depicted as a serpent or snake that has feathers? The Maya can shed some light on this.

The Maya equivalent to Quetzalcoatl is called Ku-kuul-kaan, who, unlike the other grotesque-looking gods in the Maya pantheon, is unusual in that he/she is a benevolent deity. 'Ku-kuul-kaan' is made up of the following root words: 'ku' meaning 'sacred'; 'kuul' – the coccyx at the base of the spine; and 'can' meaning 'serpent'. The whole word refers to the movement of energy up the spine (called kundalini in yoga, and 'body lightning' or 'coyopa' by shamans of the Mayalands), which facilitates travel along the Kuxan Suum. It is the shamanic flight path of the shamans that takes them into otherworlds – they see these worlds with enhanced visual abilities while in trancelike states. Fortunately, the shamans have not been blinded like the rest of the humans described in the *Popul Vuh*. When flying on the road to the sky in their altered states of vision, they perceive luminous, rainbow-like colours, hence the name 'Rainbow Feathered Serpent'.

Maya legend says the human form of Ku-kuul-kaan was a person who was white skinned with blue eyes and a beard – quite the opposite to typical Maya features. He was a powerful spiritual teacher who devised the calendar, arts and sciences. Ku-kuul-kaan is said to have disappeared from the land, sailing on a raft of serpents towards the horizon, where his heart ignited in the sunset and rose up into the sky and became the morning star. However, it was prophesied that he would return from the east. This is possibly why the bearded, light-skinned Hernán Cortes, the Spanish conquistador, was at first hailed as a returning avatar and met with little resistance from the local populations when he landed at Tenochtitlan (Vera Cruz) in 1519. It was the beginning of what was to prove a barbaric invasion of the Mayalands.

One of the main Maya centres for worship of Ku-kuul-kaan was Chichén Itzá. The huge main pyramid was dedicated to this god principle. Chichén Itzá, unlike many other sacred sites, is regarded as a 'silent city' by archaeologists, because it has no written hieroglyphs carved into the stones. However, it is rich in imagery. I remember standing in the vast ballcourt one morning as wave after wave of tourists flooded through. I listened as they were whisked past the intricately carved friezes. Stopping in front of a kneeling warrior, minus his head, they were told by the guide that his head had been 'sacrificed to be used as a ball' – quite untrue. This particular frieze, upon deeper investigation, shows seven snakes emerging from the warrior's neck that depict the energies of his seven chakras being brought into harmony, ready for the game of ball (see illustration, page 182). Nearby, two intertwined snakes biting their tails decorate the round, stone ballcourt markers. Elsewhere at Chichén Itzá are other images of snakes – for example, large, stone serpents' heads set into the Temple of the Warriors and two huge supporting columns carved as the Feathered Serpent guarding the top of the steps.

*A snake carving at Uxmal showing a human head in its jaws.*

I was excited to find one of the most striking of the Maya snake carvings at Uxmal, which is also in the Mexican Yucatan. Around the walls of the building that was the priestesses' quadrangle in the Temple of Ixchel, the goddess of childbirth, you can see a very long, carved snake. Its tail curves around almost to its head and within the gaping jaws is a human head. The intricate patterns behind the snake are of stars and the planet Venus. This is only one of many places in the Mayalands with such snake and human symbolism.

Among the few Maya 'books' that survived the burning and destruction by the ravages of the Spanish soldiers and priests were some that were made of folded bark paper covered with gesso lime plaster depicting, sometimes in hieroglyphs and sometimes graphically,

*Head and rattle of the Rainbow Feathered Serpent that twists around the walls of the priestesses' quadrangle, Uxmal, Mexico.*

other aspects of the Feathered Serpent. Within the manuscript known as the *Tro Cortesianus Codex*, the serpent that writhes across it (as part of a sort of star map) has been identified as the star Eta in Draconis – in the position that it would have been roughly two thousand years ago. Eta gave an accurate measure of the sidereal year and an indication of the precessional movement on the other stars. The *Dresden Codex*, which has been described as a sophisticated astronomical 'computer', also prominently portrays a serpent on its pages. On one of them the rattle on the tail of the serpent is in the position of the Pleiades in the sky.

The depiction of the deity Ku-kuul-kaan has multiple meanings, for it is not just representing the Feathered Serpent itself. Rather, it is a synthesis of ideas, shown graphically as a serpent with a god in human form coming from its mouth. Similar serpent imagery is used by the Maya in connection with the planet Venus as the morning star that is reborn each dawn on the horizon and sets as the evening star .

The shamanic perspective of the above 'key' is that we can see two realities: first, that such depictions show the emerging god shape-shifting between human and snake; second, that in snake imagery Venus is seen to shapeshift between being the 'morning' and 'evening' star' and is intrinsically linked to Maya concepts of Ku-kuul-kaan.

In the snake and serpent images, we can find common threads throughout the world – those of the duality of life and the potential for rebirth. The avatar that was Quetzalcoatl to the Aztecs and Ku-kuul-kan to the Maya was a wise, enlightened being who performed miracles and whose fame spread across the lands spanning centuries of time, like the ever-present rays of the sun. In the spiritual practices founded around him, people learnt how to use the power of their energy (kundalini) in order to open the heart chakra to spiritual light lensed from the sun direct from Hunab-Ku at the heart of heaven. This type of powerful solar imagery is still used today by the Maya wisdom teachers and across the other side of the world by other spiritual teachers, such as the Sufi order. It is not so dissimilar either to the ancient wisdom at the core of Christianity, Zoroastrianism and many other major religions.

As I journeyed on yet another bus, careering crazily around mountain roads, I closed my eyes and reflected that a great deal could also be gleaned by a deeper study of the hero and twins myths within these religions and by any references I could find to esoteric attributes of the sun.

You are Hunab K'u, unique cosmic deity, the creator, our creator. Good is your cosmic power! Oh Father! Keeper of our universal soul, the one whom we receive and who also receives all the beings of the universe, you that have the sky behind you when you come! When you come again, it will be the time of the beginning for humanity, of the sign of the two suns.

Great priest, Ah K'in of Cabalchen Mani, Mexico

## Practical summary of the impeccable warrior

1. Consider the hidden meanings behind the cosmic twins, the *tonal* and *nagual*.
2. How do you use your energy?
3. Is your energy drained by cultural hypnosis?

# CHAPTER 7

# Doorway to the Three Worlds

*I realized that every major image from Maya cosmic symbolism was probably a map of the sky.*

Linda Schele, artist, ethnographer and co-author of *Maya Cosmos*

## The 'mat of time'

Before the guardians fully open the doorways to the three worlds – the inner nature of this world, the Underworld and the upper worlds – one must step over the threshold of each doorway onto the doormat, the 'mat of time'.

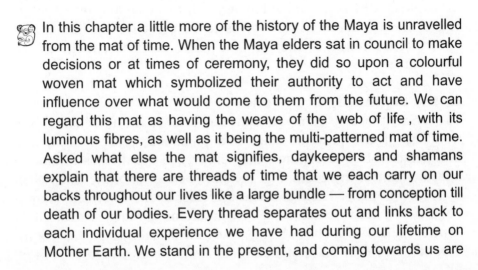

In this chapter a little more of the history of the Maya is unravelled from the mat of time. When the Maya elders sat in council to make decisions or at times of ceremony, they did so upon a colourful woven mat which symbolized their authority to act and have influence over what would come to them from the future. We can regard this mat as having the weave of the web of life, with its luminous fibres, as well as it being the multi-patterned mat of time. Asked what else the mat signifies, daykeepers and shamans explain that there are threads of time that we each carry on our backs throughout our lives like a large bundle — from conception till death of our bodies. Every thread separates out and links back to each individual experience we have had during our lifetime on Mother Earth. We stand in the present, and coming towards us are many threads of time — each being an option for us to choose. Any one of them is our possible future. The wise knowing of the shamans is to be able to travel on those threads and weave a path through time itself by selecting the time threads. We have already seen how they use the road to the sky, the Kuxan Suum, in the manner, as it were in modern jargon, of surfing the web .

It would be a great mistake to fix the Maya at any one point in time, because their cosmovision has been resonating within human minds and spanning a considerable period of known world history as well as unknown prehistory. 'We are the Lords, the travellers of time,' they say, 'We come and go, we are the same ones.'

Put another way, the present-day daykeepers and shamans are acutely aware of their inherited cosmovision. They know and carefully guard that which was seeded on Earth during their classical – what they called Baktun 10 – period. Their sons, grandsons and great-grandsons endured the 'nine hells of increasing doom' – a test beginning with the invasion of the conquistadors and ending in 1987. Now they unravel the final strands in the last days of the Fourth Creation.

The calendar shamans' continual recounting of the creation stories, together with the repetition of an unbroken count of days, keeps the time threads vibrant and alive. Western historians may spend their lives poring over dusty books, but with the Maya we still have living traditions to experience and we can ask them for their words of guidance. The Maya say that if we fix the past, surely we also fix the future? And if we do so, we limit our potential and ourselves. We become the voyeurs, instead of the voyagers of time. Now as we approach the predicted culmination of this creation, the message of the Maya is for every one of us to be proactive warriors in the history of the future so that we can weave the next pattern on the mat of time.

## In the beginning is the end

The ancient Maya explored spiritual science to understand the workings of the universe and, like pharaohs, priests, seers and astronomers of other cultures, they unravelled the threads of time to find the source, the beginning, the time before time, the time when there was nothing. Their awareness of vast aeons is evident from a number of dates recorded on stelae. According to Maya scholar Linda Schele, Stele 1 at Coba, Mexico, fixes the beginning of this Fourth Creation, through its numbering system, to 13 August 3114 BC.

Incredibly, the same stele clearly shows that the world does *not* end on 21 December 2012 (as some have predicted), because its numbers reach forward to a date of AD154,587.

That the Maya were capable of having an overview of such long spans of time demonstrates that they really were not just a primitive rainforest people. The amazing carved stones at Quiriguá, Guatemala, record events that happened some three billion years ago; they also record a single date that goes back a staggering 16.4 billion solar years. This means that it marks the Maya's awareness of a period that approximates to that given by scientists for the cosmic 'Big Bang'.

## Calendar counts and time

I began to think about the haphazard way we have measured time in Europe down the ages. The ancient Romans realized that since 153 BC the year had slipped by three months relative to the seasons. Julius Caesar ended this confusion by adding an extra 67 days into a year, and this system was introduced shortly after his death in 43 BC. Later, this Julian Calendar was again modified when a year was decreed to be 365 days with an extra day every fourth year – initially implemented by counting 24 February twice. By the 15th century, 11 March was falling 10 days later than the true equinox because the Julian year was ten minutes longer than the tropical year. Something needed to change, and it was Pope Gregory XIII who, in 1582, instituted the calendar now used by much of the world. It includes leap years, giving an average year measured over 400 years of 365.2425 days – close to the actual value of 365.2422 days.

When the Gregorian calendar was introduced, an error of 20 days had built up that was now eliminated by jumping straight from the 4th to the 15th of October in Catholic countries. Britain and its colonies, including America, did not switch until 1752, so Britain was running 20 days behind the rest of Europe! Imagine that situation occurring in the 21st century where 'time is money'. Can you also imagine how a Maya daykeeper who had kept an unbroken count of days for generations in his family would view these changing dates? He would have regarded it as an assault on the threads of time itself. By comparison with the vagaries of European calendars, ancient Maya keepers of days kept a precise record of time. They also integrated accurate timekeeping with a number of natural cycles, as well as with the spiritual pulse emanating from Great Father Sun, in the form of the T'zolk'in calendar.

Recent astrophysics has shown that not only does the sun rotate about its axis, but also the molten surface rotates at 90° to this axis in such a time cycle that the same part of the sun faces our planet almost exactly every 260 days. Precisely the same duration as the T'zolk'in calendar! This is too much of a coincidence I thought.

Time distinguishes sequential events from simultaneous events. It is regarded as the fourth dimension – beyond the three recognized spatial dimensions. According to a dictionary definition, 'Time allows the assignment of cause and effect and according to our perception, the assignment of past, present and future'. Since 1972, a precise system of time measurement known as 'atomic time' has been used for all practical purposes. It is derived from the frequency of selected transitions within atoms. Today's cutting-edge astronomer-scientists dismiss Newtonian mechanics in the nature of time and use such terms as 'parsec', 'kilo parsec' and 'mega parsec' in galactic and extragalactic contexts.

Now nearly everyone has moved from measuring time by mechanical means. Take a look at your watch: there is a good chance it has a liquid crystal display. To create liquid crystal, organic matter has been altered into a partially ordered state by applying electrical fields. It is an aspect of the same technology that enhances instantaneous computer communication, where computer networks are part of a huge electronic 'brain'.

### Diary extract: Guatemala

Mikhail and I reach the main Atlantic Highway and flag down a decrepit bus. Through the black smoke of the exhaust are visible signs revealing that the battered, blue-painted vehicle was, in another time and another place, a yellow American school bus from the 1950s. Now it is full of Maya villagers. Edging our way past colourfully dressed women, amply spreading themselves over the edges of the seats with an assortment of children, bundles or fruits upon their laps, we ask the driver to stop at Quiriguá. Some 30 minutes later we decide that since just about everyone else has got off, collecting multifarious belongings from the roof, we'd better do the same.

We start to walk along a straight, seemingly endless sand track between plantation after plantation of banana trees. This is one of the prime areas for the operations of the huge multinational United Fruit Company and Del Monte, better known to the Maya as 'el pulpo' – 'the octopus' – aptly named for their tenacious stranglehold on the economy of the region. Eventually we reach a little cluster of palapa homes and, inquiring about the way, set off along the now-defunct railway line that once carried the bananas away before better road transport existed. We pass by some of the poorest houses we've seen in the Mayalands. People sitting listlessly around the boarded-up railway station, archaic machinery rusting on the trackside, remnants of paint and old posters peeling off to reveal more of the corrugated tin wall rusting away, and the inevitable scraggy turkeys hopefully scratching hard-baked mud. Dogs and old people lie prone in any shady spot they can find, and the only activity is a surprised young man on a rattling bicycle who bumps past us 'crazy English' on the railway track as we shout at him *'Dónde estan las ruinas?'* ('Where are the ruins?').

A little farther along the railway track we come to another dilapidated habitation set among palm trees and tall, yellowing maize plants. Suddenly a small barefoot girl rushes across, pressing a bunch of bright magenta blossoms into my hands. Her eyes sparkle with the joy of giving, and I smile back, unaccustomed to such spontaneity. My shamanic experiences have primed me to watch for auspicious moments like this, so I suspect that this act is a positive sign for our exploration of Quiriguá.

## Quiriguá

Arrival at *las ruinas* is through a very small area of surviving lush tropical jungle, the only concession *'el pulpo'* made to the sacred site of Quiriguá. Myriads of flying insects, iridescent dragonflies, Monarch butterflies and mosquitoes are the guardian creatures here.

The enormous carved stones here are unique, ranking highly among a list of the most curiously amazing artefacts in the world. Archaeologists have chosen to call them zoomorphs, for want of a more apt descriptive Maya word. They are huge boulders, oval in shape (some as much as two metres/six and a half feet across and three metres/ten feet long), deeply carved with a complex array of hieroglyphs and images. Some are in the form of turtle-like creatures with human fingers instead of flipper-type feet. Others are Jaguar-like, displaying incisor teeth and claws. In almost all of them bearded human faces emerge from their mouths. The Maya are not known to have had beards, and because of weathering it is difficult to tell if these are typical Maya faces. However, in many ancient cultures the beard was the sign of great wisdom. They reminded me of the carved snakes I had seen in the Yucatan with human heads in their jaws.

I sat for many hours close to one of the turtles beneath the shade of the protective palm thatched roofs that INGUAT (the Guatemalan authorities in charge of the site) have constructed to keep the scorching sun and torrential tropical rains from their backs. I was endeavouring to clarify questions in my mind.

*A stone creature from Quiriguá, Guatemala. The left side is part turtle, the right side part jaguar. Each has a human head within its mouth.*

The next time that I travelled to Quiriguá was in the company of the shaman Wandering Wolf. He urged me to sense the energies of the turtles. They seemed to pulse with life beneath the hot stone exterior, exactly like an egg that is about to hatch, as though the human was trapped in matter – in the stone. The overriding feeling was that of a rebirth of a human from the turtle. Recall my comments in the last chapter about the significance of Orion, the Maya Turtle constellation in the sky. Imagine my surprise when Wandering Wolf said that the hieroglyphs on their backs were star maps! He told me that he could read some inscriptions but that others were in unknown ancient languages.

Later, Wandering Wolf's shamanic guidance led him to take the small group travelling with him towards a remote corner of all that remains of the sacred city beneath a lofty tree – the Great Mother Ceiba Ceremonial Place. Surely it was one of the old portals that gave access to other worlds, for he deemed this to be the place in which to invoke ancestors and to start preparations for a fire ceremony that myself and five others were to take part in. I will describe the actual process in the next chapter, for all is not revealed at once when following the ways of the shamans. The ceremony started and the air soon became impregnated with the heavy smell of the copal incense we had brought along to offer to Mother Ceiba and the star beings, keepers of this particular portal. Soon I was barely able to stand upright, such was my shift in perception. The surrounding lush vegetation became animated with murmuring voices hidden in lengthening violet shadows of the afternoon, and it seemed I was being watched from every tree. I refocused through the haze of smoke, yet still the curve of the bark of the trees took on the profile of Maya faces, complete with huge round earrings of jade. Yet was it just the mottled pattern cast by the leaves? As soon as I doubted, the faces would disappear, only to re-emerge higher up the branches as I slipped in and out of everyday rational consciousness.

Just what did this mean, I wondered, pushing my brain inextricably into its left hemisphere approach? The smoke of the fire and incense subsided a little and I heard Wandering Wolf counting the days in Mayan – 'B'atz, E, Aj, I'x...'

Diminishing smoke meant increasing mosquitoes and, with the ceremony finished, I quickly decided to move on to study the history of Quiriguá, where building began, some say, from about the year AD300. Originally, the city was subservient to the much larger settlement of Copan, just a few kilometres away as the macaw flies. However, during the rule of Ahau Lord Cauac (Storm) Sky in about 737, peaceful cooperation began to decline and Copan's ruler Ahau Lord 18 Rabbit was captured by Quiriguá. The city is now renowned for its beautifully carved stelae, first described to the outside world by explorers in the middle of the 19th century. Carefully placed around the main plaza are seven huge carved stelae, many of which show Cauac Sky's face. One of them, at 12 metres/40 feet high and weighing around 65 tons, is the tallest stele in Central America. Within the last 50 years it has been possible to decode the glyphic dates recorded on it. Clearly shown are two more amazing spans of time, reaching back to 90 and 400 million years in the past!

Why was this remote place giving me another clue to the aeons of time? With more of these incredibly distant dates apparent, it now seemed I was being shown confirmation of the origins of the universe and human life itself. I have already discussed the carved serpents that feature strongly in the Mayalands and that seem to have human faces emerging from their mouths; but was this just an assumption on my part – are the humans in fact being swallowed up? Somehow I felt that Quiriguá and the turtles with human faces in their jaws related to both our origins and our future; but what else could be made of it? I returned to sit by a stone turtle, and as I shifted my consciousness to a dream state, I began to 'journey'. I was shown the night sky and the constellation of Orion I had known since childhood. But then the tip of the warrior Orion's sword (or maybe it was his penis, I thought later) suddenly flashed with an ultraviolet light like lightning towards the three stars in Orion – Tepeu, Gugumatz and Huyubkaan (named after the three creator gods) and also known as the Hearthstones of Creation.

I asked Wandering Wolf to explain more. He replied enigmatically: 'Every moon, every day, every wind they walk and also pass. The time was come for me to praise the magnificence of the three creators – Tepeu, Gugumatz and Huyubkaan. The time was come when the cosmic measure could be found in the sun. The time was come when the gods of time, prisoners of the stars, would look upon us.' Then he smiled and said that I should not ask so many questions but continue to meditate upon the stone turtles of Quiriguá. In this way I would not 'make up' stories with anxious probing, but access the secrets of time known to the shamans, in a gentle, wise fashion.

## The turtle

The image of a turtle plays a vital part in the mysteries surrounding the beginning and end of this present Fourth World creation. The constellation we know as Orion is for the Maya the Turtle that swims in the celestial 'sea'. This is depicted in stone, on pottery, in the *Popul Vuh* and the remaining codices that record astronomical, astrological and mythical events. Linda Schele, the skilled decoder of Maya texts, says in her book *Maya Cosmos* that the phrase used in almost all classical-period creation texts is: 'On 8 Kumku *was seen* the first image of the turtle, the great god lord.' At Quiriguá the text glyphs read that this act of creation and the placing of the Three Hearthstones was not done by one god alone, but by a number who discussed and planned the great work together.

In addition to the giant, stone, hybrid turtle/human carvings at Quiriguá, there is a very beautifully made, double-headed stone turtle on the grand plaza at Copan, Honduras. A tall stele (Number C) of the Copan priest-king '18 Rabbit' (whose real name is Waxaklahun-Ubah-K'awil), which was dedicated around AD730, stands contemplating this turtle. No doubt 18 Rabbit knew of the creation story of First Father, the maize god Hun-nal-ye, being reborn from a turtle shell that split in two and who thus regarded this creature as sacred. Perhaps the juxtaposition of his image with the turtle was intended to show him personally as the reborn maize god.

In order that I should understand more about the mat of time and the turtle, Wandering Wolf told me to undertake a vision quest with the creation stories. He told me to pronounce the words '*Ix Azal Voh*',

*The rebirth of the maize god from a cracked turtle shell. Image derived from an original plate.*

which mean 'Seek the message behind what I would "see"'. I decided to do the quest in an unusual way. First I arranged an overnight stay on the remote island in the middle of Lake Yaxha, in the Guatemalan Petén rainforest. Here there is an unrestored Maya sacred site that has a very special power point within it. Armed with little but my hammock, water, mosquito net and a mirror, I embarked on the hour-long boat ride to reach it. Asking the boatman to return at the same time the next day, I started through the trees to find the place. I knew that I wanted to see the threads of time from the past behind me and the threads of time in front of me.

I lay in my hammock and used the mirror. Shifting my perception into a different 'gear' I gazed into the mirror, seeking to bring the knowledge of the past into the future. I continued to gaze as the sun dropped below the horizon: darkness fell quickly and dramatically as it does in the tropics. Fighting sleep, yet open to dreaming, I continued gazing into the clear mirror until dawn broke, greenish yellow hues suffusing my heightened consciousness as the sun broke through the trees. All night I had been calling upon my jaguar power animal, my *nagual*, to enter the dreamtime to guide me. But my rational mind was not aware of any new insights and I felt cold, stiff and disappointed. Enjoying the warmth from the gathering sunlight I peered into the dark patches of thicker clumps of palm and undergrowth. Suddenly behind me in the bushes a twig broke, a leaf rustled and close to my left shoulder I heard a deep animal sigh. The mirror clouded as I looked back at it, nothing was revealed – yet inwardly I knew more about the threads of time and that my jaguar guide had been with me all night.

I returned later by boat to the comparative civilization of the large, airy jungle lodge *palapa* on the edge of the lake. Sipping a cool margarita, I reflected upon the experiences of the night and my encounter with Jaguar, lord of the Underworld portals. I understood that the creation stories are highly complex, but the events at the start of this creation go something like this:

1. First Father, also known as the maize god Hun-Nal-Ye, was reborn from the cracked turtle shell.
2. He set the Three Hearthstones in a place called Lying-down-Sky, where it was dark. Then the image of this became visible.
3. He then entered – or became – the sky (a) by raising the World Tree; (b) by creating a 'house' in the north; and (c) by making eight partitions or cardinal compass points to the cosmos.
4. The seven gods set the Three Hearthstones into their positions.

With the World Tree raised up as the Axis Mundi, the axis of the world, all the stars and constellations appeared to move around it. I say 'appeared' because, although it seemed to be a circular movement, the Maya were also aware of the wavelike progression of our galaxy during an approximate 26,000-year cycle (known as the Platonic Year), or the precession of the equinoxes. This progression is the *spiral* that enables us here on Earth to measure time durations from the movement of the celestial bodies. For this present Fourth Creation, the movement of our galaxy and the precession of the equinoxes was a starting point for humanity to understand the significance of time in the greater plan of creation. Since the first markers were laid over 5,000 years ago at such places as Carnac, Stonehenge, Silbury Hill and Giza, the human race has been increasingly fed with vital clues to understand this portal of time into the universe. It could be said that understanding the precession of the equinoxes was, for humans, the *start of time*. Now we are very near the *end of time* and what will occur then is the subject of the last chapter.

## Medicine wheels and the three worlds

During my journeys I met a number of teachers. The right person would always seem to emerge from nowhere ready to fit another part of the jigsaw puzzle into place. Some of the most powerful events occurred when I had the opportunity to participate around the sacred fire laid out as a medicine wheel. It was always a great honour for me, a non-Maya, to be invited, especially since I had very little knowledge of the celebrant's first language, and my knowledge of Spanish – his second language – was limited. Despite this, it became apparent during such ceremonies that word recognition is not as important as listening to the hypnotic count of days and retelling of myths that are encoded within the rhythm and musicality of the shaman's voice.

To the Maya and others of indigenous nations throughout the Land of the Sun, a simple circle represents the medicine wheel. Each time the

*A Maya medicine wheel. A modern interpretation of the four directions and the four corn cobs that produced the four 'root races' of humanity: red in east; white in north; blue/black in west; yellow in south.*

Maya shamans light a sacred fire, they first draw such a circle on the ground. They orientate four arrow shapes to the cardinal compass points by observing the position of Father Sun. Normally the wheel is first divided into four sections. The *Popul Vuh* tells us the 'sky-Earth' emerged through the actions of Hun-Nal-Ye when 'the fourfold siding, fourfold cornering, measuring, fourfold staking, halving the cord, stretching the cord in the sky, on the Earth, the four sides, the four corners,' was completed.

A medicine wheel symbolically describes a movement of energy or consciousness. When its power is brought into use in a person's life, energy, whether for some practical or spiritual work, moves around the wheel in a particular way. It is always initiated by arising in the east (birthplace of Father Sun), purified in the north (place of the shaman), deepened and understood in the west (place of night and the ancestors), and released or seeded in the south (place of ripening). In this way a continual cycle of development is experienced.

Medicine wheels have certain animal *naguals* and colours connected with them. The colours and correspondences change according to the spiritual orientation of the tribe or nation, and they represent some of the guiding forces on the Earth plane of existence. On the Maya wheel the correspondences are usually:

- Red in the east – the crocodile and snake or serpent.
- White in the north – the dog and jaguar.
- Blue or black in the west – the deer, monkey and eagle.
- Yellow in the south – the lizard, rabbit and vulture.

Medicine wheels also confirm to the initiated that other hidden dimensions or worlds called 'heavens' and 'underworlds' extend above and below this world, the Earth plane. The Maya have chosen to divide the world of the heavens into 13 'layers' above the Earth plane with the Underworld below it in nine 'layers' (each of these having four directions too). The World Tree, which stands in the very centre of the wheel, sends its branches into the heavens and its roots into the underworlds. These three worlds and medicine wheels, when understood not as flat representations but multidimensionally, become doorways into other levels of understanding.

It was believed that each night the Lords of the Underworlds (called Xibalba in the *Popul Vuh*) helped the setting sun to pass through their realms and ascend again in the east at sunrise. Maya scribes and stonemasons have shown the diurnal and annual movements of the sun as snakes and also as Itzamna in his guise as a two-headed, reptilian celestial monster, encircling the Earth's surface. Contemplating this, I suddenly realized that the connection between the heavens and underworlds is not only the World Tree, but also the serpent of time that spirals around its trunk. With such numerous heavens and underworlds existing, clearly part of the Maya fascination for time lay in an endeavour to seek dimensions beyond time in any one life. Ultimately, the search took the shaman-priest-kings/queens through time to other dimensions of being.

While shamanic processes can open the portals, for many people it is vital that we enter those worlds prepared and empowered by the divine light of creation. For this reason it is important for those embarking upon a shamanic path in the modern world to learn to meditate. Regular meditation strengthens and enhances global consciousness in an increasingly dark and despondent world. Meditation is quite different to prayer, because prayer is mostly petitional, asking of something, whereas meditation is listening and making oneself available for service to creation. In this way it is possible to experience the cosmovision and worlds of the Maya shamans in a multidimensional universe, beyond this planet, where the lines of time are quite different.

## Meditation on the 13 heavens

You may like to use the following words as a meditation. Consider them slowly – they may help to bring you into harmony with Maya cosmovision.

Take a moment to move off the Earth. Imagine being outside normal dimensions of space and time and see the world as an astronaut might from beyond the fragile safety bubble we call the Earth.

Look down on our beautiful blue-green planet. With detachment from human emotion, as if you are an embodiment of the creator, gain an overview of the process that humanity is going through at this time.

Then see it as part of a much greater cosmic plan like a huge wheel spinning through many aeons. Imagine that particles of light making up a rainbow-like Earth aura at the north and south poles are charged with strands of consciousness. They swirl around, sending messages to and from the stars. Look again, with awakened eyes, see dancing lines creating patterns evoked by complex planetary and lunar orbits.

Trace these patterns as threads through time, weaving our human past with our possible futures. Listen now with different ears and hear sounds that the ancients called the 'music of the spheres'.

See our Earth held in a tender embrace by all the bright woven threads of light energy as she turns majestically. Then a dark shadow of night draws across her western face and dawn lights the east.

Hold this image in your consciousness whenever life seems difficult, for these are some of the insights of the 13 heavens.

## Practical summary of the doorway to the three worlds

1. Study the medicine wheels from a number of Central and Native American traditions and try to work with them in a practical way. For example, close your eyes and stand facing the east at dawn. The threads of time are coming towards you from your future and passing behind you to your ancestors in the west. Your *nagual* is at your left hand to the north, the place of the shamans. To your right, in the south, is the flowering fruitful earth. Understand what it really feels like to be standing in the centre.

2. Regularly use meditation techniques to support your spiritual path.

3. Contact your *nagual* and/or your power animal and ask for guidance to learn

# CHAPTER 8

# Portal of Fire

The red wild bees are in the east.
A large red blossom is their cup.
The red plumeria is their flower.
The white wild bees are in the north.
The white pachca is their flower.
A large white blossom is their cup.
The black wild bees are in the west.
The black laurel flower is their flower.
A large black blossom is their cup.
The yellow wild bees are in the south.
A large Kancol blossom is their flower and their cup.

'Wild Bees', from the Ritual of the Bacabs, the four beings that hold the four corners of the world in the measuring and quartering

## Guatemala

Present-day Guatemala is a country barely touched by materialism. Away from its capital, broad open hill tops sweep across vast areas that gave the ancient Maya living in sacred centres like Mixco Viejo an uninterrupted view of their lands towards the mysterious Central Highlands. It is a region that has some of the most impressive volcanoes on Earth. High mountains, almost always shrouded in mist, are home to brightly clothed villagers, who appear as vibrant as tropical birds and flowers. Quiriguá, with its curious carved stones, lies far to the west, nearly on the Honduran border. Farther to the north, the town

of Sayache in the Petén region is the last frontier between habitation and the UNESCO-declared Biosphere Reserve, stretching to the borders of Belize and Mexico.

In the very small reserve created around the sacred site of Ceibal on the Río Pasion, Petén, there are great ceiba trees, forest giants with buttress roots reaching up the trunks some 5 metres/16 feet or more – standing invincible despite the ravages of loggers all around. Increasing numbers of *campesinos* (land settlers), particularly along the border with Mexico, are stripping the forest bare to cultivate small fields of maize; and attempts at replanting trees are mainly with short-lived pines for commercial use, a process that speaks loudly of unsustainable land management.

Other larger areas, their forests cut down, are grazed by herds of gaunt cattle for the fast-food industries of First World countries. The National Council of Protected Areas along with international conservation organizations are endeavouring to help the situation; but village elders of these regions in the Petén explained to me how powerless they feel against the multinational logging and oil exploration companies that are ripping the heart from the forest and changing traditional Maya life for ever. The best I could do was tell the elders that I cared deeply, and that I would try to do something about it. I made a silent prayer that I would commit myself to saving the trees that they hold sacred.

The actions of land settlers and logging companies are a far cry from the Maya of the ancient cities, who operated a perfect 'permaculture system' (one that emphasizes renewable natural resources) of forest agriculture, planting food and fibre crops under the fruit and nut trees. They kept turkeys and small mammals and cultivated breadnut trees. This is in accordance with the Maya saying: 'He who cuts down the trees as he pleases, cuts short his own life'.

Journeying alone into remote areas is not to be recommended, since environmentalists are treated harshly if they campaign against the loggers or try to stop the looting of precious stelae from remote unguarded Maya cities. Two environmentalists were reportedly shot dead only days before I arrived. However, I felt safe when in the company of Wandering Wolf: we had already travelled many hundreds of kilometres together over a period of 13 days. Each day we undertook a fire ceremony with local shamans, who act as the guardians for particular Maya sacred cities and well-hidden shrines and who are familiar with the portals that have been used by their ancestors for centuries.

## Shamanic fire ceremony

Fire ceremonies may take place on just about any day. However, a particularly important ceremony called the New Fire Ceremony, Tunben K'ak, is conducted once every 52 years by Maya priests (the Ah-Men or Ah-Kij). It is timed to occur when the Pleiades return to the same place on the zenith of the horizon above the sun, and in our possible lifetimes it is scheduled for the year 2021. In times past the New Fire Ceremony was accompanied by rebuilding of temples and pyramids, the smashing of old pottery vessels and dowsing of all fires. The new fire would be carefully prepared and ceremonially lit from the light of Father Sun at midday and carried throughout the region to each important place; it was even used to relight domestic fires, which were set among the three stones in the hearth.

Guatemalan Maya regard the sacred fire as their spiritual nourishment, for it gives them communication with the creator as well as with invisible beings. Smoke from the fire and burning copal incense carries their prayers, both for personal needs and for the world, as they offer themselves to the creator. Only those elders and shamans chosen through their birth destiny ascertained by astrologers are able to perform the fire ceremony. On the day of a person's birth the elders say what qualities he or she will have: perhaps one who does good (a H'men); or one who heals or transforms negative energy to positive (a D'dzac Yah); or perhaps he or she will become a midwife, a great musician, a shaman, a daykeeper, a great artist, a healer, a fire priestess (Ix-zuhuy-K'aak), or even a much-revered man of knowledge – a Halach Uink shaman.

Within Guatemalan traditions, shamans can specialize in the calendars or as singers of chants, prayers and rituals of the calendars; or they may become marriage spokespersons, able to memorize long passages concerned with betrothal and marriage. Midwives, who are also considered to be shamans, and the healer shamans (sometimes called 'bonesetters') use traditional massage and herbal remedies. A spiritualist shaman (male or female) is considered the most powerful, treading a path that crosses the thin boundary between shamanism and its darker counterpart by confronting the sorcerer, who uses spiritual power malevolently. To ward off such possibility, various herbs are used during fire ceremonies, the most common being rue, rosemary, basil, skunk root and types of copal resin from trees. These herbs serve a protective function around the sacred circle.

People versed in old customs regard the element of fire as the way to speak to and honour the creator. Wandering Wolf told me about the ceremony, saying that the Maya do not have to use special equipment or a church, for the creator is with them wherever they are. The fire is a purifier and cleanser, it feeds their spirit and gives them guidance. Wandering Wolf added: 'Only wise men and women can read the fire. They understand the fire, how it goes, if it turns to the north, if it turns to the south, if it goes to the east, if it goes to the west. They know what it means if it spirals to the left or right, what position it forms, what kind of sound it gives off, what sparks it makes. This is the way of reading the fire. It is only wise elders who have communication like this. Anybody else might get burned. Other people see the fire and don't know what is there.'

Maya shamans are not unique in holding the fire with high regard. The Huichol shamans of Mexico say the fire is their grandfather, and the first thing they do in the morning is to tell the fire their dreams. In Lakota tradition, the fire is used in sweat lodges, where it is honoured during the ceremony. Mongolians say that the centre of their home, where the fire is burnt, is the most sacred place because it is the dwelling of the daughter of Father Heaven, Golomto. To them the fire is seen as the centre of the universe. In north European Celtic traditions the hearth is the place where the veil between the worlds is thinner and communication with other dimensions can happen, even where once upon a time, old stories were told to children around the kitchen fire on dark, stormy nights.

Traditional Guatemalan calendar shamans use an unbroken count of days as the central focus in fire ceremonies to maintain the threads of time in correct order. These threads, which tie us to the past while spinning us forward into the future, are actually seen by the shamans, intertwined with a person s own luminous fibres in the web of life. This enables them to read the threads of time during the fire ceremony in order to be able to prophesy future events. To clarify this point, imagine that the mat of creation has an overlay of the web of life representing all life on this planet. Woven through the two of them are our personal luminous fibres that are part of our auric field and the threads of time (see diagram on opposite page).

Being present at a Maya fire ceremony is a great honour, and respectful silence is required while the preparations take place. It is a rare privilege to photograph the preparation process, and to take pictures of the actual ceremony would be unthinkable.

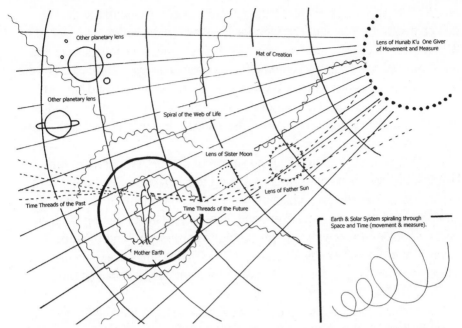

*The ceremonial 'Pop' mat of creation overlaid by the web of life, interwoven with the threads of time.*

### Diary extract: on the edge of the world, Lake Atitlan, Guatemala

From the village we were taken along a well-worn track that skirted the razor-like edge of the cliff on one side and backyards of small homes on the other. Eventually the track petered out, and, led by Wandering Wolf, we began a brisk climb over rocky outcrops and precipitous ledges, where there was nothing between sky and the shimmering lake below. Keeping up with him was more than hazardous for me: I was a mere 50-year-old, but suffering the effects of vertigo, while he was 78 years young, showing his vigour by his scrambling up the rocks like a kid goat. We reached our destination, a rockface blackened by the flames of years of sacred fires, and waited patiently while a villager finished his own fire ceremony.

Wandering Wolf and his assistants, Rosemarie, a fire priestess, and Elizabet, Keeper of the Sacred Bundle, started preparations. First they carefully cleared the area, for the villager had, much to their dismay, just sacrificed a chicken in a *brugere* (black magic) way. However, confident that their ceremony would open the right portal to the other worlds, they proceeded. The fire becomes a living, burning medicine wheel and so, to begin with, a circle was drawn on the ground in sugar, followed by a cross of the directions and arrows to the cardinal points. Brightly coloured sugar filled in each direction: red in the east, white in the north, blue in the west and yellow in the south. Rosemarie carefully laid a circle of pink forest flowers around the sugar, each flower facing inwards, offering itself to the fire. Then a pile of aromatic, *ocote* kindling wood was placed in the centre and loaded up with round pellets of copal incense. Thin, sweet-smelling candles were laid down around this centrepiece and gifts of chocolate, cigars and biscuits were scattered on top. Wandering Wolf saw that all was complete and started his prayers. As the fire was lit, each of us were handed more coloured candles, brown crystalline pieces of *pom* (incense), sugary biscuits and sesame seeds to give as personal offerings.

Carefully watching portents in the smoke of the fire, Wandering Wolf handed a lemon to everyone and told them to rub it over their bodies then throw it into the gathering flames in order to cleanse themselves and release any problems in their bodies. For good measure, he took a bunch of green herbs, sprinkled them with copious amounts of *ron* (rum) and brushed it vigorously around the circle of participants. The burning sugar, incense and candle wax began to create voluminous clouds of dense smoke as the traditional Kiché Maya count of days began.

Prayers were intoned and offerings to each day thrown into the fire by everyone present in turn as a participative act. Rosemarie explained the colours of the candles to me: red to honour the rising sun; white the air that we do not see; black the night or death; yellow the seed and the physical world; green for the world of nature; light blue the heavens; pink for love and to overcome illness; purple to assist eradication of bad thoughts; and dark blue for abundance and money. I began to find it difficult to hold my three-dimensional awareness in the circle as the fragrant copal incense opened the portals to the threads of time – the continuing count of days became a mantra that swept me along an ancient path, only returning to the worldly dimension momentarily as the word '*si k'in*' was murmured rhythmically by those standing in the circle and as sesame seeds were thrown on the fire, crackling noisily.

It seemed that my legs would no longer hold me upright and I sank to my knees. A moment in time passed and, like a vision serpent of old, a picture in brilliant colours of light emerged before me that showed the Earth in torment. Mountains were cracking apart, volcanoes and tidal waves swept over the land and I implored the creator to understand that so many people *do* care for the planet, that we want to live in cooperation with the spirits of our brothers the trees and animals and that we pray for a graceful transition at the end of this world creation.

The count of days was continuing and the time threads once again were ceremonially reestablished by the smoking fire on the world medicine wheel. I slowly became conscious of the others around me in the circle and got to my feet, purified myself and my crystals in the smoke, and jumped across the dwindling fire.

# THE FOUR DIRECTIONS OF THE MAYA
# MEDICINE WHEEL (YUCATEC)

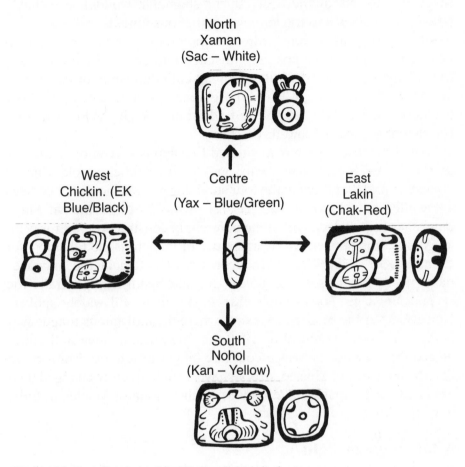

North
Xaman
(Sac – White)

West
Chickin. (EK
Blue/Black)

Centre
(Yax – Blue/Green)

East
Lakin
(Chak-Red)

South
Nohol
(Kan – Yellow)

*Glyphs of the four directions of the Maya medicine wheel.*

## Maya glyphs

Early Maya languages were written in the form of hieroglyphs – 'glyphs' for short. Present-day shamans say that the glyphs they are able to read (because some are in old languages) give various facts and dates, as well as the ancient shamans' ecstatic 'language of light', which they saw during vision-inducing rites. These visions burnt so strongly into the consciousness of the shamans of old that they were able to record them in plasterwork and stone carvings.

This description is also in accord with the Western interpretation of the word hieroglyph, meaning 'holy carving'. In Maya epigraphy, a glyph indicates a logogram, phonetic sign or compound sign. The glyphs are extremely complex because of the different ideas that they

can convey. They can be: phonetic (indicating speech sounds); logographic (depicting ideas); semantic (giving meanings); pictographic (depicting objects in the everyday or shamanic worlds); or syllabic (showing syllables and the joining together of sounds).

Additionally, as I have already mentioned about the spoken languages, when the glyphs are translated into one of the present-day Maya languages, they can often be read either forwards or backwards for another meaning. It is in these readings that today's wisdom teachers and shamans are able to understand the glyphs in a way that is different to scholars and researchers.

Epigraphic researchers who studied the glyphs carved on stone say that they are mostly written in one of three different old Cholan languages and that three of the four surviving glyphic 'books' or codices are written in a form of Yucatec. All of the 30 or so known Maya languages (not dialects) are quite different in construction to European languages: and spoken words make use of numerous glottal stops, for example 'K'in' or 'Bey t' K'an'. In present-day Guatemala, the languages have mostly been used and preserved, and Spanish is generally the second language. For example, Kiché Mayan is still widely spoken. However, over the border in Mexico, where the indigenous tongue was being lost, it was as recent as 1999 that the Yucatan state authorities agreed that Yucatec language could be taught in schools. Throughout the Maya regions of Mexico, people have even frequently changed their Maya names to Spanish alternatives, such as Juan or Miguel, in order to gain work and social respect.

## A language of light

From a shamanic perspective, some of the most interesting giant *te-tun* stones ('tree stones' or stelae) or carved panels 'announce' their story in one of four different ways. These are:

• Glyphic-encoded messages.
• Speech scrolls coming from the mouths of the person portrayed.
• A red axe symbolically piercing the third-eye, forehead chakra of inner vision.
• A vision serpent manifesting in front of the person undertaking a shamanic journey.

Such is the power of this imagery that present-day shamans who look at the stone carvings or glyphs are propelled into journeys to find deeper meaning.

All photographs in this section by MIKHAIL

1  *Typical stepped pyramid. Stairway to the cosmos. Beautiful by day, awesome by moonlight. El Mundo Perdido (The Lost World), Tikal, Guatemala.*

2  *Families may leave their villages as early as 3am to reach this typical market. Antigua, Guatemala.*

3 *"In my life I have seen much."*
*Old woman in Panajachel, Guatemala.*

4 *Ceremonial planting of Henequén, attended by Hopi, Navaho, Inuit and Maya curandero to commemorate teaching of Maya language in schools. Near Mérida, Mexico.*

5 *Maya woman in Antigua, Guatemala, carrying the Threads of Time.*

**6** *Arriving for ceremony, the Shaman El Maestro Wandering Wolf commences his sacred work by asking permission of the Ancestors to teach at Tikal, Guatemala.*

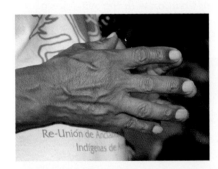

**7** *Clasped hands of Wandering Wolf express the sacred shamanic path he has walked for 78 years.*

**8** *Preparing for fire ceremony at Copan, Honduras: Shaman El Maestro Wandering Wolf, Fire Priestess and Keeper of the Sacred Bundle.*

9 Temples of the Sun and the Cross, together with the Temple of the Foliated Cross (out of sight), mirroring the three Hearthstones of Creation with the 'witz' portal mountain behind. Nah Chan (Palenque), Mexico.

10 Temple of the Foliated Cross, Nah Chan (Palenque), Mexico, showing its unique architectural features.

11 *Lacondon Maya, guardians of the tombs, selling arrows and rain sticks at the entrance to Nah Chan, Mexico.*

12 *Serpent heads at bottom of balustrades. Pyramid of Chichen Itza, Mexico.*

13 *Some 40,000 people gather each year at the Pyramid of Ku-kuul-kaan,*
*awaiting the moment when the Serpent of Light descends.*

14 *Elder Hunbatz Men, Daykeeper Itza in Mayan tradition, teaching a group of*
*Solar Initiates at Aké in 1998.*

15 *Full-size quartz crystal skull. Used in ceremony to give teachings about the light encodements in our own skulls. Chichen Itza, March 2000.*

16 *Solar Initiate Directors from seven of the worldwide Maya Mysteries Schools on the temple steps, after the Serpent in the Sky activation. Aké, near Mérida, Mexico, 1998.*

**17** *Bat carving, approximately 75cm tall. "The Lords of Xibalba demanded that the Hero Twins survive for a night in the terrible House of the Bats". Percent sign on its pectoral may be a reference to our sun crossing the Dark Rift (Xibalba) in 2012.*

**18** *Two entwined serpents adorn the ballcourt marker at Chichen Itza, Mexico. At one time in history, the ballgame was a sacred ceremony in which the ball represented our Father Sun.*

19 *Lake Atitlan, Guatemala, mirror of the sky, ringed by active volcanoes.*

20 *The Feathered Serpent appears in the sky at dawn near Tulum on the Caribbean coast, Mexico.*

21 *Medicine wheel painted by the author showing corn cobs of four directions representing the four root races of this Creation emanating from the Galactic 'G' spiralling outwards from Hunab K'u.*

22 *Example of stone creature (zoomorph) at Quirigua, Guatemala. Measures approx 3.5m x 2m x 1.5m.*

23 Close-up of bearded face emerging from the jaws of a stone creature (zoomorph), Quirigua, Guatemala.

24 The Monkey scribe carried wisdom from the previous Creation. Part of an initiatory path at Copan, Honduras. Note 'T' and emanations from the copal incense censor being held in left hand.

25 Preparations completed, with the fire laid in the form of a Medicine Wheel. Fire ceremony about to commence. Copan, Honduras.

26 *Sacred fire before lighting. Offerings include biscuits, chocolate, sweets, incense and cigars. Rum, sesame seeds and other appropriate 'payments' are made as the ceremony proceeds.*

27 *Author's personal 'bloodletting ceremony' as wild macaw (symbolically Father Sun) has more than a 'word' in her ear!*

28 *Thirteenth of the dynastic Shaman/ Priest/Kings Uaxac Lahun Ubac K'awil. Main plaza at Copan, Honduras.*

29 *Shamanic initiation at the platform of the double-headed Jaguar, Uxmal, Mexico in 1995.*

30 *Morning mists dancing across the mirror-like water of Rio Pasion, Guatemala.*

31 *Numerous 'T' carvings in and around the temples of Nah Chan (Palenque), Mexico.*

32  *Two of the four winged Balaams from the Pleiades. Part of an awesome restoration project recently completed at Balaam K'u, Mexico.*

33  *Stone turtle-like creature over 2m long in main plaza of Copan, Honduras. Note human-type fingernails.*

34  *Ballcourt at Mixco Viejo, Guatemala. Macaw bird ballcourt markers symbolise Father Sun.*

35  *Magic of the forest at Ceibal, Guatemala.*

I also became aware of other connections beyond the obvious ones that the Ahob (rulers) had with the cosmic Maya when I examined many examples of special stone benches with glyphs for the planets carved upon them. They are known as 'sky-band benches', and there are some beautifully presented and restored examples of them, particularly in the museum at Copan in Honduras. The Ahob depicted on painted pots are frequently shown sitting upon such benches, indicating their close association with these planets and how they drew their power from them.

In most of the large classic-period cities (AD300–900) glyphic inscriptions were recorded on the *te-tun* (stelae). Epigraphers are gradually decoding those that have survived robbers and the rigours of time. Modern shamans and wisdom teachers understand them in a different shamanic way. Gradually we understand what they have to tell us because the glyphs speak to each one of us in a way we can comprehend. For example, to the shamans they reveal visions of light, other worlds and what has existed and what is yet to exist. To the epigraphers and archaeologists they show dates and dynasties. We each see what we need to see. Certainly my experiences of drawing glyphs from weather-worn stones have been profound. I entered into the hearts and minds of the sculptor scribes after sitting for many hours in searing heat with beads of sweat threatening to drop onto my paper.

## An ancient teaching

During my journeys in the Mayalands, several exceptional people have been my teachers. Some were the old and sick I saw begging in the streets of Mérida (the capital of Yucatan); others were the smiling women and respected Maya council elders who greeted me at the beginning of ceremonies, particularly at Chichén Itzá. Other inspired shamanic teachers who can be named are: Wandering Wolf, with whom I journeyed in Guatemala, undergoing many of the experiences in this book; and Elder Hunbatz Men, who initiated me into the Solar Sovereign Order of Chichén Itzá and gave me solar initiations in the temples of Yucatan and Chiapas. One of Elder Hunbatz Men's frequent sayings is: 'We must understand the past in order to walk into the future'. With this in mind, I shall give you an idea of what a shamanic journey could have been like in the past. To undertake this journey, just read the following paragraphs slowly, every so often closing your eyes and taking yourself into the time-thread-tapestry of images I am creating, by opening the portals of your own imagination.

## Snake-eye stones: a shamanic journey

Cast yourself back in time and prepare for an initiation into the underworld through the portals at Nah Chan (Palenque). High above you, on the green slopes are many people dressed in simple, loose white tunics walking up towards the Temple of the Cross. Its innermost temple, the *pibna* or 'underworld house', contains a beautiful image of a Maya cross, which is watched over by a shaman at the entrance, ceremonially dressed in jaguar skin and smoking a sacred pipe. Standing behind, as his double, is a carved image of a shaman. Next to him is a stone panel showing the World Tree at the centre of the world supporting the heavens and rising from the red-masked Great Earth Monster. Twin branches of the tree hold the double-headed serpent bar, one of the primary symbols of kingship, with the Celestial Bird, Itzamna, perched on top. You see, even at this distance, luminous golden threads of energy emanating from the shaman's forehead, seeming to tell you not to follow the masses up to this temple to watch preparations for a ceremony but to seek your own underworld initiation.

You pass by some workers still building a square platform of great cosmic significance between the three temples on the hills, each adorned with stucco reliefs painted with natural pigments of red, green, yellow, black and blue. You have seen these dazzling colours vibrate in harmony with the brilliant hues of tropical animals, birds, flowers and butterflies by day, and dancing shadows of lamps, fires and moon by night. As you start to walk up the long flight of steps to the vast palace, a young woman takes your hand, offers you a dark, sticky *balché* drink from a gourd cup and leads you past residential rooms, draped with woven cloth and echoing with the sweet sounds of children playing. You are taken into a maze of corridors and rooms deep beneath the palace. Walking through them is disorientating as the corridors twist and turn and the stones underfoot become slippery with damp. In the dim light you can see that some of the walls are painted and richly decorated with masked faces of ancestors, jaguars, toads and crocodiles.

Now alone, for the young woman has vanished, you eventually reach a passage, painted green, that spirals into the shape of the letter 'G'. You know that this green colour signifies the very heart of heaven, the most sacred portal under the palace, and you stand shivering in an unaccustomed chill. A beam of light pierces through a crack in the masonry high above your head, catches your attention and illuminates a thin, black, venomous snake with orange markings. Shocked by its sudden appearance, you stand frozen, not daring to move a muscle as the eyes of the snake piercingly fix you. Unexpectedly it makes a quick withdrawal into a very narrow fissure in the stones and for some moments you remain transfixed.

Then time and space have no meaning as you are reduced to the size and shape of a snake and drawn into the fissure; and then you experience the roughness of rock alternating with damp lichens that, through your snakelike eyes, you see as a myriad colours. You turn and twist uncomfortably in your new body as you are pulled deeper into the rocks beneath the palace. You know it would only take a small shift in the dimensions for you to remain in this place forever, crawling in the underworlds, locked in the stones. But by a supreme effort of gathering all your energy together, you assert your humanness and as quickly as you entered the rocks you emerge into the beam of sunlight again. The ingredients in the *balché* drink that the young woman gave you now give out their secondary effects and you are able to reflect upon your experience with heightened human superconsciousness. You have entered the Underworld and, like the Hero Twins of myth, have returned alive. You have tasted death by becoming a snake and have risen through it to an understanding of the heart of heaven.

Walking as quickly as you dare, you ascend the sloping tunnels. You are exhausted and finally allow the sacred drink to sedate you into a dream state. Sinking into the corner of a small stone room and drawing a woven cotton cloth around your shoulders, you feel you are wrapping yourself securely in the threads of time themselves.

## Power of the nagual: how to increase and hold energy

The shamanic initiation in the last section will have given you a clue about how capturing the full essence of humanness can counteract the pull of the underworlds. People who are on a spiritual path are able to use techniques that they have learnt in their training for whenever times are difficult or a supreme effort of will is required. Their aura or luminous cocoon burns bright. They know how to gather its luminous fibres into coherent patterns of light that stream through and enhance their chakras, in turn energizing the physical body. They also know how to hold their assemblage point in altered positions and still have enough energy to return it to its normal location when they have finished their shamanic journeying or undertaken difficult tasks.

We can capture energy in a number of different ways – bodily, mentally and spiritually – from the food we eat, the way we breathe or the spiritual focus we maintain. Shamans from a number of different cultures also say that when we are born into the world we come with a predetermined reserve of energy that has been influenced by the way we were conceived. If we were conceived in passionate love then our energy levels will burn strongly; but if our conception was without love and care, then this will militate against a high energy reserve.

In the shamanic initiation, seekers become their power animal or *nagual* – they do not fight against it initially, but when too close an association begins to feel dangerous, they summon all their human energy power to bring them out of the Underworld. Travelling between this world, the Maya nine underworlds and the 13 heavens using the threads of time is a path that is difficult for most. But some travellers have made such a burning impression on the thread that they can move along it at will. Why do we remember Pakal Votan today? Or why do those interested in Egypt remember Tutankhamun? Even through such long periods of time the impression they made on the thread remains strong and it carries their memories into the present and on into the future. It was for this very reason that Pakal Votan had the so-called Telektonon, or speaking tube, installed in his tomb. As a physical reminder of the thread of time from the Underworld and the Nine Lords of Time who adorned his tomb, it connected him to the past. The Telektonon was, and is, also the path from his present to the future. It was specially constructed for him to travel through the small temple atop the Temple of the Inscriptions. Thus it gave, and gives, access to the stars, the 13 heavens and the future of the immortal part of his two-part soul, enabling its ascension to the 13 heavens after a sojourn in the underworlds.

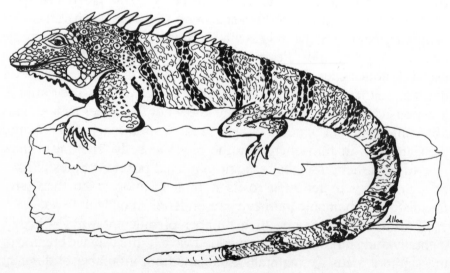

*The guardian animal of Uxmal, Yucatan – almost one metre/three feet long from its nose to the tip of its tail.*

Another interesting pointer to the ability of ancient peoples to transcend death is strong anecdotal evidence that on the occasion of the Tutankhamun Exhibition at the British Museum in London in the 1990s, a black panther was seen a number of times in the nearby city streets. A black panther is Tutankhamun's *nagual* and so it was that he shapeshifted into this creature and passed forward through the threads of time to the future. The amount of energy required to do such acts beyond the portal of death is phenomenal. How many of us will even be remembered in a mere 500 years time? However, we each still have the potential to achieve this kind of development, but it requires total commitment of the highest order to achieve the heightened levels of vibration that enable shapeshifting, especially of the physical body.

One of the main ways that we lose energy is what can be described as cultural hypnosis — that is the conditioning that is imposed on us by the society in which we live. If we rely upon society, the outside world, for a sense of identity, rather than taking guidance from our inner soul, it gives away an enormous amount of personal power. Such cultural hypnosis can take several forms, any one of which will cause energy loss. They include:

1. Observing social norms in order to be part of the in group and be accepted.
2. Religion.
3. Social structures and politics.
4. Sex.
5. Family image and responsibilities.

Be aware that some elements of the above may be necessary for you as an individual, and that some may not. If you wish, there are numerous ways that can be used to change cultural hypnosis in order to increase personal energy. Below are a number of suggestions for achieving liberating amounts of energy expressed in modern shamanic terms.

- Primarily increase your energy levels by living an authentic life close to nature.
- Devise personal ceremonies.
- Follow medicine wheel teachings.
- Use the 13-day count of days or an alternative calendar such as the T'zolk'in.
- Regard death as your ally – living every day as if it was your last.

- Honour your ancestors.
- Stop the demands of the world and dream a new reality – use shamanic journeying.
- Contact your power animal or *nagual*.
- Find a new vision and purpose – undertake vision quests and meditations, especially in nature.
- Associate with like-minded people who do not drain your personal energy levels.
- Step into your own power – find your soul purpose.
- Use drumming, trance dancing, singing, dancing the four directions/elements, ecstatic sex, and teaching and sharing your wisdom with others.

Undertaking ceremony and ritual creates sacred space and time, increases personal energy and, by enacting a rite in the outer world, it gives inner power to the soul. A time-honoured method among the Plains Indians from the Land of the Sun is to build a sweat lodge in which to do a sacred cleansing ceremony. It is usually a low, round structure of bent wood covered with blankets or canvas in which has been dug a small central pit where red hot stones are placed. Large quantities of water and herbs are sprinkled onto the fire during the ceremony to produce copious amounts of steam. It is customary to set up an altar outside the door to the east.

To these indigenous people the sweat lodge represents the body of the turtle that swims across the heavens (as the Orion constellation) and the altar is regarded as the turtle's head. At the same time, the lodge is experienced as the womb of Mother Earth and participants often describe a feeling of dying and being reborn during the course of the ceremony. The Maya today also use steam and herbal sweat baths, but not in the same ceremonial way. Their appreciation of the meaning of the turtle for the most part, with the exception of the wisdom teachers and shamans, continues to be locked in stone, their heritage having been taken from them traumatically during the times of terror and hardship caused by the Spanish conquest. Their social disempowerment and cultural hypnosis is still largely maintained through domination by non-Maya people.

## How to capture energy from the sun and moon
The power of meditation is increased if you first make the sound 'K'in' by sounding a strong explosive 'K' followed by a harmonious long 'in' sound. The word *'K'in'* can mean 'the sun' or 'one day' or 'our relations'

(as in the English expression 'kith and kin'). Repeat this word seven times (in the way that some yoga practitioners repeat a mantra), to link the energies of humans and the sun together and to help you capture some of the sun's energy that is needed to sustain all life on Earth. It is for this reason that the Maya regard the sun as father, Earth as mother, and moon as sister. The worship of the sun is still observed by the Hau K'in priests, who are called the 'sons of the sun'; they give solar initiations and continue to instruct people about the sun in numerous pyramid centres throughout the Mayalands.

Elder Hunbatz Men teaches that Father Sun imposes a condition upon his sons and daughters when they face him to worship, namely that they must call him by the name that is traditional in their culture – for example, Tonatiu in Mexico, Ra in Egypt, Arev in Armenia, Inti in Peru and K'in in the Mayalands (or if the worshipper has been initiated by the Maya). In times past, in the temples of Uxmal, Yucatan, women were also taught how to work with the cycles of the moon in order to gain knowledge and to utilize moon energy. Priestesses instructed them for a period of seven years, from the age of seven until 14. After that they were free to marry or to become priestesses themselves – if during the Emk'u puberty ceremony their destiny was found to be in this direction.

I continued with my search for the meaning of time, confident that the fiery sun had much to teach me about the nature of energy. Every morning I greeted the rising sun with the words:

> Father Sun give me strength
> Father Sun make me wise
> Father Son make me into a seed
> Father Son make me Eternal.'

From *Solar Meditation* by Hunbatz Men, published by Comunidad Indigena Maya, Mexico

## Practical summary of portal of fire

The keys to this portal are simple, yet vast in their implication:
1. Honour the natural world. Know and accept in love the natural flow of things – which the Maya call Ix Otzil.
2. Honour our connection to the stars, planets and sun.

# CHAPTER 9

# Temples of Ritual and Ecstasy

When you have the knowledge, when you walk inside the
intuition, so the doors will be very easy to open. There exist
the natural doors in many places but you need to be very
sensitive to see and touch that door. In the physical aspect it is
very complicated because you need more discipline to go up
to that door. There exist dangerous situations – some people
go inside and it is difficult to come back.

Elder Hunbatz Men, March 1998

## Opening temple doors with the key of vibration

I stood by the doorway to a tiny ruined temple. A group of workmen
carrying long, sharp machetes were walking home on the narrow
forest path below. I made a slight movement that caused the last in the
line to look up. His eyes caught mine and he walked up. His face had
strong, typical Maya features and his black hair was drawn back. He
looked as if he was an embodiment of Pakal Votan.

'In lak'ech,' he said, greeting me with the Maya phrase meaning 'I am
another yourself'. 'Do you want to go inside?' he continued, 'Do you
want a door opened?'

'Really inside?' I asked.

'Yes, but you must prepare yourself well to enter such a powerful
place.' He pulled a few small, fresh mushrooms from his top pocket.

'I'm really very prepared already,' I said. 'Thank you, I prefer to be alone.'

With that he fixed me with his dark obsidian eyes. Suddenly for a moment they became transparent and I saw beyond him into another world. He smiled and was gone.

Settling down I contemplated the way the Maya communicate with the supernatural. It is very similar to what we now call trance mediumship or 'channelling'. I knew that when shamans talk about doors or portals, they generally do so in a guarded manner, for while portals may be opened relatively easily, it is vitally important to know the code of conduct to close them (as in the quote at the start of the chapter). This is particularly so if any of the sacred plants or drinks such as *balché* are used. Marijuana, sacred mushrooms, peyote cactus and even tobacco can enhance experiences and understandings if used ceremonially. The shamans refer to these ecstatic experiences as 'flying'. But there are other ways that rely upon your higher consciousness being able to open the channels through the resonant lenses of the planets as I explained in Chapter Five.

I started to realize the significance of the snake and serpent imagery in the temples. Today s Western healers and homeopaths identify, sense and measure frequencies of the body — literally vibration. The preparations they use bring the vibrations of muscle, tissue, organ or other body parts back into natural harmony, and therefore the body into good health. However, if you were a shaman in past times wanting to explain vibration, which even by today s scientific apparatus is relatively difficult to measure, how would you do it? You would use a line that zig-zagged, that moved up and down, that twisted and spiralled. You would describe it as the movement of the snake, or you might draw it as a snake so that your audience would understand.

Vibrations exist at higher (or faster) levels of the electromagnetic spectrum than light, x- or gamma rays. They are of a cosmic nature and phenomenally faster that those of the human body. They are lensed and transduced in intensity in order that they do not totally fry us! Mystics of most traditions would agree that the rate of vibration of your body is relatively slow and that the rate of vibration of your spirit is fast. When you know your body enough to realize that it is merely a vehicle for your spirit then you can raise its vibrations until they are equal to those of spirit. Your body will not be heavy any more and at that moment you become winged – you are able to fly shamanically.

The eagle or, to the Maya, the Celestial Bird, has picked you up and together you go on a journey. But while the bird appears to carry a serpent or snake, it is really your own immortal soul energy that has been lifted out of your physical body. So, too, at physical death (what I prefer to describe as 'excarnation', ascension or an event horizon), the soul is freed from the outgrown snake skin and leaves the physical vibrational level behind.

## Blueprint of the gods: becoming one with Hunab K'u

It was inevitable that sooner or later during my journey through the Mayalands I would be confronted with blood sacrifice, but it was not in the way I could possibly have dreamt of. A newborn baby was crying inside a village *palapa*. The midwife emerged and ceremonially buried its placenta under the nearby ceiba tree. Wandering Wolf tapped me on the shoulder and said, 'It's a girl. If it was a boy she would have hung it in the tree.'

*The shaman's dance, inspired by a vase from Altar de Sacrificios, Guatemala.*

The Temple of the Liquids, part of what is misnamed the 'church' at Chichén Itzá, is currently used by the healer shamans as a teaching temple; for an important aspect of the cosmic Maya 'university' was once here. Above its entrance, carved in stone, is an illumined Maya priest who 'taught in the path' – as Hunbatz Men once told me as we reverently entered the temple together. Through this portal the questor, with sufficient preparation over the course of a lunar month, is able to go into a dimension where understanding the healing of body fluids takes place. These are the sacred liquids of the body – blood, lymph and bone marrow. It is the first of these sacred fluids that has been the subject of much debate ever since the Spanish conquistadors, returning to Europe, gave accounts of Aztec blood sacrifices that apparently far exceeded their own horrendous acts. Note that I say Aztec, not Maya. Present-day Maya wisdom teachers deny that there was widespread human sacrifice among their ancestors, even during the classic period that predated the conquest by a thousand years. Such accounts given later by soldiers, priests and friars were wildly exaggerated to justify their own actions. Archaeologists and students of the Maya seem to have condensed more than 5,000 years of history and seized upon the few, rather more gory, depictions of the fate of captives.

There was certainly ritual self-sacrifice of blood in the Mayalands. This took place in order to access visionary states that we would call shamanic journeys. This personal letting of blood was shown on stelae precisely because it was a momentous event that accompanied some important occasion.

The birth of an heir, succession or death of a ruler, or a good omen for battle, were all considered times that required ceremonial bloodletting. Epigraphers have been able for the most part to identify precisely what these events were by reading the accompanying glyphs. Again this is an instance of where the actions of a person, way back in history, have burnt such a strong thread on the weave of the mat of time that we still remember them to this day.

Sacrifice of blood has a number of meanings, including a deep esoteric aspect – the very word 'sacrifice' (literally 'make holy') does not mean a person has to die in the process. It is well illustrated on artefacts that personal bloodletting by Maya rulers induced ecstatic vision. To the audience of perhaps several thousand people assembled on the plazas at the sacred cities, the ceremonies involving blood letting were understood in a particular way. The shaman-priest-kings/queens undertook personal blood sacrifice, sometimes in full view of their subjects, in order to ensure the continued presence of solar energy to benefit them and their people and symbolically nurture Mother Earth. However, on another level, the shamans realized that bloodletting allows the portals to open as a way to return to the cosmic light of Father Sun through the vision serpent. I came to realize that something more was hidden within the ceremonies. From my work with light and colour for healing I knew that 'living essences' captured from sunlight through food we eat and air we breathe find their way into our blood and every cell of our body, nurturing our life-force energy. Without sunlight we could not exist on this planet.

Next I looked at the latest scientific discoveries that show the possibility that these same cellular encodements are 'captured' in our DNA and carried within our blood. Perhaps this was the great mystery that emerged like a blueprint of creation in the classical Maya period, making a very special 'sacred star essence', derived from the cosmic Maya, directly accessible to the royal lineages. This star-born essence was the secret of the real origins of the human race. Even today shamans experience the movement of kundalini and *pranic* energy within the blood (i.e. *coyopa* or 'body lightning'). This *coyopa* was the vehicle in the body for the star-born essence. It was carried by the ancestors, most particularly through the royal lineages, and the shamanic prowess of the rulers was apparent. The star-born essence was, and is still, accessed by those shamans who undertook ceremonies to invoke the vision serpent. To enable this to happen, the establishment of lines of rulership was carried to great lengths. For example, from glyphic texts we know the Votan line – of which Pakal Votan of Nah Chan was the most important member – was composed of three distinct strands on the mat of time.

The first strand of the lineage came about on 13 August 2305 BC, when the royal personage, named by the epigraphers as Lady Beastie, was crowned at the age of 815 years! According to the inscriptions at Nah Chan, she was born in the last years of the previous creation. According to Linda Schele, in her book *A Forest of Kings*, the glyphs (which she brilliantly decoded) say that 'First Mother [also called the Mother of the Gods and Lady Beastie] was the First Being to become a ruler in this creation. She also taught the people how to offer their blood to nourish life, to maintain the social order, and to converse with their ancestors in the otherworld.' Chan Bahlam, son of Pakal Votan, to justify his own accession, contrived to make her the founder of his prime lineage – because her birth date held the same destiny pattern as his. Later, two other females carried the encodements in the royal bloodline: female rulers were appropriate for establishing provable lines of succession, since it was obvious to all who the mother of a child was, whereas paternity was more difficult to prove. So, the second strand began with Lady Kanal Ikal, Chan Bahlam's great-great-grandmother; and the third strand began with the accession to the throne by Lady Zac Kuk, White Resplendent Quetzal, Chan Bahlam's grandmother. Pakal Votan, son of Lady Zac Kuk, was in this third lineage, ruling from the age of twelve. There is some speculation that when unexpected breaks in the male royal succession happened, enabling the women to rule, other factors took place – for example, that divinely procreated people came into being, or that 'soul planting' occurred. Certainly the shamans undertook ceremonies by which the soul of an ancestor was 'planted' in the womb of a pregnant woman.

Serpent Wisdom used by the travellers in time was carried as a DNA imprint and formed part of *coyopa*. This DNA encodement in the sacred blood of the Maya serpent lords and ladies entitled them also to be regarded as divine shaman-priest-kings/queens. There are similarities here to the way lineages of pharaonic succession were established in ancient Egypt. It was vital that the bloodlines remained pure. Awakening and passing this serpent wisdom on to Maya royal heirs was done by mythic ceremony enactments, shamanic ritual, soul planting and self-induced bloodletting to honour both the human s Earth origins and star connections. Such ceremony took the participants and the royal successor flying , in the shamanic sense, to his or her star-born inheritance.

Eventually the royal bloodlines became, we could say, somewhat diluted. But to this day the recognition of a particular lineage carrying a special pool of knowledge is carried on through the method of choosing the shamans and calendar wisdom teachers. Their spirit chooses to reincarnate for a particular purpose and they are recognized because they are predestined for their work (in much the same way as the Dalai Lama is in Tibet).

However, to return to the end of the classical period, the great cities in the Yucatan had not succumbed to whatever caused the demise of cities in the other Maya areas. But between the 10th and 12th centuries, the more warlike Toltecs invaded the relatively peaceful society of the Maya (albeit one that engaged in numerous intercity skirmishes), which was governed by a royal elite. These Toltecs enforced an era of great change. Throughout the Yucatan, great Maya royal rulers were removed and replaced by governing councils. Subsequently, with the ending of the ruling lineages, the Maya's serpent wisdom knowledge carried in their *coyopa* was withdrawn. It could no longer regroup in what was a hybrid Toltec-Maya civilization that eventually became centred at Chichén Itzá in the Yucatan: the Maya's star-born essence of *coyopa* became impure with the 'blood of destruction' through the process of interbreeding with a more violent people.

Present-day wisdom teachers still refer to the esoteric wisdom known as the 'opening of the heart' – meaning the heart chakra energy centre. At some time in the course of the degeneration of royal rulership during Maya history, these teachings were taken literally. The Maya royal Ahob (rulers) held the true serpent wisdom knowledge together with the real meaning of time. The degeneration that ensued caused these teachings to be dispersed into the Maya collective unconscious, where they were held by the cosmic Maya, who awaited the time when they could reappear.

## Goddess Ixchel and the ecstasy of childbirth

Until this chapter, you may be forgiven for thinking that all of Maya society, past and present, was dominated by males. Today this is clearly not true, for Maya women are respected members of their communities and village councils, and they are the driving force in most families. In times past, as has been discussed, shaman-priestess-queens carried vital spiritual encodements in their blood lineages.

Seeking the feminine aspects of Mother Earth in the Mayalands has been a challenge. The only goddess that is readily apparent is Ixchel (pronounced 'Eshell'), who represented the divine feminine to the Maya of old and who continues to be worshipped alongside the Virgin Mary in hybrid ceremonies to the present day. Whenever the prefix 'Ix' appears with a word, you can be sure it has a feminine connection.

Honouring Ixchel ('she of rainbows') dates from the times of the royal lineages, for she had an important presence in the birth preparations of the inheritors of serpent wisdom. At Tikal, for example, there is a small, hidden temple to Ixchel and Mother Moon, Ix-Ma-Uh, where moon phases are inscribed on the stone of the stelae. Tulum, once called T'Zama, City of the Dawn, on the Caribbean coast of Mexico, has birthing temples where Maya women came by canoe on the trading routes around the coast. They would call at the islands of

Cozumel and Isla Mujeres ('Island of Women'), where there were other temples dedicated to Ixchel.

Can you envisage the ceremonies that would have taken place? At the sandy beach a pregnant woman is helped from her canoe and slowly makes her way to the small temples that offer shelter from the burning sun. Two groups of women gather: one with the Ix-Zuhuy-Kaaks fire priestesses to prepare a sacred offering fire for a successful birth; and another with the Ix-Zuhuy-Has water priestesses. The mother-to-be is cared for by midwives and given strong herbal drinks to soothe her pain. Meanwhile the Ix-Zuhuy-Has intone long prayers and ask for blessings from the great waters of cosmic rebirth to favour the coming infant.

In a nearby temple dedicated to the rising sun, the shaman day-keepers recite their long ritual count of days to keep the threads of time vibrantly alive for the coming child. Then the ecstatic timelessness of birth comes, and for the mother, deep in a trancelike state, this moment is as potent as ritual death. The cord is cut with a sharp blade made of a freshly flaked-off piece of black obsidian, and the child is immersed and cleaned in the waters of life drawn from the nearby sacred *cenote* or water hole. Suddenly across the city the conch shells sound like trumpets, announcing the birth. Astrologer priests complete their considerations of star charts, and divining the destiny of the baby girl, proclaim she will be a gifted temple dancer. Young girls, trainee priestesses in their own right, carry armfuls of bright red hibiscus flowers and offerings of maize bread to the round altar at the foot of the steps leading to the Ixchel temple. Setting them down they thank:

Ixchel: goddess of childbirth and rainbows, she of pure and radiant energy.
Ix-Zak-Ek: First Mother of the Milky Way.
Ix-May-Ek: goddess of stars and sky.
Ix-Ma-Ux: Mother Moon.
Ix-Mukane: ancient and wise grandmother.

Then carried on a soft zephyr from the sea, come their sweet songs to Ix-Kay, the goddess of singing and dance; to Ix-le-Ha, 'she of the trees'; and to Ix-Nicte, spirit of the flowers. As the ceremonies end, the midwives emerge from the birthing temple, immerse their hands in a blood-red liquid made from ground cinnabar and print their hand images on the walls of the temple in a kind of symbolic finality, indicating that their work is now complete.

*Depictions from the temples of Tulum, on the Caribbean coast, Yucatan, Mexico, showing the birth cord of the physical birth and the small face of the sun being born simultaneously with the descending god consciousness, which occurs at the moment of birth.*

## Royal Copan, Honduras, city of ritual temples

The remains of Copan hold many secrets of the cosmic Maya, those star beings who guide from other dimensions. The wild setting of the Copan River Valley, overlooked by Macaw Mountain, was once home to an enduring lineage of shaman-priest-kings/queens. Copan's ceremonial stairway has the longest recorded glyphic text (carved onto the risers of the staircase) so far discovered in Central America. There are more than 2,200 glyphs, but unfortunately they cannot all be read coherently, for weather erosion and a number of earthquakes during the last 1,250 years since its construction around the year 750 have taken their toll.

The staircase rises up from the gaping mouth of a vision serpent in stone. Close examination shows its mouth is upside down and the Ahau Smoke Shell, according to archaeologists, appears to emerge from it. But, I reasoned, if one wanted to show what happens during a vision quest or depict a ceremonial release of the vision serpent, it would be necessary to show someone being drawn into the vision. This is exactly what this hieroglyphic staircase is showing! The Ahau is *going into* the vision, not coming out of the mouth, and the other five life-sized carvings of rulers on the steps are his ancestors, also going into the vision through the portal that he has activated for them. According to Linda Schele in *A Forest of Kings*, they are identified as Smoke Monkey, 18 Rabbit, Smoke-Imix-God K, Butz Chan (Smoking Sitting Snake) and Moon Jaguar.

*Glyphs of the Bolontiku, the Nine Lords of Time, based on a carving in Pakal Votan's tomb.*

I sensed that the Underworld is ever-present at Copan. Tunnelling inside the giant stone structures under the hieroglyphic staircase led archaeologists to a phenomenal discovery. Through one and a half kilometres/one mile of underground passageways, they came upon two beautifully ornate temples once painted in brilliant colours of red, green and white, with an almost oriental appearance. One, informally dubbed the 'Rosalila' ('lil' means 'vibration'), is known as the Temple of Red Vibration. Shamans say it holds supernatural keys that the kings and queens of yesteryear could turn in order to understand time past and time future. Something inside this temple, hidden beneath the portrayal of the huge vision serpent, allowed the divine lineages of god-kings/queens to continue. It was a sacred place that only the reigning Ahau could enter in order to commune with the ancestors and release the destiny and cosmovision of the Maya. It was the Ahau's own private temple of ritual and ecstasy. The mystery of the temple deepened every time it was used, its portal becoming increasingly potent.

## The shamanic art of stalking

In Chapter One I discussed the actions of a warrior. Now, at this point in my shamanic quest for the meaning of time, I found that events or energy, still lingering in Copan from almost 2,000 years ago, were continuing to affect Mikhail and me when we entered certain parts of the city. The techniques of a specialized warrior, the stalker, were required to bring some meaning into these strange happenings that I will recount in the following diary extract. The shamanic term 'stalking' is most likely to make one think of hunting. If we wanted to trap an animal, we would first have to take up a hidden vantage point and quietly watch in order to observe its movements and routines to help us to trap it. This kind of stalking is based on observation. Shamanic stalking, too, is a way to disengage from the ordinary self, the usual mind clutter, and to shift yourself into really observing all the qualities of what you need to achieve. Continual internal chatter keeps the mind occupied with trivia and keeps the assemblage point fixed in one mundane place. The shamanic way of stalking is to observe and at the same time control actions so that one is unaffected by outside factors over which there really is little control. This enables shamanic stalkers to have more energy to give to things they are observing.

Stalking is also an aspect of second attention concerned with body awareness – symbolically referred to as left-side awareness (an appropriate term since the actions of the left side of the body are related to the right side of the brain). So how can one understand second attention? In practice, it is a way of noting what *all your senses* are telling you beyond the basics of food elimination, temperature, and the like. It is how your body reacts when it is in the presence of certain other people, a certain place or how it feels when it is completely alone. Your body has the ability to continue to re-live, at a cellular level, everything that has happened to it in its life.

This is why at the point of death it recapitulates all the major events, places and people it has experienced, even way back to childhood, focused into a few moments of time. Shamans say that this is the cleaning and the clearing of the body by the soul just at the moment of death, and they liken it to an eagle eating the heart that contains inner awareness of the body. This is why images of an eagle or a jaguar eating a heart are fairly common in the Mayalands. It is *not* the heart of a sacrificial victim being thrown to the bird or animal. The warrior seeks this ultimate act of second attention and ability to recapitulate as at death. It leads to a state of high awareness and freedom that is the goal the warrior stalks. In the following diary extract, you will see two examples of stalking.

*The jaguar, as symbolic Underworld creature, eating a heart in order to take the inner awareness of the body into the Underworld prior to the release of the soul to the 13 heavens. From Chichén Itzá, Yucatan, Mexico.*

## Diary extract: Copan, Honduras

I stopped at the entrance to the main plaza beneath the shade of a large tree hung with vines and with bromeliads cascading from its forked branches. Just above my head a vividly coloured macaw was sitting – it was a large adult bird displaying plumage painted in primary colours of red, blue and yellow with green back-feathers. It eyed me haughtily, unmoving and I recalled my last encounter with a semi-wild macaw that suddenly alighted on my shoulder as I stood sketching under his tree. That bird had tried to peck off my earlobe with its large hooked beak – I wasn't willing to hang around for a similar occurrence!

With my customary approach of appealing to the hidden guardians of the site for guidance now rather abbreviated, I walked quickly on and got out my metal dowsing rods from my daysack. Now some people just 'feel the vibes' of a place, but I need assistance. So, going across to one of the now-familiar, carved stone stelae, I concentrated on the founding cache of precious objects that each one of them has interred beneath its base. As a soft breeze swept across the sun-baked earth, many eyes seemed to be watching my every movement, but they were only ancient blank stone faces I told myself. I was 'led' to a particular stele, which had a complicated and deeply cut, ornate carving of a long-passed Ahau wearing full ceremonial regalia and holding the serpent bar and a jade pectoral. He cradled something, a face of sorts, in his hands. A voice told me to seek the connections of this 'tree stone' and, with the dowsing rods, I was able to establish that its energy fields contacted a number of other standing stelae positioned some metres away across the plaza. Suddenly, with a whoosh, the macaw swooped low across my head and alighted on the top of the stele. I went into 'stalking mode' and felt convinced that this was a key to the energy of the sacred city and that the other macaw had pecked my ear because there was something I had to hear.

I refocused on dowsing questions. Walking backwards, I established a line of energy going some distance. Stepping back, I almost fell down a steep and eroded stone staircase. Recovering, I spoke out loud: 'Does the energy of this stele connect with other stelae on this plaza? Does this stele connect with other stone markers in the Copan Valley? Is it connected with Quiriguá?' Each time the answer was in the affirmative. I heard it loud and clear in my head and echoing around the grey glistening stone steps of the plaza. I went on asking more and more questions, progressively going farther away from Copan: 'Does the energy of this stele connect with all the Earth, the moon, the planets?' The answer was 'Yes'. 'Does it connect with the galactic source?' – 'Yes!' The ancient stone was clearly focusing an energy channel lensed through the cosmos from Hunab K'u.

I returned from my stalking consciousness, feeling elated and excited by this discovery. Hurrying to find Mikhail, who I knew had gone to meditate in the West Court, I saw him sitting on a rock beneath the huge stone head of a Pauahtun, one of the four beings who holds up the corners of the world. Mikhail was clearly distressed. 'I have been speaking to Butz Chan,' he whispered. Butz Chan, I thought, is portrayed on the stele I had been looking at – so how could he have been speaking to him?

Michael again whispered: 'He told me to go through the small entrance door covering the tunnel into the Rosalila Temple. It's another world in there – the red walls seemed to dissolve – I was back in the time of Butz Chan and his name means Smoke Sitting Snake. He was preparing to give blood sacrifice and he was old, as old as me. He was so sad because his life was almost finished and he wanted to stay with his young wife and child, but then he wanted to show me where he was going. The smoke of an incense burner increased and curling around formed into a snakelike form. It spiralled and turned around me, drawing me up and out of the solid walls of the temple. Butz Chan took me on a long shimmering path of light, leading through the resonant lenses of the planets and we looked back on our world together. It was awful, really awful, for all around the Earth hung a black pall of pollution and hatred. Little points of light that were baby souls waiting to be born couldn't get back through it to Earth. And Butz Chan was so distraught about the fate of his grandchildren and his grandchildren's children.'

Mikhail went on, his voice and expression changing: 'I, Ahau Butz Chan, Smoking Sitting Snake, saw harmony with animals, birds and trees all around my great city when I was living here. All was peaceful, my people felt the power of their hearts filled with deep happiness. In my time of destiny my body was recharged from the fire of Hunab K'u whenever I walked into the red underground place. In there my voice sang softly, curling upwards, backwards and forwards around the moist walls. It was for my voice that I was given the name "Smoking". My heart was filled with love for my queen. Those who keep my time thread alive knew how to record my love. The stele carving shows woman in my heart cradled by hands. Son of mine, whom she bore, made certain that the violet lightning would continue for my people's sake. You may take up my time thread any time you wish – just watch for me in the smoke of ceremonial fire.' A moment passed, the chattering of a troupe of spider monkeys brought Mikhail back with a start.

He turned to me. 'What can I do?' he asked in his normal voice.

'You must ask the shamans here to do a fire ceremony and make offerings for Butz Chan [a Copan ruler who lived for 64 years and brought great stability to his people] and the destiny of the world,' I replied.

## Practical summary of the temples of ritual and ecstasy

1. Practise the warrior's art of stalking by placing yourself in unusual situations that require you to use second attention.
2. Meditate on the power of the cosmovision carried by the Maya Ahob (sun kings/queens).

# CHAPTER 10

# Path of the Animal Shaman

The rattlesnake is your *nagual* – the fire is your spirit.

**From the *Chilam Balaam of Kaua***

### Diary extract: *Ceibal on the Río Pasion, Guatemala*

Somewhere in the distance, seated among the forest canopy, howler monkeys began their mournful cries. Deep in the heartlands of Guatemala I was exploring yet another overgrown sacred site. In some places the once carefully laid stones of the temples were split in two by the strength of the roots of colossal trees. I stepped warily through the undergrowth for fear of snakes and not wishing to disturb the natural lushness. Unless you have been alone in a rainforest, you maybe won't understand that everywhere is truly alive and must be respected.

As I walked on, pushing deeper through the vegetation beneath the towering ceiba trees, I really felt I was breathing in harmony with the forest, and all fears of encounters with snakes, tarantulas, scorpions or jaguars left me. I came upon a clearing and rested in front of an amazing, uniquely carved stele. It showed a person festooned with snakes. There they were, wrapped all around his body. I counted seven snakes in all – and my mind was instantly struck with the words 'the seven chakras'. I started to ask the hidden guardians of the place what I could learn from this, since this stele or 'tree stone', like many others, was clearly both a teaching and a portal. As I sat there contemplating, about to get out my drawing materials to record it, I was taken into another dimension. Each of my chakras expanded, responding to an in-rush of golden white light in a spiral snakelike form. I breathed deeply, remembering my shamanic training to send down 'roots' through my feet for fear of not returning from such an instantaneous initiation. Then I was propelled through the stele and seemed to look out from the other side. I could see a ceremony taking place and many people were gathered around a group of elders preparing a sacred fire.

'Heart of the heavens, heart of the Earth, heart of the fire, heart of the air, heart of the water ... ' – the words of a Maya prayer drifted towards me as the ceremony began to unfold. First an equal-armed Maya cross and circle were drawn on the ground with honey. Large pieces of pom incense were placed at the points where the cross intersected with the circle (in the four directions). More incense was piled in the middle and each quarter of the directions on this medicine wheel were filled in with coloured wax. One by one, dark, mysterious-looking shamans stepped forward, wearing heavy, round, green jade earspools and old, red coral necklaces. They were holding sacred objects and enormous head-dresses, each portraying a different jungle animal. Beneath this heavy regalia they were clad in simple, clean white tunics with bright red woven bands wrapped around their waists. They quietly placed unlit candles around the medicine wheel. Dusky young women in short white robes approached the circle bearing flamboyant tropical flowers that they laid around the intended fire. A scattering of sacred tobacco and cacao completed the offerings. As the fire was lit and the kindling took hold, elders and shamans watched the flames and smoke intently. Swaying in a trance, they began to speak the predictive messages written on the threads of time as the fire crackled and smoked. I could hear each person in turn honouring the count of days as they threw offerings of flat incense, which were quickly consumed by huge, crimson fire serpents now appearing from the flames.

I was an observer of a very ancient rite that had once taken place here, for as I looked beyond the shamans I could see walls and plazas of the original city stretching below me towards the bright curve of the river in the distance. Each building was intact and bore colourfully painted decorations along impressive façades. A bright humming bird flitted across my line of vision as I watched some musicians. The sound of drumming on their *bahbinob* clay water drums brought my attention back to the fire, a *zubak* bone flute played a haunting melody. Then, unexpectedly, a resounding series of seven deep notes played on large conch seashells reverberated through my chakras and slowly, as if in suspended time, each chakra curled inwards and became still, like snakes at rest. I withdrew through the stele and was suddenly back in the ruined city. Looking around I saw it was overhung with voracious strangler vines, like some strange parody of my chakra snakes. By now, of course, I was truly disorientated.

## Walking the path of the animal shaman
You will already have started to understand why the shamans of

indigenous cultures worldwide respect animals and creatures of the natural world. They enter into a seemingly strange liaison with them, for part of the shamanic process takes them out of their human bodies and into the body of an animal. What I am stressing here is that this process is not just thought projection into an animal, but an actual transformation or shapeshifting into the creature itself. Throughout the Mayalands, on carved stelae, pottery and temple façades, shamans are shown wearing masks of animals or birds, leaving us a record of their ability to shapeshift into these creatures. Of all the power animals connected with shapeshifting, snakes are one of the most awesome. I began the chapter with them because they are prominently displayed and easily recognized on so much artwork. Vision serpents, ceremonial serpent bars held by Ahob, and bodies and huge mouths of mythic serpents forming doorways are all still found at nearly every sacred site – despite the ravages of time.

Archaeologists tell us that many of the illustrations on carved stelae represent people in ceremonial dress and that they are wearing animal

*The façade of this temple at Tabasqueña, Campeche, Mexico, opens a portal through its jaguar-mouth doorway.*

masks. But we cannot expect archaeologists (although there are exceptions!) to understand or fully explain the extent to which life between 'worlds' was entered into by the shamans. However, what we are being shown are shaman-priest-kings/queens (and other elite people) taking up the form of their animal *nagual*, such as a jaguar, eagle, dog or deer, during vision quests. Often a vision serpent is seen emerging from the smoke of incense and/or engaging in personal bloodletting, displaying within its jaws the head of a *materialized* ancestor, who guides the seeker. Wherever the serpent's mouth is open, it represents the path by which ancestors, cosmic Maya and gods of the otherworlds can commune with the Ahau, who is in trance, by pushing an open channel through the very forces of nature and time. A decorated bar made of wood and woven matting and known as a 'serpent bar' is frequently shown being held by Ahob (rulers) as they dance. Usually there is a serpent head at either end of the bar, representing the Ahob's ability to overcome the duality of this physical dimension.

The serpent bar was part of the Ahau's magical 'regalia'. Every time he went into shamanic dances or trance states holding this sacred object it would remind him about myths of duality, such as stories woven around the opposition between night and day. One such myth of times long past told of two gods, Jaguar Paddler (night) and Stingray Paddler (day), who paddled a canoe across the 'primordial sea' of the heavens bearing the Ahau's soul. The reigning Ahau and his people were told this myth from childhood and realized that whoever held the serpent bar also held power beyond this Earth plane. Additionally, ancient codices containing astronomical information portray these old gods in their canoe as the movement of the stars across the ecliptic (the apparent path of the sun's annual motion among the fixed stars, as seen from Earth).

The serpent bar therefore symbolizes the ruler s ability to overcome duality as well as his authority because of deeper cosmic connections beyond the confines of this planet. For this reason the serpent bar is one of the keys to travel in time.

Further insight into the serpent bar is provided by Linda Schele, who says in *Maya Cosmos* that when the Ahob held a serpent bar it was an aspect of K'awil, a one-legged god with a foot in the form of a serpent (recall that Pakal Votan in Chapter Two was described as having a foot like a snake). K'awil appears as a companion spirit who was called up during ritual acts in order to grasp the path to otherworlds and was the means by which the path was opened. 'K'awil' is also used to describe 'lightning' and the 'lightning in the blood' (*coyopa*) that is experienced by the shamans, who have described it in terms of their bodies being attacked all over by the little stone axe or sharp flint that K'awil always carries.

From the evidence of the glyphs, the Maya Ahob had colourful names, many of which are associated with the animal that is their *nagual* or guide or, in Maya languages, '*way*' (plural '*wayob*'). The names include: Great Jaguar Paw, Lady Jaguar, Smoking Frog, Curl Snout, Spearthrower Owl, Kan Boar, Smoke Monkey, One Macaw, Sun Jaguar and 18 Rabbit. For the most part in this book, I will continue to use the term *nagual* to describe an animal guide since it is more familiar. Kiché Maya are given their individual animal guide from birth; for others, the *nagual* is an ancestral one, passed on through their lineage from parents to child. The word '*way*' in written glyphic form is closely linked to the words meaning 'to sleep' and 'to dream', and there are particular altars and structures of the classic Maya period that are '*waybil*' – that is, shrines for the housing of the animal *nagual* or companion guide. Maya people are aware that illness can be caused by the loss of the *way* and that the illness may have been precipitated by an intentional act to 'steal' another person's power, resulting in possible death.

*By choosing this powerful water jaguar as his way, a ruler of Ceibal on the Río Pasion, Guatemala, indicated that he had overcome the perils of Xibalba, often seen as a watery underworld, in order to attain his position.*

## Raising your vibration to shapeshift

By now I was wondering how it is possible to know not only our *nagual*, but to be able to choose to shapeshift into it. A shaman once explained to me: 'Our *nagual* must become as familiar to us as our other aspect, the *tonal* of our everyday lives, has become. You must stalk your *nagual* in order to be able to really understand it and move yourself into its consciousness and world. Then, when you muster all your energy and focus with clear intention you will have the ability to fly or shapeshift.' For some this will be a journey in the mind. For other accomplished adepts, it will be an actual cellular shapeshift, achievable because they burn such strong lines of light on the mat of time. They can use their own luminous fibres to take them along different time threads, seek the animal that is their *nagual*, shapeshift into it – and return!

Your ability to shapeshift and return will depend upon your being able first to move, then to fix your assemblage point in another location at will. Never allow another person or drugs to do this for you. Wait until you are ready and have the support and guidance of a wisdom teacher working with pure spiritual energies of light. Or, you may practise doing it when you are in a very relaxed dreamlike state – by knowing that you are in the dream and moving yourself within it.

John Perkins, in his book *Shapeshifting*, comments that fear is the greatest factor preventing people from being able to shapeshift. He says that the fear is to do with exhausting one's energy and in consequence being unable to return to one's original body: 'If people believe this then they probably cannot cellular shapeshift... In a way you have to shapeshift yourself out of it [the fear]. But that shapeshift is one of those cultural, institutional ones, and therefore maybe not quite so difficult, not as frightening. You have to accept that you already *are* the same as the thing you're going to shift into – that your separateness is only an illusion. You also must believe that there is no hierarchy, that you as human being are no higher on some evolutionary chart than you as tree or jaguar.'

## Serpent wisdom

Complementary to your *nagual* is serpent wisdom. It is one of the profound 'seedings' of wisdom teachings for humanity, potent today as it ever was. I have been constantly reminded of how not only the Maya but other traditions knew its secrets. Its alchemy was used in the Egyptian, Greek, Indian Vedic as well as the Western 'mystery tradition'. From what remains of ancient Maya teachings, it is clear they knew of its meaning on physical, mental and spiritual (otherworldly) levels. Serpent wisdom might best be described as a 'wise knowing' that is founded upon universal truths. This is a kind of inner knowing provided through an insight that is equally heart and mind based.

In many parts of the world, serpent wisdom has been hidden from ordinary people, cast out as evil, cloaked in secrecy and symbols, so that seekers have to rely on their own inner sources of knowing. For example, aspects of the symbolism behind the serpent are the four elemental qualities of earth, water, fire and air. It is easy to see that the lowly snake is associated with the earth, because it literally crawls upon it, and also, the snake can change its form and become a mythical creature moving between the underworld of caves and crevices and this world. As a sea serpent in tales from many cultures, it represents the element of water, as well as the element of fire when it is a dragon, and air as the Rainbow Feathered Serpent (Ku-kuul-kaan). Esoteric tradition also names spirit as the fifth element. When spirit rises through the elements of earth, water, fire and air, it becomes awakened and arises like a snake charmed by the playing of a flute, but the tune is the music of creation, calling you to return home.

Serpent wisdom can be subtle; but if it is ignored, it can lead us into a dangerous sliding and slithering as we probe and scratch beneath the surface of our lives. It can prompt us to shed old 'skins' of misunderstanding and ego, and move us from the consciousness of a snake hiding in a dark hole to a mythical snake that flies in the air – Ku-kuul-kaan, as the Maya call this mystical union of matter and spirit. Choosing to explore further, we find it is serpent wisdom that feeds us from the World Tree – provided we reach upward on our path of knowledge.

**Exercise: Finding your '*way*' – your *nagual* or animal companion**
By now my quest was showing me how to be just in the moment and let things happen. However, you may like to use the following as an exercise that combines a number of the shamanic teachings encountered so far.

Shamans say that a spirit ally is necessary to help understand things that other humans could not possibly know. The ally may be a physical 'outer' or 'inner' teacher; it may be the higher consciousness of a living person that you know. Your allies have probably already appeared to you as spirit guides, or helpers in dreams and fantasies. In childhood, your allies were perhaps 'imaginary' friends, or a favourite teddy bear to whom you could tell all your troubles. Now you are going to find your animal ally, or *nagual* in shamanistic terminology.

As you have gone through life, it is likely you have already gained an affinity with a certain animal or creature. Unfortunately, unlike the traditional Maya, you will not have inherited an animal companion or animal name. So you might consider searching for one. This could take you to distant shores or alternatively to a place in nature that you can most easily reach – it may even be your local park or back garden. Wherever it is, you need to find a quiet spot where you will be undisturbed for a considerable period of time.

1. Spread a mat or blanket on the ground, as the Maya did, to represent the weave of the mat of time.
2. Draw a circle around yourself, either on the ground, or in visualized light. Scatter an offering of herbs, tobacco or flower petals within the circle. Sit on the mat and carefully unwrap your bundle containing any sacred power objects that you have collected over the years – maybe you have crystals, musical instruments, arrows of intention – and place them nearby. What you need to do now is make yourself attractive to the energy of the *nagual*, your *way* guide, who is currently in the form of an animal or creature. It is probably wisest to ask your first *nagual* experience to be with a gentle mammal rather than enter the worlds of insects and strange creatures.
3. Breathe out deeply, relaxing on the outgoing breath, allowing space for Great Spirit to lead the *nagual* to you.
4. As an animal first appears you may feel a barrier come up, something that is stopping you proceeding. Identify it, go deeply into the fear of it, and *then let it go*. Do your fears require you to put further protection around yourself? Will your fears stop you from experiencing?
5. Watch from an inward space what is happening to your body.
6. When you are ready, begin to call the animal companion closer. Where do you feel the power of your body? What animal senses come as you move into your power?
7. Feel any changes that happen to your body if you start to identify with the animal.
8. Imagine now that you *are* the animal *nagual* and give your ordinary self a message.
9. Finally thank the spirit of the animal for being your ally and gently return to normal consciousness. You might find it helpful to have a personal prearranged signal to do this, such as tapping your arm with your fingers or clapping your hands sharply together three times.

10. Afterwards, you may want to record your experience. Pay particular attention to what your body was telling you and exactly what the animal *nagual* looked like.

## White bird *nagual*

The previous exercise showed you how to seek an animal ally as your *nagual*. On other occasions it can be sought by observing unusual events particularly connected with real animals, which act as guardians of special locations in the natural world. During my travels in the Mayalands I have repeatedly encountered hidden guardians of sacred places. Let me give an example: .

Early one morning my husband and I were on the wide Río Pasion, Guatemala, with a boatman steering our craft – a dugout canoe (complete with Japanese Honda outboard motor!). We were travelling to the ancient city of Ceibal, once called Saxtanquiqui, a Maya name for a white bird. The river began to enchant us. It was wide and deep, and it appeared to move like a very slow ancient snake. Little eddies and currents told of its secret tides beneath a dark, oily-seeming surface. We tried to peer down into its depths but this was impossible and we just had to trust that this twisting, green river snake was bearing us in the right direction. The river wound all the while deeper into the otherwise impenetrable forest. We looked for crocodiles along the water's edge, unsure if 'logs' had moved in the murky shallows under the overhanging trees.

It felt right to trust the waters, from which mist rose like smoke, since we became aware that we were being given a sign of power. The mesmerizing whisps of mist parted overhead as we heard the wingbeat of a large bird. We saw its flight curving first to the right then to the left of our small craft. It was a large, grey-white heron, wings stretching across a full two metres/six and a half feet, gliding effortlessly overhead, leading us, watching us intently. Obviously knowing this part of the river, it acted as our guardian bird and companion, and so we implored this shapeshifter of water and air to lead us well. Upon our canoe taking a wide turn into a tributary, it disappeared, only to be replaced by another bird, swooping low over the three of us in the boat. This happened time and time again on the 90-minute journey, and as our next bird guardian took the lead we finally approached a small landing stage.

Sometimes you just attract the right animals to appear, on other occasions you need to call upon the animal spirits and ask their permission to venture into their territory. At *all* sacred sites worldwide, there is always a special point on the entrance path that you will be able to identify because it feels as though somehow you have made a transition in the process of passing through it – like a door or portal. Often there is a discernible shift, a resonance, such as heightened awareness, or flashbacks to other times, at the location of this portal. The best way to describe it is to imagine a stage with a heavy curtain. This stage curtain is the density of our three-dimensional physical existence and when it is pulled back, even very slightly, another dimension is revealed. It is here at the entrance portal that you do your first work: asking permission to enter and being open to guidance – because you will not go further until you have affirmation from the inner knowing of your higher self.

This process immediately brings you into synchronization with specific energetic qualities unique to the place, so that you may learn from the animals, insects, trees, stones, mountains, water, buildings and people that you will encounter. Sometimes you may be guided to make special offerings, as the Guatemalan shamans do with their fire ceremonies; or a particular part of the site will call you to sit in meditation there and learn its secrets. The magic of the sacred sites is that they have been ceremonially used for millennia. They were most likely chosen by Stone Age inhabitants of the area and/or peoples of earlier world creations (according to Maya mythology), who established power centres to seek ancestors, animals, gods and goddesses. The imprint remains – as the spirit of the land – still available to enable profound shifts in consciousness, so that genuine seekers may access time threads within the overall matrix of the web of life.

## Snake walk and double-headed jaguar throne
Entry into the teaching paths of the shamans is often accompanied by ritual. Traditionally, they received their position through an event that projected them into the other worlds. For some it was severe illness, perhaps fever or a near-death experience; for others it was through personal blood sacrifice. As with all esoteric paths, years of preparation and apprenticeship would follow. Today's shamanic teachers endeavour to shift the consciousness and assemblage point of initiates by gentler means. For example, I have encountered ceremonies in the heat of the midday sun in Central American latitudes that can easily cause hallucinations. Other methods use repeated chanting of ancient sacred words during lengthy rituals, utilizing first and second attention as already described in Chapter Two. Doing something quite out of the ordinary also shifts the consciousness. Try walking at night without a

light, walking and running backwards, observing shadows of objects (instead of noticing light and colour), or listening to natural sounds and observing the rhythm of silence between them. Another way is a 'snake walk', which is done by a group of people walking in single file, each placing his or her hands on the shoulders of the person in front, and taking exaggerated sideways steps, first with one leg, then the other and following precisely the pace of the person in front (as I experienced at Aké).

I once watched as a group of initiates performed the snake walk up to a small raised platform at Uxmal in the Yucatan. A young shaman was being given teaching. The maestro shaman, in full ceremonial dress, stood behind, directing him to kneel before a stone shaped into a life-size jaguar – but a jaguar having two heads and forming a throne or seat! He performed a series of movements with his hands, much as a spiritual healer might do. All the while, the initiate's hands rested on the two stone heads of the jaguar. What was happening here? Was the maestro behind him moving the threads of time coming from the past? Was the initiate creating a bridge of understanding and coherence between the right and left side of his brain while his hands lay on the stone jaguar heads? Or was the jaguar his *nagual* power animal, and the shaman was reminding him of this by travelling with him to retrieve his soul's purpose?

## The World Tree – the Wacah Chan ('raised-up sky')

To this day, the indigenous Maya still use trees to build and to provide shade, fruits, dye, incense, drinks, food and medicine. It is no wonder that they still call the trees their brothers. This is one reason why the majority of those living in the forest are anxious to ensure their land rights. Every villager there would traditionally have had access to forest materials, collected on a sustainable basis. In order that this balance of sustainable life continues, it is essential that those areas already designated as nature reserves – Biotope Reserves – are fully protected. In an ideal world it would mean continued international recognition of them and full legal guardianship given to local people to resist corporate interventions of roadbuilding, logging and oil extraction. Unfortunately, what is happening falls far short of this and the shadow of the conquistadors still dominates these people; but this is not an appropriate place to pursue this matter.

I met Elder Hunbatz Men in the Yucatan many times. He has given numerous teachings about trees. He began one teaching with the words, 'T is for Tree' – it will become clear over the page why he did so.

In the *Popul Vuh* it is written: 'At the beginning of time ... in the heart of the Lake... in the heart of the Sea... the Maker of the blue-green plate, Maker of the blue-green bowl... allowed the sky to be lifted from the primordial sea...' By interpreting what remains of sacred texts, we can understand how the World Tree (the Axis Mundi) brought about the mythic action of sky lifting. In this, the fourth time our world was created, the sacred World Tree was raised to align with Polaris (our pole star, which indicates the direction of true north). Some 4,600 years ago, because of the precession of the equinoxes, the pole star was not Polaris but Draco. Three early races give us clear evidence that at the sites of La Venta (Olmec), Teotihuacan (Toltec) and Monte Alban (Zapotec), many structures constructed *before* the classic Maya period of building were deliberately sited and aligned on the ground with Draco. Some of these buildings were later rebuilt in the classic period and realigned to compensate for precession. John Major Jenkins, in *Maya Cosmogenesis 2012*, says that because of the 'slippage' of the stars due to precession, the Maya invented the Long Count in order to keep accurate track of lengthy periods of time. Once they realized that precession would cause a different pole star to be in place down the ages, they decided upon a more stable reference point. Consequently they identified the galactic centre. It is the hub of our Milky Way galaxy and the source of the sacred raised-up World Tree, where the ecliptic crosses the Milky Way near Sagittarius.

The Maya came to understand the galactic centre as the true cosmic centre, the womb of all, which it is prophesied will renew the world in 2012.

Around the majority of ancient city sites are giant, buttress-root ceiba trees that provide the soft bedding material known as *kapok* from their seed cases. Ceibas frequently grow as 40-metre/130-feet 'brother' guardians, standing with trunks straight and strong before bursting into a horizontal living 'medicine wheel' of the four directions and playing host to creatures of the rainforest canopy. To the Maya, the ceiba is equivalent to our concept of a 'national tree', sacred because it is an earthly representation of the cosmic event of sky lifting.

One day under the welcome shade of a small grove of trees below the Temple of the Inscriptions in Nah Chan, Hunbatz Men began to teach me about the tree spirit. He said, 'The Maya use the word "*Teol*". "*Te*" translates as "tree" and "*o*" as "spirit". By this word every tree is recognized as a living spirit.'

He went on to tell me more about the significance of the tree. He said that to the Maya of the 16th century the cross and the 'T' symbol of the tree were central to their cosmology and beliefs about creation. During the advance of the conquistadors, the people were astounded by the Catholic imagery of a man being tortured and suffering on a cross. For them, seeing such a sacred symbol used in this way created great confusion.

Elder Hunbatz Men has made a special study of Maya writing that has double as well as reversed meanings, and 'T' is a good example of a glyphic symbol representing a word or sound with a multiple meanings. When referring to the wind, 'T' is pronounced as 'Ik' or 'Eek'; when used to mean 'divine breath' it is associated with one of the 20 faces of Great Father Sun in the T'zolk'in calendar. One day we walked slowly across to the 'palace' of Nah Chan, where Hunbatz Men showed me where Maya architects had incorporated T-shaped wall openings in the building. Artists also used this shape on masks and painted or carved figures to refer to 'breath' and by implication 'life'. The 'T' was depicted on intricately made jade masks used to cover the face of a deceased person (a practice of both the Maya and Aztecs). It signified the idea that with our first breath we connect with the wind, the sacred breath of life, and with our last breath we lose our bond with the body. When archaeologist Alberto Ruz Lhuillier found the famous sarcophagus of Pakal Votan with a skeleton inside, being aware of its significance, he respectfully replaced a T-shaped carved jade stone that had fallen out from its original position between Pakal's teeth.

I was amazed that so much symbolism could be incorporated into such an ordinary thing as a tree. Not only in the Mayalands, but throughout the Land of the Sun, there are writings and symbols of the 'T', all of which in some way refer to or represent the sacred tree. But of all these peoples, the Maya have depicted perhaps the most dramatic – and much-analyzed – sacred tree on the slab that forms the stone lid of Pakal Votan's 'tomb'. Emerging from a human navel, this tree has a bird sitting upon it called 'Itzam-Yeh', which is symbolic of spirit. At first sight, the meaning could not be clearer: the image shows the integration of the divine with the human. But look again and you will realize that the tree is also the 'raised-up world tree' and the bird is a celestial bird, sometimes called a serpent bird, identified with the pole star. Pakal Votan, while appearing to fall back into the Underworld, is actually looking up into the World Tree – ready to follow his destiny on the road into the sky leading to the stars. The inscription reads: 'Och bih' – 'He entered the road'.

*The lid of Pakal Votan's sarcophagus at Nah Chan, showing Pakal dressed as the maize god and being transformed as he prepares to enter the 'road to the sky' through the World Tree.*

## Weaving the mat

My journeys in the Mayalands were drawing to a close, and I needed to return to the UK to study the Maya further and to tidy up my drawings for publication. On the day before the flight home, I sat on the veranda of my favourite 'watering hole', drinking coffee and trying to assemble hundreds of pieces of paper containing hastily scribbled notes. I reflected on so many undreamt-of experiences, each a little part of the story in what seemed a never-ending Maya dreamtime. I gave silent thanks that I had entered and left through many portals under the protection and guidance of great spiritual warriors. I had accessed portals with keys that gave clear indications of what I might expect before opening them.

Having read this far, you will probably have realized the numbers of each chapter form part of the shamanic count of 13. This chapter, number ten, has a resonance to Day 10 or to any other count of ten. So if you recall your work with the 13-day diary from Chapter One you will know that for Day 10 the advice is: 'Manifest your vision, your dreams of the work you need to do'. So now, I was near the end of my quest. I intended to manifest my vision and summarize how I had pieced together the jigsaw puzzle of this Maya creation, what I had learnt and what else I needed to achieve in order to understand better the weave of the mat of time. Picking up my notebook I set out a clear list of the main points of my findings so far.

- The ancient Maya shamans, as well as those of today who follow similar paths, have an incredible understanding of dimensions beyond the physical world.
- They have the ability to enter those dimensions by opening portals to them through the use of ceremony to shift their consciousness.
- They are able to do this because they have mastered a number of shamanic techniques similar to those of other shamans throughout the world. They include:

First and second attention.
Psychic protection.
Communication with the world of nature.
Being a hunter and stalker.
Stopping internal dialogue and releasing cultural hypnosis.
Understanding the subtle energies of the human body.
Capturing energy.
How to undertake a vision quest and shamanic dreaming.
Being a spiritual warrior.
Understanding the *tonal*, *nagual* and ally.
Shamanic flight and shapeshifting.
Stepping out of time and dimension.

- In their work, the shamans have always been supported by other respected members of their society, such as healers, midwives, calendar daykeepers, astrologers and scribes. Indeed, in earlier times the ruling Ahob were the state shamans in their own right.
- The shamans used decoration on their buildings, folded paper-bark books and pottery as teaching tools.
- In particular the images of serpents or creatures with humans in

their mouths show not only an interesting aspect of the shaman's vision quest but also – more vital to this present time – clues as to where exactly in the vast possibilities of the starry cosmos human beings originated.

- Portrayals of zig-zags of snakes that substantiate the above.
- Images showing the Maya's understanding of souls and reincarnation abound in remaining original artefacts.
- They left many calendars unlocking the meaning of time itself.
- The Maya shamans were concerned for more than personal goals. Those of the past and those of today carry a clear eco-spiritual message, calling us to right the wrongs in our relationships with nature and the worlds of the cosmos.
- Maya spiritual warriors are constantly battling to empower human cosmovision, which they believe was taken away by the creator gods (according to the *Popul Vuh*) to enable us to see through the resonant lenses to the stars.

So my vision of the shamans was clear enough. But just what they were trying to achieve was deeper and more mysterious than I could have ever dreamt. I have already explained that the royal lineages carried a special essence encoded in their blood. This essence was linked to the name Votan. The intense spiritual focus became personified and known as Ku-kuul-kaan or Quetzalcoatl to others living in the Land of the Sun. This spiritual focus must not be underestimated when trying to pull meaning from the threads of the mat of time, for many clues have been left for us to unravel as follows:

The serpent: often the shaman's *nagual* or *way*, manifested in smoke and appearing as the Vision Serpent in visions during powerful rites where energy was 'woven' on the mat of time. Along with strong beliefs that such rites would benefit their people and the fecundity of Mother Earth, the shaman-priest-kings/queens undertook to maintain the secret of human origins from star encodements and vibrations represented by snake imagery. They were guardians of the soul portals for their subjects, occupying positions of unchallenged power through their royal lineages. At the height of their prowess, whatever the Ahau desired was realized. If he wanted to emphasize the mythic stories, they would arrange huge musical and dance performances to create an air of dramatic happenings. They also organized the building of stepped pyramids, which became taller and grander with each rebuilding, like a grand backdrop in a play. Level after level of narrow steps constructed, and placed on the most sacred part at the very top was the *pibna*, a small temple that would usually hold only 13 people at most. From that great height, sometimes on the tallest pyramids, which rose way above the rainforest tree canopy, the Ahob held the position of supreme power, overlooking their people and lands. But more importantly it was from there that they could invoke the vision serpent, travel in time and 'fly' to the 13 Maya heavens, for it was a temple kept rigorously clean and used solely for that purpose.

The jaguar: People feared the jaguar, the *balaam* that stalked between this world and the nine hellish underworlds of Xibalba, when it hunted stealthily by night. However, the shamans and Ahob, as a sign that the jaguar was their *nagual* and that they had a close relationship with it, used to turn the pelts of these beautiful creatures into ceremonial cloaks. The cloak was an indication that they also had power over the underworlds and could survive life-threatening tests there, just like the Hero Twins in the *Popul Vuh*, in order to be reborn as stars in the night sky.

Two carved jaguars appear on late classic-period friezes near the ballcourt at Chichén Itzá with human hearts, dripping blood, in their claws. Contrary to the lurid interpretations of tourist guides, Hunbatz Men states that this is a representation of the ego being destroyed in order to release us on a path of ascension into higher consciousness (see illustration, page 147).

The astromythology of the Maya shows us how their myths, although speaking in archaic pictorial language and images that the common people of the time could understand, nevertheless also had other layers of meaning encoded within them. Decoration of text, pottery or building was never purely for aesthetic effect. It was always a way of embellishing history, the divine right to rule and connections to the stars. Much imagery is now known to portray astronomical events in a pictorial form. Breakthroughs in decoding these drawings and glyphs have gone on simultaneously with, but quite separate from, the interpretations of wisdom keepers, shamans and daykeepers who are speaking out to the world. One aspect, or thread, is of an environmental nature, and this will emerge in the countdown to 2012 (it will be highlighted in the remaining chapters). A second thread forms the backcloth to the weave of the mat of time and connects every human on the planet to their origins in the stars that the Maya identified in their works.

## Practical summary of the path of the animal shamans

1. Learn some breathing techniques (for example, those used in yoga).

Breathe out to allow space for Great Spirit to enter before starting any shamanic work. Seek your animal guide (*nagual*), while retaining your own power.

2. Contact the life force within trees, plants, rocks and crystals.

3. Attune to Earth energies such as ley lines and magnetics. Notice the change in energy as you enter any place that has been used, either now or some time in the past, for sacred work, and note its effect upon you.

4. Do something completely different to practise shifting your assemblage point gently into another dimension. (Remember, it is that aspect of yourself that frequently keeps you fixed in one reality, clouding your inner vision).

# CHAPTER 11

# Portal of Light

All matter is frozen light.

**David Bohm, physicist**

## Changing personal history to a human *be-ing* instead of a human *do-ing*

What strange fate had caused me to cancel my flight and bring me back to 'the lake at the centre of the world'? The calls of my computer and easel had to wait a few more weeks, for I knew there was more that I must discover here.

From the shore of Lake Atitlan from Panajachel to Tzununa, the lake shimmers in the late evening sun. The primordial scream of elementals of earth, air, fire and water echoes through the encircling ring of volcanic fire mountains. Surrounding steep cliffs cast long reflections across the lake's surface, which begins to be kissed with soft pink sheets of light, as ever-changing shades of pink- and magenta-coloured clouds seem to descend into its dark liquid depths. I remembered a little old Cakchiquel Maya woman in the village telling me that the souls of her beloved family inhabited such pink clouds. Father Sun had indeed wielded his magical brush over the sky tonight! Stopping to rest on a sunbleached log lying on a patch of sand at the waters edge, I heard a rustling sound behind me. Suddenly a large frog emerged, leaping from the vegetation to escape its pursuer – a small but quick-witted iridescent lime-green snake some 80 centimetres/30 inches long. As if it were an athlete propelled by a pole, the frog vaulted across the sand and landed in the water, sending an ever-widening circular ripple of light-topped wavelets across the lake. Amused at it opening this 'portal of light', I sat a little longer, contemplating humanity's interdependence with all life.

The present-day Maya realize this interdependence. Their usual greeting *'In Lak'ech'* means 'I am another yourself'. Unlike some people in more materialistic societies, they know there is a need to have their feet in the soil to see the stars. The Maya shamans I have encountered frequently talk about their star families, the Mishule, and their ancestral home in Atlantis. In their hearts they know the materialistic industrialized world has become so out of balance with the natural world and that urgent action is required to redress this imbalance. Their ancestors, seemingly obsessed with time, watched for signs in the night sky recording the unfolding drama of the planet and its human population, preparing for this very time in which we are living – the final years leading up to 2012.

I walked on, the light fading now, waiting for the display of stars in the night sky, which, being closer to the equator, has a particular brilliance – every night revealing a tapestry of pin-points of light punctuating the velvety, deep blue sky. The ancestors of the Maya had observed stars reflected on the still waters of a lake or from carefully constructed, elaborate observatories. A sense that I was witnessing a far greater drama swept over me as I watched starlight mirrored in the lake, just as the ancestors had done centuries before. Many 'star platforms' and elaborate observatories have been discovered throughout the Mayalands of Guatemala, Honduras and Mexico. Each one that I have visited includes its own special 'mystery feature', often overlooked by historians and archaeologists but known by the living wisdom teachers and shamans. The observatory, normally sited within the central group of temples, was built with great care and astrogeometric precision, enabling the astronomer-priests to make outstandingly accurate records of star and planetary movements by taking sightings from key points. Light phenomena would frequently be built into the design so that sunlight filtering through small openings would illuminate carved panels, for instance at equinoxes and solstices.

I continued along the edge of the lake remembering something a friend with intense psychic insight had said. One starry night, she said to me: 'Locked into the hewn stones from which the Maya sacred cites in the Yucatan and Guatemala were constructed are powerful presences of ancestors, crystal elementals, and nature spirits as well as devas or guardians of the landscape. Encoded within the stones are centuries of mythic ritual and shamanic practices that have strong connections with Atlantis and the stars. It isn't surprising to discover such presences guarding and guiding serious questors in search of dimensional doorways. For some, all that is needed is to rest the palm of their left hand on a carved Maya glyph to receive a cellular-level, starlight encodement that is not necessary or desirable for the brain to interpret.'

Carrying on walking along the lakeside, barely leaving a footprint in the hard sand, I hummed a tune from my childhood and mused that even the traditional English children's song, 'Twinkle, twinkle little star,/How I wonder what you are?/Up above the world so high/Like a diamond in the sky...' keeps some sort of a cosmovision alive and helps a child to link to his or her cosmic ancestry.

Eventually, with the stars already twinkling brightly above me, I arrived in Tzununa. I was seeking Don Pedro, who had spent many years in this village. Originally from Arizona, he once told me he had left the USA for good. He had conversed with many local shamans and wisdom teachers across the Americas. Once I was settled down on his terrace with refreshing 'Dos Equis' beer in hand, he started to explain his personal quest to me. He was in search of changes that would break an ego-driven past and enable him to reinvent the self inside. 'You must have seen the way people always make excuses for themselves,' he said, dipping half a lemon into salt, a tasty way to rehydrate oneself. 'Time after time they may say they want to change but always put obstacles in the way – they have excuses like, "It's too late, I'm nearly 60 years old" or "My family need me" or "My health isn't very good". Every time they say this they fix the past and don't allow change to occur; they become an item labelled "best before" with an end date. They also avoid their real, inner-core self by rushing around – the actions of a human "do-ing", instead of a human "be-ing".'

'So how can we change, reinvent ourselves and move forwards in a shamanic way?' I asked.

'Well,' said Don Pedro, a Buddha-like smile changing the seriousness of his face, 'it's really very easy. I will tell you in a form that can be remembered – as five peas growing in a pod.'

'The first "p" is for personal past: your personal past readily feeds your ego, giving an inflated image of yourself. Be selective; don't reveal your life history to strangers. Create a mist of invisibility around the sacred bundle of personal time threads you carry.

'The second "p" is for power: change your power to empowerment. Don't give away your power by mixing too often with people who drain you physically, emotionally or spiritually. Choose your friends wisely on the basis of them increasing rather than depleting your power so that the dynamic between you is one of mutual empowerment.

'The third "p" is for please: this is how to resist the "please-tell-me people" who try to demand unnecessary explanations or apologies from you, creating dependencies. The impeccable warrior does not need to justify his or her actions.

'The fourth "p" is for physical appearance: alter your appearance and undertake challenging things you wouldn't usually do. Shock your physical body with a daily surprising action to prevent somnambulism.

'The fifth "p" is for personality: change your interests and find something that nourishes the personality of your new self. This will give your luminous fibres coherence, as first your chakras, and then your physical body come into balance with a new harmonic vibration.

'When you have changed all the peas, discard the shuck that was your past, for like the snake that sheds its skin, you shed your past and open the door to your cosmic ancestry that will guide you forwards. In the way of the impeccable warrior you will be able to go through portals of light and enlightenment in the coming age.'

I thought about ways to release cultural hypnosis, which I have referred to in Chapter Eight, and started to explain it to Don Pedro, for I wanted to hear his reaction. Letting me ramble on, he finally interrupted me and said, 'You really have missed the point, haven't you?'

You are chattering away , Don Pedro continued, like one of the monkeys from the previous creation and you are jumping from branch to branch to try to get the best fruit. You are acting like a human do-ing, instead of a human be-ing! Like so many people with the materialistic habits of the First World countries, your mind and internal dialogue is never still. You are always talking to yourself in your thoughts but of course as you know with meditation or shamanism, such as on a vision quest, you have the opportunity to silence your mind. This has been the goal of the oriental practices, too, like yoga, Zen and Taoism, for all of them seek a state of no-mind in order to reach mindfulness. Have you ever read the Carlos Casta eda books about the shamans of central Mexico?

Yes, I replied. He called it stopping the internal dialogue and it is the key to the door between the worlds.

I looked along the terrace and I saw, carefully painted in rainbow colours above a door, the words: 'I am my own limitation. Without my own limitation – I am.' Smiling, I pointed across to it and Don Pedro gave a knowing nod of his head. 'Yes, those words have changed many people who have come here.'

## Synchronicities: where more than one thread of time joins with another

The word 'synchronicity' seems to jump out at those of us interested in time. It comes from the Greek word *'sunkhronos'*, which includes the stem *'khronos'* or 'time', and it usually refers to simultaneous events that appear to be related but are not consciously planned – and therefore seem more interesting than chance happenings. From a shamanic perspective, synchronicities happen when two or more events in a number of people's lives converge and knot together on the threads of time – exactly what shamans call portents or omens. I wonder just who is playing this game, who is tying the threads? What cosmic force is at work to make us aware of synchronicities? Who or what are the weavers?

The Maya wisdom teachers frequently refer to the cosmic Maya who guide and give special emphasis to the stars of Orion and the Pleiades. I have been shown examples of how their configuration in the sky is repeated in the design layout of temples at Tikal and Nah Chan, highlighting some profoundly significant connection. I have also been privileged to see specific 'extraterrestrial' landing places; one of them, a flat-topped pyramid – the location of which is not revealed in this book – has been the subject of many UFO sightings and unexplained lights upon the summit. Such disclosures echo Wandering Wolf's words that present-day village Maya, particularly those dwelling in the forests, see many things that cannot be explained to the rational minds of the authorities, but are shared in their indigenous councils. Bizarre as it may be to some, there are rational people who talk of star ships and galactic lords as if they were a reality. Actually, for those who have inner vision, they are a manifestation from another dimension, just as the cosmic Maya come to the invisible council meetings to strengthen the cosmovision of the Maya.

Just as certain as the existence of the cosmic Maya are other beings of light with whom we can choose to communicate or, more correctly, who may choose to communicate with us! There is a growing consciousness around our planet, awakening us to the end of this world creation. Many souls are being dragged down because they find they have become prisoners in bodies controlled through mental processes – impeded in the growth and learning they were incarnated to experience. Their lenses for light transmission have been damaged, shattered or closed down, leaving only those linked to the lower bodily chakras concerned with physical functions to be fed and satisfied by the old part of the brain and having nothing to do with serpent wisdom.

But this is exactly why the serpent has to fly – why it is shown as winged or feathered. It *will* fly if a person's power is enhanced – if people recognize synchronicities for what they really are and are prepared to change their intrinsic vibration to one of higher-colour frequencies of light, so that all the colours of the light spectrum resonate in their luminous fibres passing through their auric field.

It is us that will become the Rainbow Feathered Serpent!

## White Flower Soul Keeper and the Jaguar God

Maya people such as the Zinacantecos, Yucatec and Kiché say that the soul consists of two parts, and they have numerous names for it in their own various languages given to them by their ancestors. A glyphic word that has fairly recently been decoded is '*sak-nik-nal*' referring to soul as 'the white flower thing', or a 'white blossom on the Tree of Life' – perhaps an echo of the flowers that open high on the branches of the ceiba trees in the forests around sacred cities. A creation myth describes how, after First Father raised the great World Tree, all that was needed was the creation of human souls. So White Flower Soul Keeper pulled maize corn dough into a huge conch shell and there she moulded human flesh. Next, First Mother made the white flower souls in Precious Shell Matawil – the place in the sky where she dwelt with her children – and they were hung on the branches of the World Tree to await birth.

*Precious Shell Matawil (K'an-Hub-Matawil) from the Temple of the Foliated Cross, Nah Chan.*

*An example of the white flower glyph for the soul from Dos Pilas, stele 25.*

On a number of occasions, Elder Hunbatz Men has said that spirit is a 'vibration of the cosmos'. He is referring to the union of *nagual*, our free soul, and *uxlab*, our breath soul. (It is important to remember that *nagual* can also mean the spiritual essence of a person, plant, animal, stone; or place/spirit-guide/soul of an ancestor; it also has the sense of a person's 'guiding force'.) The *uxlab* enters the body at birth and stays in the heart during life. According to Douglas Gillette in *The Lost Resurrection Teaching of the Ancient Maya*, 'The Maya, along with many of the world's spiritual traditions believed in the pre-existence of the soul, a soul that is far more ancient and enduring than the brief span of our lifetimes on Earth.' He is also talking about the two parts of soul: the *nagual*, which is everlasting, and the *uxlab*, which leaves upon death. Some say that the white flower souls came into being in the night sky at the place called Xibalba, the place of death. Xibalba was also where the roots of the World Tree became a reflection of its branches. This would mean that as well as being in the sky, the tree could also be located below the Earth. Again, there is a long tradition that says caves are the entrances to Xibalba and some people, such as the Kiché, believe that below the Earth lies a pool of souls. Other aspects of the *nagual* guard these souls in the Underworld, manifesting as plants, animals or ancestors. (Because of the importance of the *nagual*, when a child is born shamans will observe what creature crosses its path to determine its guiding *nagual* animal.)

While not directly related to the idea of the two-part soul, teachings of Elder Hunbatz Men include references to Venus being another aspect of the Earth, almost as if the planet herself has a two-part soul or a twin. He has said that: 'Venus is our duality. When your body loses strength in its vital fluids and bones, seek Venus. Venus will help you.'

Once, back in history, the Maya Ahob and astrologers, aware of this strengthening aspect of Venus, normally arranged that local warfare between cities and regions began during the transit of the planet across the heavens. (This was a custom that appears to have been introduced from contact with influences originating in Teotihuacan, supported by the dual-nature Tlaloc/Venus war god, who is portrayed with goggle eyes like an owl.) To the shamans, Venus was the *nagual* of the Earth, and its transit was an auspicious omen and time for an honourable death. Warriors went into battle with big circular eyes painted on their faces to make them look like a screech owl known as the Muan owl, the mysterious bird of the night, and to absorb its prowess as a stealthy hunter. Additionally, in consort with many Tlaloc images in the Mayalands, the serpent again makes an appearance as Waxaklahun-Ubah-Kan, the great double-headed war serpent, wearing a mask of Tlaloc. On a graphically detailed panel from Yaxchilan, Guatemala, glyphs referring to the *nagual*, soul companion and the house of the World Tree (the 'wi ch'ok te'na' or 'root-sprout tree house') are shown together. Meanwhile the war serpent looms overhead as Lady K'abal-Xok scatters her blood on the dancing platform in the centre of the plaza. Clearly the Ahob used all the magical power available to them in various ways; to create authenticity for their lineages as on the panel mentioned above; to commemorate the ascension of a ruler; and to access supernatural powers in battle.

Take yourself back to an event some 1,500 years ago. The city of Yaxchilan is crowded with people who are aware that the stony ground of the plaza is symbolic of the primordial sea of creation. A small, square, stepped platform in the centre becomes the focus as brightly clad drummers beat a hypnotic pulse on *bahbinob* (water drums). To the rhythmic count of days, calendar shamans tend the sacred fire. From the large, flat clay pots of burning incense, heavily perfumed smoke from the resinous copal twists upwards in ephemeral blue spirals into the clear air. Conch seashells are sounded as Lady K'abal-Xok, weighed down with her ritual dress, bird mask and heavy jade earflares, is carried on a litter from her palace. She is already weak from days of fasting and her rational mind awaits with apprehension the coming accession ceremony of her husband, Ahau Shield-Jaguar.

Father Sun rises higher, noon approaches, and the heat causes onlookers to slip spontaneously into trance states, opening their consciousness to the solar lord. The lady is helped up the steps and sits, preparing herself for the ritual at her husband's side. This she does by breathing deeply in harmony with solar energy, causing the rise of not one, but two kundalini snakelike movements up her spine – the twin energies of the snake, the duality of life. She has been expertly trained and knows this secret teaching that the ruling Ahob have preserved since Atlantean times. When the kundalini opens her heart chakra centre, she smiles in rapture, with smoke from incense momentarily clouding her vision. Overhead, Father Sun's rays hide the movement of Venus; but knowing it is there, she implores the Night Owl, bird god of Tlaloc, to assist her. A shaman since childhood, she is well prepared for the next part of the ceremony. She allows her own daughter to pull her tongue forwards and suddenly pierce it for her with a sharp stingray spine. Drops of blood fall onto bark-paper in an offering bowl, and through her pain, a vision of an ancestor uncurls within the gaping jaws of a serpent of light. The ancestor holds his flint-tipped lance as if to pierce her third-eye chakra of inner vision – just as sometimes the one-footed god, wields his red axe for the male shaman's visions.

Turning to the crowd, Lady K'abal-Xok ceremonially burns the offering papers, throwing the ashes to the ground of the plaza. Almost like a great sigh, the sound 'Ah, Ah, Ahau' ripples among the people. In the branches of a fine, tall ceiba tree covered in tiny blossoms and overshadowing the plaza, a quetzal bird sits, the *nagual* of the lady. Its plumage reflects the colours of her dress – deep green and magenta red. The iridescence of the feathers caused by polarization of sunlight creates a glow that appears as an emanation of its own aura to the eyes of the initiated in the crowd. They see a bright flash of the two complementary colours as the bird, its long tail trailing, suddenly takes flight into the surrounding forest and Lady K'abal Xok slumps forward unconscious into waiting arms. The other shamans, deep in trance, are ready to read portents from the natural world all around them. Gazing up, onlookers catch sight of a circular rainbow around the sun as the

Rainbow Feathered Serpent rises there and opens a portal to the Ahau Kines, solar lords.

But in the north, rain clouds begin to gather. An unearthly sound sends a sudden chill down the spines of the watching, inquisitive children as howler monkeys announce coming rain from the treetops. For Lady K'abal Xok, despite her ritual offering, clouds in the darkening skies shape up into a portent of the Jaguar God, the Rainbow Feathered Serpent's black twin, and impending doom for the royal lineages.

## The end of the weavers of light?

A sift through 3,000 years of Maya history reveals the problem of the influences of the Olmecs (c.1300-300BC), the Toltecs (c.AD500-1250), and the Aztecs (c.AD1325-1525), each overlaying their particular threads on the mat of time and making it a challenge to draw solely upon the Maya threads. Incomplete references in old records, literature and historical accounts easily lead readers into confusion, especially since most information about this great culture was either hidden, burnt or rewritten at the time Catholicism was introduced. Add to that our interaction as people from the present-day First World, with all our bundles of time baggage on our backs, and you can see that our interpretations of what the Maya of Central America were about needs to be looked at afresh. This book aims to give some of these alternative interpretations, but occasionally, to set the scene, I must revert to generally accepted historical happenings.

In keeping with my reference to the sudden demise of the Maya culture throughout most of the Mayalands at the end of the classical period, all recording of images or dates stopped about this time. This happened, for example, by AD808 in Yaxchilan in Chiapas, Mexico, and by AD810 in Copan, Honduras. Various theories have been proposed for this (see Introduction, page xii). From that time onwards, organized social habitation of the great Maya cities by royal lineages ceased. Maya society then became centred in the Yucatan peninsula, mainly in a large area around Chichén Itzá. This city is called by archaeologists 'silent city', for it has no glyphs; but as described in Chapter Four, it has much to tell us shamanic questors about the nature of time and serpent energy. In later, post-classic periods, the royal lineages at Chichén Itzá were removed and it was governed by a confederation like a council with predominantly Toltec influence. The great Ahob had served their purpose and there were no longer controlling dynasties of shaman-priest-king rulers.

These last inhabitants were distinctly Itza Maya ('*Itz*' means 'dew' and can refer to the *coyopa* movement of subtle energy in the blood). Like an undulation of the serpent, *Lil* – the 'vibration' – was changing, the age of darkness was approaching. The Itza Maya began to focus more and more on the reenactment of cosmic events through the ballgame in the huge ballcourt, largest in all the Mayalands, and upon time encodements within the Great Pyramid of Ku-kuul-kaan, completed in the latter part of the 11th century. The old Maya lineages of Nah Chan had already preserved a record of creation in the Temple of the Inscriptions for future generations – forwards to the date of 23 October 4772. There they even interred their greatest Ahau – Lord Pakal Votan – as their messenger. But perhaps the later Itza became more adept at reading the threads of time and knew that time was literally running out for the whole human race; and also that life might be unsustainable beyond the 'end times' of this Fourth Creation.

As we approach these end times in the first quarter of the 21st century, the phenomenal light serpent that the Itza built into the Pyramid of Ku-kuul-kan is becoming an event attracting thousands of people annually at the spring equinox. It calls upon our personal superconsciousness to be present, even if we cannot be physically there. To meditate upon its implications raises subtle energy levels of the major human chakras in order to lens incoming planetary and solar influences. But note the twin connection that was known of in Atlantis times: for here the twins occur again, since the light serpent is not just one serpent, but two! Of the two balusters on the pyramid, one carries the light serpent, the other is the dark twin. Likewise, the twin serpents appear on the ballcourt marker. These are Atlantean teachings that became diffused across the planet when the cataclysmic happenings caused forced migration of survivors to many lands. They continue to be held in human consciousness, arising as serpent wisdom, which, I emphasize, has nothing to do with our so-called 'reptilian' brain (cerebellum) or fantasies of extraterrestrial lizard or reptilian people.

At a deep soul level, two realizations emerge: one is that the sun is a living entity; the second is that Ku-kuul-kan, the Feathered Serpent of Light (or Rainbow), is not just something outside us. These realizations enable us to reach back to our source and simultaneously forwards to a future with Hunab Ku in the heart of heaven. The modern American prophet Edgar Cayce declared (in channelled readings during the first half of the 20th century) that in the future when the consciousness of people reached the appropriate level of the initiate, three repositories containing vital information about the Atlantean civilization would be revealed. He said that one of these lies in the lands of the Maya.

The Itza Maya also left many carvings that unfortunately are still misinterpreted by archaeological guides, despite what the present-day wisdom teachers are telling those who care to listen; for they show the possibility of the ascension of human consciousness, the triumph of spirit over matter, not the mass, gruesome events told by the unknowing. The Chichén Itzá craftsmen and women graphically depicted esoteric understandings. Directed by visionary shamans, they had to work hard to preserve the time threads, and they decided to do it in a way different to that of earlier peoples in an effort to reach prophetically into the future – into the time predicted by their calendars in which we now find ourselves. We are poised upon the thread of time, which once again is in danger of being lost as we rapidly approach year 2012.

*A cosmic ballgame player from the ballcourt at Chichén Itzá, Yucatan, Mexico. Wisdom teachers say this depicts the seven-fold flowering of superconsciousness, not a decapitation.*

In the next chapter, the portents of doom held on the time threads will be explored with the light of our present-day understandings. As my husband, Mikhail Baker, once wrote: 'It is not "history" that calls up the past, but the past that returns for healing.'

## Practical summary of the portal of light

Cutting-edge research into the properties of light has found that polarized monochromatic light (one precise colour vibration measured in nanometres) can be manipulated with laser-type technology. Explorations by those concerned for health and spiritual aspects of science have resulted in the development and application of a 'field generator', a machine producing a field of coherent light that is both beneficial to the physiology of the human form and auric field. It has also revealed time anomalies, still to be explained. From a shamanic perspective these time anomalies are shifts of the assemblage point of the person standing in the field of coherent light into different time coordinates.

1 Study the work of mystics who have said they can create light through sound, as well as current scientific research on the properties of light in all its forms. Some key words are: 'biophotons', 'coherent light', 'polarization', 'lasers' and 'astrophysics'.

2 Increase your own inner light through clarity of intention during meditation.

# CHAPTER 12

# Serpent of Prophecy in the Sky

In a very close future the Maya temples will return to the true Guardians of time.

Elder Hunbatz Men, speaking in Nah Chan (Palenque), October 2000

## A strange encounter

One early morning, I was at Tikal (original name Yax Balaam, 'Tree Jaguar') in Guatemala, walking past colourful flocks of grazing, wild, oscellated turkeys, vociferously taking their customary breakfast of grass and grubs just beyond the parked tourist coaches. A water tanker drew up, billowing out choking diesel fumes into the pristine crispness of the morning, ready to deliver the only source of water for the two jungle lodge hotels. Whole families of Maya traders emerged sleepy-eyed from behind their *palapas* ready to set up pistachio nut stalls and hang up racks of colourful woven clothes to catch the acquisitive eyes of visitors. I noticed at the side of the old airstrip, on the sun-scorched grass, a small experimental apparatus housing a clear quartz-crystal sphere. Looking closer, I saw that it appeared to be a time-measuring instrument.

While musing at the appropriateness of its site here at Tikal, a bearded young man wearing a bright rainbow T-shirt and red macaw feathers in his hair, came up to me and, pointing at the quartz-crystal sphere I had been meditating upon, said: 'Hi, would you like to know more about this?' I replied with a faltering affirmative, somewhat taken aback by the intensity of his voice.

He turned to me face on and studied me with care. 'Well, do you know why we see in colour?' He paused for my reaction. 'I want to tell you that the light we see is scattered light, because the lenses of the sun transduce pure white cosmic light, changing it into a coloured light experience for us on Earth. What do you think would happen if we used a beam-splitter to split and project light as a hologram at frequencies above visible light?' His voice then lowered conspiratorially. 'I think we could travel in the light,' he continued with quiet conviction.

'Hey, who are you?' I asked, looking into his strangely blue eyes sparkling within his face, which had features typical of a Maya but a much lighter skin.

'Sorry, hello, I'm José – some call me Jake. Been studying astrophysics for a few years – I came from the east,' he said nodding his head in that direction. 'Now I'm here to find out what the Maya discovered.'

He held out a welcoming hand and continued, more relaxed, in a knowing voice. 'To the ancient Maya, with no modern technology, the only light they saw was the sun, stars, moon and fire. But this simplicity helped them see and use inner light. Their inner-light technology was far superior to ours, for just about all of them could see auras around living things. I have recently been experimenting with mystics who can project their inner light into a laser. Wow, you should see that! But I can't tell you more, there are those who want to use this in a corrupt way.'

'Is this some conspiracy theory?' I asked.

'Lady, this ain't no theory,' he whispered, suddenly looking agitated. 'I can tell you about the Maya shamans, though; they projected their inner light so that it became coherent – that is with all the particles going in one direction. It was a kind of laser. They did this in their secret temples where the crystalline stones held vibrational resonances that enhanced their abilities. Every time they projected their inner light they got better at it and lost their "blindness". They believed that it was Father Sun who had blinded them and who needed to be placated and understood. When they were able to project their inner light and go through the portal of the sun, they did so by what I call "moving as a fractal within a hologram".'

This last comment made me very curious, but he would not say more about it. Instead he continued: 'If you wish to learn more, look at the natural world, study a newly shed snakeskin. Look closely at the delicate coating – you will find that even the skin covering the eyes has been sloughed off and that metaphorically, for the snake, the punishment of the gods of the *Popul Vuh* has been rescinded.'

'Yes,' I said, 'the Maya royal serpent also has something to tell us. The rattle it shakes at the end of its tail has a little image on it, looking just like the Ahau glyph of the sun. The shamans carry a rattle too; usually a gourd filled with dried corn. They use it to agitate and move the threads of time towards Great Father Sun.'

I thought about how, on Earth, the mat of time comprises woven threads of 'warp and weft', held in a kind of matrix.

'Do you think that beyond Earth dimensions the mat of time becomes like liquid crystal in its movement?' I asked Jake. 'And do you think the stars shine through its lenses in a holographic pattern of the creator's mind?'

'I'll ask my buddies about that,' he replied, smiling and inclining his head to the sky.

'Thanks Jake,' I said as he strolled off towards the jungle path, 'but when shall we meet again?' I called out.

'See you around,' he said. But I never did.

## Prophecies to guide the children of the sun

Maya shamans and wisdom teachers have a long tradition of prophecy, accessed by their ability to travel in the dreamtime on the threads of time. Their cosmovision gives them the ability to 'see' the threads and select those of the future. Sometimes they share their prophecies. The following is the prophecy of Xnuc K'in of Mani. It was released by Elder Hunbatz Men and is here reproduced with his commentary and permission:

> Some prophecies have already been fulfilled. Others are yet to be fulfilled because the wise one of Mani pronounced them in her time. She was a real person, who lived in that legendary town in southern Yucatan, Mexico, last refuge of the powerful Maya of Tutul-Xiu. Her prophecies are famous throughout the land of the Mayab.
>
> It is said that as the sun set behind the forest that surrounded the town, the Xnuc K'in of Mani would sit in the shade of a ceiba tree that grew near the door of her hut. In this manner she would begin to prophesy. Not only the Maya of the town but also many others of the surrounding communities would gather to hear her prophecy. She would make her pronunciations with great serenity as she raised her hands as if

inspired by the gods of the universe. Xnuc K'in of Mani possessed the science of divination. She could read occult knowledge of the stars in the folds of the sky and even that which is in the depths of the Earth. She knew what we do not know. She knew that her wise words were light to illumine our way. It is said that one of her prophecies mentions the destruction of the trees. She prophesied this in this manner:

"To all the people of the lands of Mayab, know ye that a time will come which will rent your soul and your flesh until you are torn with pain; the day will come in which your tears will fill the rivers because on that day which I mention to you the bird 'E-BUC' will fly in combat upon the bird 'E-PIS' in a horrible fight. This will be a great and horrible fight in which they shall each rend each other's wings until they have bled. Their blood shall flow until they are wading in it. One of these birds shall die. The other will fly wounded and with great difficulty shall reach the last tree. In this manner both bird and tree, wounded, shall die embracing each other. Then the Earth without the tree shall be without skin, desolate, without life. In these times the Maya will cry with such great anguish that they will lose themselves in their desperate lamentation."

We always desire that prophecies that help humanity live a better life in spiritual and physical levels be fulfilled. But when a prophecy like the one by Xnuc K'in of Mani appears, one should meditate upon its pronouncement. For, by what one can see, the destruction of our brother tree on this planet causes one to reflect upon the possibility that this prophecy is upon us. I believe sincerely that it is within our reach to do something so that his prophecy might not be fulfilled. However if this prophecy should become a reality, this will indicate that we should never have been categorized as humans; because it will be written in the Akashic Record that we were a bad experiment on this planet Earth.

## The prophecy of Wandering Wolf

When I heard Hunbatz Men give this prophecy it caused me to remember another prophecy, spoken by the Kiché Maya wisdom teacher and shaman Wandering Wolf. He was addressing an audience in London at the end of 1997. As he spoke to them, he held in his

hands a full-size, quartz-crystal skull (similar to the famous one found by Anna Mitchel-Hedges in Belize and, at the time of writing, preserved in Canada despite the Maya elders' request for its return). This is what he said: 'Children do not forget us or our memory; we have left you healthy reasoning. We were those of yesterday, we are those of today and we shall be those of tomorrow.

'Quartz stones [such as the crystal skull he was holding] always have communication with the living, and the living should practise their true traditions for communication with the dead. The skulls are the teachers and have knowledge from thousands of years ago.

'This is what we have come to tell the world. Awaken everybody, do not sleep in ignorance. Look at your mountains, your rivers, your lakes, which are drying up. Where is the beauty of the natural world? It is time for the new day and the work shall be finished; the work we have to finish before this period, this sun ends. The period of the Fourth Sun will end on 21 December in 2012. The Maya count began many thousands of years ago. We know how the first, second and third cycles of the sun ended, and now we are in the fourth cycle of the sun. In 2012 this count will end, the sun will darken for 60 or 70 hours, but do not be afraid. Those who are children of the sun, of time, of fire, will be the survivors because in this period until 2012 there are more and serious events, great illnesses, great earthquakes, great volcanic eruption, great hurricanes, and there will be more.

'And after 2012 we will enter the new millennium that is the fifth sun and there will be peace. There will be no borders, no more inequality; remember how the rich laugh at the poor and the poor cry and they are hungry; but this land is for everyone, it belongs to the creator and he has given it to us while we are alive. This skull I am holding means that although we might be dead, we have to give testimony through the centuries. These are my words for you, my brothers and sisters.'

The audience was enthralled as they listened to him. Many were in tears. He went on:

'The Mitchel-Hedges skull is the most alive and sacred skull. It is thousands and thousands of years old; it came from the Pleiades.

'The Maya are the voyagers of time; they are the space voyagers because they are "interplanetary travellers". They do not have any machines, but by means of quartz stones they see what is happening. The carbon layer went up against the crystal layer – you call it the ozone layer – and it was broken with rockets and pollution.'

He finished by telling us, 'More than 20 years ago I began to walk among the Americas. I tried to make the world conscious.'

I marvelled at the way great teachers and shamans like Wandering Wolf can journey on the threads of time to understand the past and the future. Yet, upon reflection, I perceived that every one of us has that ability too. All it needs is to maintain the focus of second attention, allowing 'space' in your mind for your *nagual* to guide you. As you already know, ceremony or ritual will assist the process of second attention and take you into the dreamtime. Or it will propel you into a spontaneous shamanic experience, such as the following in this diary extract that also turned out to be a prophecy.

### Diary extract: a shamanic experience with Pakal Votan during a solar eclipse

A solar eclipse is ending, the strange darkness is retreating and birds, which were just a few moments ago weirdly silent, begin to sing as if it is dawn. Ahau, Great Father Sun, is released from Ux, Sister Moon, and his flaming cross spins before my eyes, turning into a solar wheel. Cascades of sparkling light, great streamers of consciousness, spill from its centre, as if 10,000 tails of comets have exploded before my eyes. The solar emanations totally fill my inner essence with light ...

I begin to say aloud the mantra 'K'in, K'in, K'in, K'in, K'in, K'in K'in ...' Toning it out loud in seven sequences of seven, I feel sounds take my soul essence to the portal of Father Sun.

I stand before the flaming 'doorway' and without hesitation take three steps into the sun ...

The pulse of the solar flares beats a rhythm of incredible intensity deep in my consciousness and I am propelled through the lens of the sun into the heart of heaven. Suddenly all becomes still; 'I am that I am' echoes softly again and again in my heart. I hear a voice: 'I am the one you call Pakal Votan. I have a message for the world. I need to make the world conscious, help its people out of their sleeping nightmares and remove the mists from their eyes. I come and go through the ages and the creations. Listen to my prophecy. Soon the Earth Mother will become dark for three days – whether the light will ever shine again is up to each and everyone of you on the planet.'

## The Hearthstones of Creation

I found these prophecies quite disturbing, and I felt I needed to know more and give myself opportunity to understand at a deeper level. It was not enough to study them in an academic type of way. So I then started to consider extending my stay in Nah Chan (Palenque). It has long been my favourite and most challenging sacred site. As you will see, the arrangement of temples there has something to say to all of us

present-day seekers, if we can look beyond the obvious with second attention.

In European folk tales, the hearth of the open fireplace in a home has long been regarded as an intermediate place between the worlds. This association emerges in another form in a Maya house. First, here is some background information about Maya traditions – including cooking! Go into any village and you will see the traditional sight of women bending over a hot, rounded, cooking iron, which is balanced on three large rocks or hearthstones, with the fire in its middle. A thin pancake tortilla of maize dough is cooked upon the stone in just the way their ancestors did. Maize, a plant that requires human intervention to remove the seeds from the sun-dried cob in order to replant them, is known as the first food provided by the gods. The women preparing the daily food are also in reality acting out a recreation of how a human being was made from maize dough. I remembered a wild-looking shaman at a seed-planting ritual in a *milpa* (maize field) waving his planting stick in the air and telling me that the

*The sun as a jaguar shield, from the Tablet of the Sun, Temple of the Sun, Nah Chan. This ancient war shield of the Ahau shows the jaguar god aspect of the sun in the Underworld and crossed spears with stone spearheads emerging from snake bone mouths.*

hard kernels are sometimes called little skulls. He said that their continued cultivation means that we will be reborn as long as maize continues to flourish and grow.

At Nah Chan, three temples built by Chan Bahlam, the son of the great Serpent Lord, Pakal Votan, stand in front of Yemal-K'uk'-Lakam-Witz ('Descending-Quetzal-Big-Mountain'). The surrounding area of forest runs virtually uninterrupted from the Pacific coast on the west to the Caribbean on the east, forming a sea of green – the Lakam Ha ('Big Sea' or the primordial waters of creation) mentioned in the creation story. On this sea of forest green, the magical temples of Nah Chan seem to float – beautiful, mysterious and intriguing. For the thousands who visit annually, the temples leave them with their most lasting impressions. One of these temples, which I have already explored, is the Temple of Inscriptions. As well as being the burial chamber of Pakal Votan, it contains four massive stone tablets recording the now almost completely deciphered history of creation. By relating this temple to three other ones at the site and to the mythic hearthstone stars in the sky, the words 'as above, so below' take on an uncanny significance. The other three temples are:

- The Temple of the Cross: this gives the events of creation and the history of the dynasty. The inscription begins with the birth of First Mother and First Father before the present creation on 7 December 3121BC and 16 June 3122BC respectively. It records that in the north, First Father 'entered the sky' by raising the World Tree from a sacrificial plate. The Maya believe his act caused the movement of the star fields, making them travel through space in the precession of the equinoxes. On the inscribed stone tablet is a picture of a decorated tree as a cross. It is draped with the double-headed serpent (known here to refer to the ecliptic) and Itzam-Yeh (Seven Macaw) as the Big Dipper constellation sits on top.

- The Temple of the Foliated Cross: this has another amazing carving showing a different World Tree cross. It sprouts leaves depicting 'first tree precious' as a maize plant, signifying the rebirth of the maize god and humanity.

- The Temple of the Sun: this contains a carved tablet about the accession of Chan Bahlam. On it is recorded that he 'became the sun' in the company of an ancient god during shamanic initiations and ceremonies there.

One afternoon, after the tourist crowds had left Nah Chan, I rested on the parched flat grassy area between the Temples of the Sun, Cross and Foliated Cross. My eyes focused on a small and relatively insignificant stone platform in front of me, and in spite of exhaustion, I felt I had to get up and go to sit there. It was 'calling me'. Suddenly I remembered the hearthstones that I had seen in Maya homes – the three large rocks in triangular formation, upon which to balance the 'tortilla' cooking iron over the fire. To me this was just too much of a coincidence: the three rocks in a Maya home supporting the cooking iron; the three temples surrounding me as I sat on the small stone platform; and the three bright stars of Orion in the sky, which, according to the creation story of humankind, are the Hearthstones of Creation. A shiver went up my spine as I realized I was sitting within an ancient powerful portal. In the final chapter I reveal astounding evidence to transform this creation myth into creation fact and give predictive guidance on choosing the time threads between now and 21 December 2012.

When viewed together from above, these three temples are positioned on the ground in an unusual configuration, mirroring the positions of the three stars of the Hearthstones of Orion in the sky. They are arranged around the low square platform of stone. This platform is the most potent portal in Nah Chan. It was there that the sacred shaman s fire was lit and the dance of time enacted.

Now the clouds of confusion and mystery that had surrounded me in this adventure really began to lift. At last all the pieces were fitting together. The shamans had already shown me how Chan Bahlam, Pakal Votan's son, had constructed the Temple of the Inscriptions: on only one day of the year, the December solstice, Great Father Sun sends a piercing beam of light through a notch on the mountain ridge behind to illuminate the panels in the Temple of the Cross, depicting Chan Bahlam as First Father of this creation. Each time this happens, up to the critical solstice end date of 21 December 2012, we can use and interpret its message about creation. As if this was not enough of a clue, there was also the fact that standing together nearby were the three temples, deliberately constructed to be the hearthstone stars that the *Popul Vuh* names as the source of creation. Elder Hunbatz Men had given me a profound lead to all this when he said of the Temple of the Inscriptions: 'There is something hidden in there, it has been deposited there for the Ages.'

*Tcaloc, the goggle-eyed god of war. Based on a panel from Nah Chan.*

## The messages of the Kogi and Hopi

The Maya are not alone in prophesying difficult times ahead. The few remaining Kogi people of Columbia have said that the signs they see all around them in nature indicate that the world is dying. The Hopi of the Arizona plains say that humans are the caretakers of all life on the planet, which is seriously out of balance. To describe this state of affairs they have a word *'Koyanisqaatsi'*, which roughly translated means 'gone mad'. Their prophecy takes many days to tell and many lifetimes to understand fully. The most chilling part of it is about the atomic bomb, a 'gourd full of ashes', and a final stage of life on Earth.

At the end of 2001, the Elders of the Hopi Nation, at Oraibi, Arizona, released the following message:

> You have been telling the people that this is the eleventh hour
> Now you must go back and tell the people that this is the hour
> And there are things to be considered:
> Where are you living?
> What are you doing?
> What are your relationships?
> Where is your water?

It is time to speak your truth.
Create your community.
Be good to each other.
And do not look outside yourself for the leader.
This could be a good time!

There is a river flowing now very fast.
It is so great and swift that there are those who will be afraid.
They will try to hold on to the shore.
They will feel they are being torn apart,
And they will suffer greatly.
Know the river has its destination.
The elders say we must let go of the shore,
Push off into the middle of the river,
Keep our eyes open, and our heads above the water.
See who is in there with you and celebrate.

## Practical summary of the serpent of prophecy in the sky

1. Widen your vision to the greater plan of life, your understanding of cosmovision; and approach all your life interactions and events as if you are already an impeccable warrior of light.
2. In your shamanic work, use crystals, particularly clear quartz crystals to access the 'over-lighting' presence, the world mind, or the archetype of all quartz, to understand better the significance of the crystal skulls.

# CHAPTER 13

# Turtle of the Cosmic Sea

Only through the solar initiation can the sleeping body of
mankind be awakened. The reincarnated teachers of the New
Age of Aquarius implore for the sacred human race to
awaken, so that in this way it can fulfil its sacred destiny,
which is to be the true sons and daughters of the Cosmic
Light. The time of knowledge approaches, the light in the
centre of the pyramidal house of Hunab K'u will flash like
lightning that will pierce through the shadows that envelop the
human race. Let us prepare to receive the light of knowledge
that comes from Hunab K'u and transcend into the memory
of the creator and become beings of eternal luminosity.

Part of a sacred text released by Hunbatz Men in 1995 through the Center for
Maya Studies, Comunidad Indigena Maya

## This pivotal time

I spent the last few days of my stay in the Mayalands in Honduras. I
sat in my hotel room in Copan Ruinas, Honduras, trying to meditate.
Next door the thumping beat of music was blaring out from a radio. I
then wondered whether we, as human beings, have mislaid our real
'radio transmitter'? Was it finally switched off, maybe 5,000 or so years
ago, as the signal got weaker when the priests of light vanished from

Europe or, as the Tuatha de Danaan, from Proto-Celtic Britain or from Kharsag, Sumeria, where 'heaven and Earth met the heavenly assembly and the great sons of Anu descended'? In those times and places, as in other areas such as Polynesia, Mexico and Colombia, the fading signal was still discernible through the semi-divine shaman-priest-kings. The imprint they carried in their blood was strong but not clear enoughfor others to follow in their steps as fully awakened initiates and adepts. Confusion and blinding of humanity's insight denied connection to the light, as great forces in the unseen worlds gathered around our planet to arrest evolutionary processes from taking place at spirit and soul levels.

Now the beings of light, the cosmic Maya, have taken the decision to regain contact, rousing humanity to the urgency of the times in which we live. Even at this moment, as our Mother Earth swims through the cosmic sea like a turtle, the Maya, along with other indigenous nations, from the Inuit of northern Canada to the Wichí of Hoktek T'oi in Argentina, are united in their condemnation of the destructive path humanity is taking with complete disregard for our Mother Earth. Yet such is the illusion created by the orchestrators of materialism in this world that everyday life goes on with uncaring environmental degradation and war. No wonder the Maya, Hopi and Kogi are shouting at us. Can we still avert the disaster that's coming? We are Mother Earth's highest intelligence and yet we have the stupidity to reach the brink of becoming an unsustainable life form – a cancerous growth.

Not only is it apparent that disaster may occur physically, but also that something more profound is becoming obvious to those who 'see' the time threads coming from the future. Whereas souls have until now been able to reincarnate to learn further and to enable cosmic evolution to take place, this may not be possible for much longer, with both physical and psychic pollution reaching alarming levels. Wandering Wolf said that the crystal layers of the Earth have been damaged. We would call it the Van Allen Belt or the Earth's aura. Astrophysicists are mystified as to the reason why our planet's outer atmosphere is disappearing at the rate of approximately one kilometre, or just over half a mile, every ten years. If this continues we will lose it completely and the Earth will become a dead planet, like Mars. Because of this, the threads of time upon which the Earth's Akashic Record is written are being damaged, allowing degrading astral levels to find their way into human consciousness. The inevitable prognosis is that beings of light will have no option but to leave the Earth plane.

Maya ancestors were masters of time and vibration. Every stele and glyph contains encodements of a multiple vibrational nature. Maya ceremonial centres, like those of their European counterparts, have their own 'time switches': sometimes the entire centre is active, buzzing with energy, and sometimes it is passive, linked in some way to cycles of time and original encodements not yet revealed. I have recounted a number of personal happenings at these places, both strange and seemingly unreal. That they happened, I have no doubt. My brain, like yours, is a vast 'living library'. Development of your 'living library' through use of shamanic teachings will unlock individual portals of perception. This gives the brain a 'superhighway' link to the collective human awareness anchored on this planet, which in turn has a 'superhighway' to the cosmic mind of Hunab Ku. The mysteries of any tradition imply that they cannot be accessed without considerable effort on the part of the questor. That in itself is part of our test; but it is a hard pill to swallow for some who are in need of immediate solutions, and it caused me to recall some words I had heard a long time ago: 'Not 'til the fire is dying in the grate do we look for any kinship with the stars.'

## The celestial peccary and celestial tapir

I returned to my study of the Maya shamans' cosmovision, the noise of the radio next door subsiding as the heat level rose. Scents of flowers and freshly baked tortillas pervaded the air; life went on. Once again, I was struck by the profound, enigmatic account of creation described by the myths in the *Popul Vuh*. The initiatory tests that the Hero Twins had to undergo contain a message that we too need to overcome vast obstacles to help in the creation of the next age. I mused upon more aspects of the symbolism behind their astromythology: both First Mother, who was seen in the night sky as the stars of the celestial peccary, and First Father, the celestial tapir, together invoked powerful processes to cause this present Fourth Age to be created. How can we learn from their actions?

- Primarily they used enraptured visioning (sometimes called suprarational vision) to dream the world.
- Sacred word caused the genesis of creation and gave the beings that came into existence their ability to use words and languages.
- First Mother, who wove the cosmos on her celestial loom, as well as the sages and sky artists who worked to 'paint the stars in the sky', used powerful artistic expression. They were the inspired sculptors, the makers and modellers who created the world.

- These gods used sexual reproduction coupled with the divine creative force of serpent power kundalini. (Phallic imagery is depicted alongside serpent wisdom and bloodletting at many sacred cities.)
- They regarded the process of birth as a sacrificial act akin to death.

These actions call to us from the dreamtime from which worlds are created.

Synchronistic threads bind these gods and goddesses, travellers in time, inextricably to the present day. Since the Maya say that the ending of one cycle of time strongly influences the beginning and continuing nature of the next, then what happens at the end of this age is vital for all the human race. In their calendars, end days are known as seating days that colour the next period. What we do with our lives right now will influence the times to come. Are we

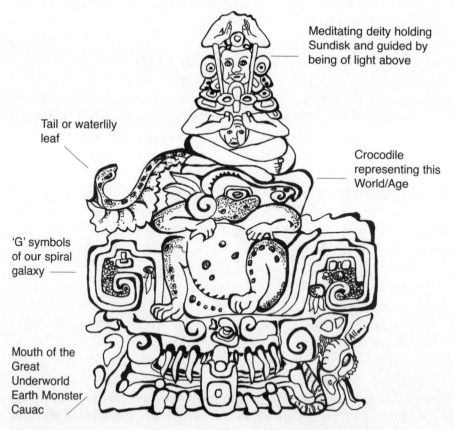

Meditating deity holding Sundisk and guided by being of light above

Tail or waterlily leaf

Crocodile representing this World/Age

'G' symbols of our spiral galaxy

Mouth of the Great Underworld Earth Monster Cauac

*The creation of the worlds and ages. Part of a large frieze, recently discovered on the wall of an original pyramid carefully covered by a later construction. From Balaam K'u, Mexico.*

content to sit back, comfortable and well fed, or will we be impeccable warriors of light, hungry for change, fighting for our souls?

I packed up my study papers and drawings, ready to walk the short distance to *las ruinas* from the little town of Copan. The walk was uneventful and I decided to take another quick look at the excellent new museum to clarify a detail on a stone, sky-band bench that I was sketching. Settling down to sketch, my eye caught a large stone relief of a bat, which seemed to jump out at me from its position on the wall above. The bat was one of the main symbols used by the Maya to signify death. I saw this as an omen urging me to go to the crumbling unrestored remains of the Bat Temple on the east side of the principal courtyard of the sacred city.

Ten minutes later, pausing at the entrance, I asked that I might learn from the *nagual* of the bat. I made the fairly arduous climb, in increasing humidity, down the decaying stone steps edging the courtyard, which had been racked by countless earthquakes, to the remains of the temple. Presently, seated on a rock in a dim corner, my nostrils sensed the acrid smell of a present generation of bats emanating from the spongy moss covering on the stones. Below me, the Copan River twisted in serpentine undulations through the hazy heat as occasional glints of light in the late afternoon sun. A soft breeze relieved the still, dark secrets of this small hidden temple, moving them along the threads of time from the past to my future. I contemplated just how the whole of humanity could challenge the bat-knell of death, wrought through the destruction of our own natural environments.

Something was telling me we would be wise to do as the Maya shamans have done: learn how to weave those very threads of time from the past that we metaphorically carry on our backs with the threads coming to us from the future. We must bring primordial magic back into our lives; feel the fire of *coyopa* in our bodies, dance with the vision serpent and ward off the bat with a wild exultant affirmation of life. This is a collective fight for our lives. Like the creator gods of the *Popul Vuh*, our creative force must be enhanced if we are to begin anew in 2012. Raising our vibrational levels of being will cause 'chu'el' soul force to gather in the light threads of our luminous bodies and sustain us into this coming Fifth Creation.

I left the Bat Temple and made my way towards the large ballcourt, convinced that the deep past from before the present creation is also a dreamtime that the cosmic Maya wish us to bring into the future. Each of the previous creations had ended cataclysmically because the beings created by the gods were unable to honour them. Then, by some strange quirk of fate, they made our 'lot' very difficult, blinding most of us from seeing our true potential! But, of course, we are as blind as bats! Our real destiny is to be part of a greater galactic plan, to fulfil our destiny and to learn how to care for a planet. So what lies deep within the Maya message? Was it as Douglas Gillette said in *The Shamans' Secret*: 'When in imitation of this divine creative ecstasy, the Maya shamans produced their own works of art, they believed they were participating in the ongoing creation of the cosmos, "giving birth" to God, and guaranteeing their own eternal lives'?

## The ballcourt and the lords of Xibalba

I climbed down to the flat area of the ballcourt, just a short distance from the Bat Temple. Cosmic imagery is rife; on the centre marker set in the ground, First Father's severed head peered up at me from the Underworld, tied on the stem of a calabash vine. To each side of the ballcourt, three strongly carved images of macaw heads looked down haughtily, reminiscent of the proud and vain macaw Vucub-Caquix of the *Popul Vuh*, who thought he himself was the sun and moon. This ballcourt, like all others, is the primordial sea of creation made manifest. On either side the ballcourt slopes upwards like cosmic shores, their stones sparkling green and pink in the light of Great Father Sun and Solar Grandmother, Ix Nuc K'in. The court is shaped like an 'I' with open ends and stepped walls and is symbolic of the dark rift in the Milky Way, the place of creation. Once the ballplayers, or *ah pitz'lawalob*, used just their buttocks and elbows to strike the rubber ball, to re-enact the movement of the sun and planets across the primordial sea of creation.

On occasions, dark forces of the underworld lords of Xibalba undoubtedly reared up strongly through the active portal of the stone floor of the court, to be countered by the ball, itself symbolizing the awesome dominating powers of the sun. For a period of perhaps 15 centuries the ballgame (*pitz*) was played by generations of Ahob and lesser lords to challenge the Underworld. In a similar way, the priest-king-shamans, too, ceremonially placated underworld powers as they gave the precious liquid of life, their own blood, in personal sacrifice. This was the potent supernatural world of the Maya that empowered their soul force, the *chu'el*, and ensured the survival of their *nagual* soul.

Now the consciousness of humanity has moved on. While it would not be desirable to re-enact the ballgame at the end of this creation, we can learn from how it focused the intense power that opened portals between life and death. Perhaps what we have discovered is that we can envision our own empowerment today as peaceful impeccable warriors in what is called shamanically 'the way of the heart' of the enlightened human being.

I left the ballcourt for a slow, thoughtful walk back to the town.

## The shamanic art of recapitulation: second attention in action

My journey was nearly finished. I, a traveller in time of the 21st-century, was reminded again of Wandering Wolf's words of prophecy, learnt from his ancestors: 'We are the travellers of time – we are the ones of yesterday, we are the ones of today and we are the ones of tomorrow.'

I recalled how once, with six other people, I was taken to a remote cave to take part in a Maya fire ceremony. We made our tortuous descent into a vast cavern, where bats, aware of our presence, restlessly screeched overhead, and glyphs that were over 3,000 years old adorned the walls. Flames from our fire made an eerie connection to those ancient people still lying in hidden rock tombs...

My recapitulations continued... time, and the greater cycles, were on my personal agenda, so I revelled in the way time seemed to stand still as I travelled by boat to an island on a blue-green lake, where, standing within a healing temple, I was shown stelae with star maps on them. Maybe these maps were made in memory of those great travellers, the four Balaams, who came from the Pleiades so long ago and can be seen to this day in the ancient city of Ek ('Star') Balaam.

My companions and I – the voyagers of the dreamtime – went on to the splendid desolation of Yaxha, and the temples of Uaxactun, all our dreams filled to overflowing with experiences. Then we came to the dream beyond all dreams: 'el Mundo Perdido' – the 'Lost World' of Tikal. Guided into the rainforest, we pushed our way through moist leaves and hanging vines until we came to the Temple of Ixchel, the outline of her image still visible at the entrance to an initiatory tunnel in the womb of Mother Earth. There we paused in a moment of spontaneous silence to acknowledge her role as goddess of childbirth and healing. Nearby on the main plaza, the sun and moon are embodied in the names of two towering pyramids, while a huge, reddened mask of Chaak, god of the rain and fertility, looks on.

My journey to Ceibal, in the company of giant herons, was along the

green, snaking River Pasion that flows endlessly past the steep steps leading up to the ancient city. Gigantic ceiba trees guard this river entrance, and howler monkeys announce the arrival of visitors. Little is visible beneath the undergrowth except a cleared area with a small platform, where I received a shamanic initiation watched by a collection of strange carved figures on attendant stelae. Later, back in the town of Sayache, I learnt about the questionable activities of loggers in the Petén region, with large areas of rainforest being cleared as massive hardwood trees, including the ceiba and mahogany, are felled. Never again will the jaguar stalk, the monkey play in the overhead canopy, or the tiny hummingbird flit from flower to flower. Intensive maize planting and overgrazing will quickly turn the land to dust, and pine tree monoculture will deplete the exposed thin soil forever.

My recapitulation reminded me that I had been on a journey around the medicine wheel, with experiences at every turn. I remembered sitting, drawing in the hot, dry, sun-scorched plazas of the Yucatan, Mexico, and the refreshing coolness when I finally returned to the sacred lake of Atitlan to discover hidden Maya altars perched upon rocky ledges and smoke-blackened cliffs, testifying to centuries of sacred fire ceremonies. Thankfully, I reflected, the Maya still offer their prayers for Mother Earth – let *us* pray that they will be heard.

## The end of the journey is but the beginning

Amid the confusion around the year 2012 emerges one main question: does it signify an end of the world – or a beginning? The answer is either, or both!

All the present understandings about the end of a Maya time period say that the last days, or years, create an 'end naming' and set the tone for the new cycle by what is known as the 'seating' of the coming period. What this actually means is that birth happens at the *end* of a spiral process or cycle. All the omens indicate that we are undoubtedly living in the end times. We are in the last years of a 13 Baktun calendar cycle, a period of 5,125.36 years, whose beginning was envisioned by the calendar shamans. They did this by setting the day of the beginning of this present creation to, as we have seen, a date that equates to 11 August 3114BC, amazingly making allowance for the precession of the equinoxes, so that the count ends precisely on 21 December 2012.

In the lead up to this potent date, a rare cosmic event takes place. The winter sun will slowly converge to align with the dark rift of the Milky Way at the end of the Great 13 Baktun Cycle of the Long Count.

On 21 December, the Wakah Chan, the Milky Way (the raised-up World Tree) will lie all around the horizon at dawn. The primary act of tree raising that took place at the beginning of the creation will be reversed, and the cross in the heavens, upon which creation hangs, will fall. This falling movement prepares the dark rift of the Milky Way in the centre for the principal player, Father Sun, to rise out of it at dawn on the solstice. Precisely this occurrence has been portrayed and envisioned by the Maya shamans throughout the ages. They clairvoyantly saw the threads of time from the future and left us the 13 Baktun calendar as evidence of this in order that humanity would have sufficient time to choose a powerful and positive 'seating' for the next creation. It was the very reason they built their observatories, counted the days, ritually gave their blood and invoked the power of Hunab K'u, lensed through the sun. By contrast, some of us, struggling with the death throes of materialism, sometimes find that the action at cosmic levels is so vast that it is difficult to comprehend, and we appear to 'lose control of the ball'.

However, all of us are vital players on the world ballcourt. Exactly what Great Father Sun arises to illuminate is up to everyone, for clearly we have now entered these very end times for which the shaman-priest-kings/queens waited, watching the stars.

## Born in the stars

We know that the stars called the Hearthstones of Creation were at the zenith point at dawn on the creation day that equates to our 13 August 3114BC. Forming the belt in the constellation of Orion, these three stars – Tepeu, Gugumatz and Huyubkaan – are often depicted as three stars on the turtle's shell and form an incredibly special portal. Beneath them and within a triangle of stars locked into place below lies the most potent point in the sky. The Maya were not the only dwellers in the Land of the Sun to accord great significance to these, for the Aztec name given to Orion's belt means 'fire drill' – that is, the stick used to start a new fire. Fire was the prime generative force for all ancient peoples.

The Maya left numerous messages on the mat of time for us to read in the future. Artists, scribes and sculptors worked tirelessly to tell us about their understandings of light and vibration – in the form of the Rainbow Serpent of Light, Ku-kuul-kaan (Quetzalcoatl). Their wisdom teachers hid sacred folded tree bark and vellum books in dry caves and encoded quartz-crystal skulls with messages of inner light, some of which are still accessible. daykeepers continued their count of days, passing their accumulated knowledge down through their families, from ancestors to the present day. What for? So that we understand the portents in the sky, the movement of the stars, the coming of comets and the 'wandering planet' – and know that they are messengers, but not the message. The message for each of us is at soul level: to understand our origins and our future, and thereby be able to take an easy transition on 'the road to the sky' in the next creation. Within the Hearthstone stars lies the 'smoking fire' – still called in the Kiché language, *Q'aq* ('fire') and *Je Chi q'aq* ('dispersed fire') – which astronomers know as the Great Crab Nebula M42. Astrophysicists have recently discovered at this very place the great light – the great brilliance where Hunab K'u built his house in the 13 heavens and created life, giving us an incredible confirmation of the sacred knowledge carried by the Maya shamans.

The message is to look to the stars. An international team of astronomers found that a rare form of ultraviolet light arises from the M42 Nebula. Reported in 1997, they said that sources of ultraviolet light in the cosmos are very unusual. Coming from the very place of the smoke of the fire of creation in the Orion Great Turtle is an emanation that links to the amino-acid building blocks of all life on Earth (forming DNA). This ultraviolet light is circularly polarized and as such determines chemical reactions that create molecules with a predominant directional spin. According to scientists, the polarization appears to be all right-handed and it accounts for the left-handed spin of amino acids on Earth.

As we approach the end of Maya time, Hunab K u has allowed his emanations, the ultraviolet light I referred to above, to be measured by science. The vital message of the Maya shamans is that the birth of the new Fifth Creation awaits all on this planet. This right-hand-spin-polarized ultraviolet light is carried by extraterrestrial magnetic, or otherwise unknown, types of fields. Such fields must surely be the lenses, linking us to Hunab K u, which the Maya knew of so long ago.

The vital message of the Maya shamans is that the birth of the new Fifth Creation awaits all on Mother Earth. We are secure in the knowledge that Hunab K u s great light, the great brilliance, will sustain us from his pyramidal house in the heavens so that a new humanity may be born.

# THE HOUSE OF HUNAB K'U

In this matter Hunab K u placed in the centre of his pyramidal house in the heavens, in the constellation of Orion, Huyubkaan, and told him:

**'You will set forth the breath so that
all will begin to take life'**

And so it was that there became a beacon of great light, the Great Brilliance . It was flushed with multiple colours that harmonize with the cosmic, celestial music of the heavens.

**Hunab K'u established that the human being could spiritually enter this sacred temple for ever.**

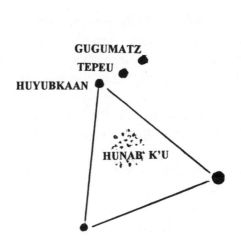

*The three Hearthstone stars in the constellation of Orion.*

**To Tepeu and Gugumatz he said: 'Stay together always. You, Huyubkaan, will also live at the highest point of my pyramid, as will Tepeu and Gugumatz. Each one of you will be a star.' Hunab K'u continued: 'Take care of the light that I leave within my temple, for within, humans will find the light they need for eternal life.'**

With this knowledge of the imminence of Hunab K'u's great light, the prognosis for life on Mother Earth is positive if we can envision the Fifth Age in a particular way – not as a new golden age, as some have said. The vibration of metallic gold is too slow and heavy. The range of light colours coming from the cosmos goes beyond our imagining, and the new awareness will carry a raised vibration not seen as gold in the form of a precious metal. Within the scale of electromagnetic vibrations in a spectrum, this faster vibration will be seen more like a sparkling silvery light. It is this light to which we need to attune our vibrational frequencies in the last days of this creation.

With the incoming Fifth Creation, Maya shamans prophesy that humanity can evolve spiritually. This phase of evolution will occur if succeeding generations of family lines *consciously* seed new life with mindfulness of the creator. Procreation is a sacred act. Children will be born with increased cellular vibrational rates because they have been procreated when both partners are alive with kundalini (serpent wisdom) surging through their bodies, with deep love and respect for each another and the planet. As this intention is achieved, certain bloodlines will produce highly evolved human beings. The increased light we will see on the planet, including inner light during meditation and shamanic visions, will strengthen their physical bodies within a very few generations. It also has the potential to enhance levels of super-consciousness. If the new age of the Maya Fifth Creation is perceived as a 'golden age', using old words and outdated thought forms about linear time, then raising of consciousness will not take place.

In the coming age, cellular vibrations of children in these family lines will be progressively quickened – as a 'fast-track' human evolution. Parents will have a responsibility to ensure they guide their children into enhanced consciousness for when the latter decide upon parenthood. The new light vibration, the *coyopa* of the shamans, is held in the spinal fluid running through the central nervous system as kundalini, and then principally distributed by the blood. This again substantiates the insistence and tenaciousness of the Maya shamans, who persisted in depicting snakes and vision serpents as the symbols of cosmic energy, ready for these future travellers in time.

We are all destined in the greater plan to become beings of light, in resonance with a higher visible light band of vibration, only part of which we understand at present. Within the upper, faster frequencies of the light spectrum, normal visible light reaches into the ultraviolet light range. Frequencies of this spectrum can be beneficial or destructive. The slowest part of this ultraviolet (UV) range is beneficial to plants, animals and humans. Until now our planet has been shielded by the ozone layer from what science describes as UVB (ultraviolet B) and UVC (ultraviolet C), which are, on one level, highly destructive to life on Earth. The planet's upper atmosphere and ozone layer are lenses to transduce the faster vibrations, such as ultraviolet, that our physical bodies are otherwise unable to cope with. At the present time, our bodies are not designed to resonate beyond visible light frequencies. But our soul or spirit is becoming more able to 'bridge into' our super-consciousness and assimilate rapid frequencies that would otherwise destroy our physical bodies. This is the path of light that was developed by those ascended masters, priests of light and cosmic Maya in times past, who were aware of the source of creation within the Orion Hearthstones.

The threads of time continually move us on in spirals of evolution. In the Fifth Creation, many more people will be able to access the faster light frequencies than at present. Pakal Votan left a message in the Temple of the Inscriptions alluding to dates way back in the past and into the future. He ensured the survival of his own time thread, leaving it for any of us to pick up and weave into our possible futures. The mat of time was woven with care by the 'serpents of light' – the raised vibrational frequencies. Its emanations caused the ancient Maya scribes to explain their cosmovision in myths of the stars. The Ahau lineages of Copan and other royal cities sustained their faster frequencies of light within secret temples, using shamanic visions to manifest the vision serpent. They manipulated these faster vibrations to travel in the worlds beyond time, commune with the beings of light and return to record their ecstatic experiences in glyphs and upon stone panels. In their altered, heightened states of consciousness, they travelled through ancient portals, sanctified by aeons of use, on the Kuxan Suum, the route to the centre of creation. There they saw the raised-up World Tree, its branches hung with flowering souls awaiting rebirth.

In the coming Fifth Age, it is unlikely that everyone will be able travel this route while still in physical form, but the actions of the Maya shamans have ensured that once they enter the 'road to the sky' they will return to Hunab K'u, transformed into their light bodies as 'white flower souls'.

While I was at Copan, a friend stopped me as I closed a gate. She asked me why the ancient Maya rode the undulations of the serpent of time, and how they knew about the exact place of creation in the nebula within the Hearthstones of Creation – and whether the Maya shamans could shapeshift and were really travellers in time?

I answered like the shamans would have done: 'We come and go, we are the same ones. We are the lords, the travellers in time. We are those of yesterday, those of today and will be those of tomorrow.'

**A path strewn with orange marigolds – flowers of the sun – guides the soul home.**

# Epilogue

## Extract from the sacred manuscript of *K'altun*

'HUNAB K'U said: "From my House in the heavens, I imagined all the creation on Earth. You will be the moulders, the caretakers of what I will create." HUNAB K'U built his house with a pyramidal shape and, at the top, he set Huyubkaan and told him: "You will blow and everything will come into life." In this way, everything was created in the house of God in the heavens. HUNAB K'U placed the constellation of Orion in the centre of his pyramidal house in the heavens, so that it could bear the great light, the great brilliance. This light was flushed with multiple colours that harmonized with the cosmic, celestial music of the heavens. HUNAB K'U decreed that the human being could spiritually enter this sacred temple forever.

'All this was accomplished by HUNAB K'U in seven stages of time. He said to Tepeu and Gugumatz: "Stay together forever. You, Huyubkaan, will live at the top of my pyramid, as will Tepeu and Gugumatz. Each of you will be a star." HUNAB K'U continued: "Take care of the light that I will leave inside my temple. When you create the human beings, teach them to venerate my house, because there they will find the light they need for their eternal life. Also teach them that if they get lost, due to their errors, vices or ignorance, then I, HUNAB K'U, will reclaim my beloved beings and will take them to my temple of wisdom and feed them back again with my light which is in the heavens. Then, together, Tepeu, Gugumatz and Huyubkaan, and I will perform purification rituals using that brilliant light for the benefit of my beloved creatures, whom we created and moulded, so they can live in the light of eternal wisdom.

"The human race will have to see, in the coming years, the path of initiation on Earth and in heaven, and watch a new HUNAB K'U's pyramidal house and, in spirit, visit Tepeu, Gugumatz and Huyubkaan. The human race may then be led into the house of God and together they will pray, meditate and work with the sacred light of the brightest star of Orion. Through this initiation they will be able to see the luminosity of Great Spirit. When this spiritual initiation is completed in the house of HUNAB K'U in heaven, the spirit of each initiate will be illuminated. Then, it will return to Earth to awaken its body and take it to the pyramids. Chichén Itzá, Uxmal, K'aba, Edzna, Nah Chan (Palenque), all of these sacred Maya centres have a specific function in every part of the body to awaken the seven chakra powers contained in it.

"Only through solar initiation can the sleeping body of mankind be awakened. The reincarnated teachers of the new age of Aquarius implore the sacred human race to wake up, so that they can fulfil their sacred destiny of being the true Sons and Daughters of the Cosmic Light. The time of knowledge is approaching, the light in the centre of the pyramidal house of HUNAB K'U will flash like lightning that will pierce through the shadows that cover the human race. Let us prepare to receive the light of knowledge that comes from HUNAB K'U, transcend into the memory of the creator and become beings of eternal luminosity."'

Reproduced by permission of Elder Hunbatz Men

# Appendix I

## The 20 day signs of the T'zolk'in calendar

The following are the 20 days signs of the traditional Kiché T'zolk'in calendar and their associations. The beginning of this calendar was the start of time when the One Giver of Movement and Measure breathed creation into being.

*(Note: Yucatec Maya names are in brackets.)*

**B'atz' (Chuen)** The monkey. The thread of time. Weave the good things of the world. Marriage, divination, continuity with the past.

**E (eb)** The road. Personal destiny. Invoking protection from danger. Good fortune.

**Aj (ben)** Corn. Day of the sacred bundle (of cosmic knowledge). Work issues – with oneself, with others.

**I'x (ix)** The jaguar. Day of the Earth – woman/Mother Earth. Fertility. Day for animals.

**Tz'ikin (men)** Serpent bird Gugumatz. The eagle. Day for petitions. Abundance; good things. Sesame seeds offered to the sacred fire on this day.

**Ajmaq (cib)** The vulture. Reconciliation day. Family. Power of forgiveness.

**No'j (caban)** Incense. Wisdom and knowledge. Meditation. The seven senses; the seven-headed serpent.

**Tijax (etznab)** Obsidian blade. The flint. Surgery or healing. Forces of divisiveness through quarrels.

**Kawoq (cauac)** The storm. Family, authority and ceremony. Listen to elder. Destructive power of karmic past.

**Ajpu (ahau)** Day of the sun and human beings. The ancestors. Ceremonial day. Power of the ancestors. Houses/homes.

**Imix *(imox)*** The crocodile. The healer. Telepathic day. Earth and animals. Vision or madness.

**Iq *(ik)*** The wind. Air, breath, imagination. Raw power of anger, strength, wildness, violence. Destructive power of the universe.

**Aq'ab'al *(akbal)*** The night. Always a happy day. Opening of things closed. Seeing future well-being.

**K'at *(kan)*** The lizard. A net for fishing. Abundance. Avoiding/overcoming things.

**Kan *(chicchan)*** The snake. Spirit of air/water, especially rivers. Equilibrium. Justice. Cruelty. Cause and cure of illness. Kundalini.

**Kame *(cimi)*** Death. Very favourable and specially sacred day. Marriage and the female side of life generally. Day to commune with the ancestors.

**Kej *(manik)*** The deer. Day the four Balaams came from the Pleiades. Shaman. Divination. Personal power.

**Q'anil *(lamat)*** The rabbit. The seed of everything. Day to ask for rebirth, regeneration, ripening, harvest, abundance. Yellow.

**Toj *(muluc)*** Water. Thunder. Power of the moon. The day to pay. Payment of karmic debts.

**Tzi *(oc)*** The dog. The day of authority. Destruction and inequilibrium. Reconciliation. Corruption and uncertainty. Sex.

# Appendix II

## Maya calendars

**T'zolk'in** (also called Chol q'ij) Main 'sacred round' calendar of 260 days' duration. Holds a harmonic relationship between us, Great Father Sun, the solar system and Hunab K'u, Giver of Movement and Measure. Also relates to human gestation period. Together with the Haab it forms the 52-year calendar-round loom of time and short Pleiadian cycle (see Muchuchu Mil).

**Haab** The main secular calendar: 365 days of 18 months x 20 days – and five days at end of year.

**Long Count** (see Appendix III) A linear time count. According to NASA its accuracy is a mere variation of 0.00000001 to the atomic calendar clock, being but one day out over 180,000 years. Used on monuments to project unique dates far into the past or future. Related to Oxlajuj Baktun – a 5,200-year x 5 cycle that marks the development of each 'world' in human progress on Earth (making up the approximate 26,000 years of the 'Platonic year'), the Fourth World Creation being due to end in 2012.

**Lords of the Night** Repeating nine-day cycle. When used in combination with the calendar round it gives a date that will not repeat for 467 years.

**Ixim Tun** A calendar for natural cycles, important to the Maya for agriculture. A time cycle of 130-day duration, exactly half the T'zolk'in.

**Mom Tun** A 180-day calendar benefiting agriculture. Its observance enables the Maya to understand insect fertilization. A half cycle of the Tun calendar.

**Tun** A 360-day rhythm perfectly relating to solar system, planets, stars and galaxies.

**Tz'otz Tun** A 364-day calendar of prophecy. The 13 months of 28 days are known as the 'bat cycle'.

**Ix Tun** A moon calendar used on monuments. Counting days of

lunations and therefore relevant to water (tides) as well as women's cycles.

**Kiejeb** A prophetic calendar of 400 days used by some of the present-day Maya, of which little has been revealed as yet.

**Muchuchu Mil** Calendar of the Pleiades. A 52-year calendar cycle synchronizing Haab and T'zolk'in calendars and providing each human being with a full life experience from which eldership status is reached. It marks the short cycle of the Pleiades and on completion all fires are extinguished and a new fire ceremony is enacted. The next time this becomes due is 2029.

**Chol Tun** A 260-year calendar working much the same as the T'zolk'in but on a macro level.

**Ku Tun** A 520-year cycle to observe and measure the 'collective influences' on humanity.

**Tiku Tun** A calendar divided into two specific cycles: (1) the Belejeb Bolon Tiku cycle of darkness – nine periods of 52 years, equalling 468 years in total; and (2) the Oxlajuj Tiku cycle of the 13 heavens – 13 periods of 52 years, equalling 676 years in total. A prophetic calendar.

**Ajau Tun** A prophetic 20-year cycle – of particular interest to archaeologists.

**Ekomal Tun** A 520-year cycle marking masculine and feminine radiation from our sun. Gives information concerning humanity as a whole.

*Note: there are five further calendars that as yet only serve the needs of the Maya.*

# Appendix III

## The Long Count

| | | | | | |
|---|---|---|---|---|---|
| | | 1 kin |  | = | 1 day |
| 20 kins | = | 1 uinal |  | = | 20 days |
| 18 uinals | = | 1 tun |  | = | 360 days |
| 20 tuns | = | 1 katun |  | = | 7,200 days |
| 20 katuns | = | 1 baktun |  | = | 144,000 days |
| 13 baktuns | = | 1 Great Cycle (5,200 tuns) | | = | 1,872,000 days |

# Glossary

**Ah Nab**  Waterlily people (i.e. nobles).

**Ahau (pl. Ahob)**  King, emperor, prince, great noble.

**Ahau Kines**  Solar lords, priests of the sun.

**Ah-K'in**  Diviners (Ah-Q'ij in Kiché).

**Am**  The moon goddess.

**Balaam**  Jaguar – the shaman's *nagual*.

**Balché**  Sacred drink that includes bark of a tree fermented with honey and prepared in a *pib* or underground oven.

**Brujeria**  Follower of tradition – a shaman.

**Cahal (pl. Cahalob)**  Person of noble rank.

**Can**  The number four. Energy. Serpent. To teach.

**Ceiba**  Large sacred tree symbolic of the World Tree and four directions of the medicine wheel.

**Cenote**  Sunken water hole.

**Ch'ul K'awil**  Sak-Hunal – the jester god.

**Ch'ulil/Chu'el**  Soul force of the universe.

**Chaak/Chac**  The rain god.

**Cahal**  Lesser noble or governor.

**Chak**  Red.

**Chakla  Chakra** – subtle anatomy energy centre.

**Chilam Balam**  Name of some twelve or so books, mainly post-16th century, thought to have been salvaged from earlier glyphic texts destroyed by the Spanish.

**Coyopa** (Kiché)  'Body lightning'. An inner psychic energy from which to draw power.

**Cresteria** (Spanish)  Stone roof-comb found on temples atop pyramids.

**D'dzac Yah**  He who heals or transforms negative to positive energy.

**G** (pronounced 'ge')  The Milky Way. Zero. Egg. Essence. Aura.

**Gugumatz**  The middle of three stars in the belt of Orion. The second of the three kings bestowing a gift at the birth of this creation.

**H'men**  He who does good. A shaman in present-day Yucatan.

**Haab**  The 365-day secular solar year calendar.

**Hearthstones**  Three stars in the constellation of Orion.

**Hun Nal-Ye**  First Father as maize god.

**Hunab K'u** (Yucatec)  The One Giver of Movement and Measure. The Absolute Being. Known as Hachakyum to the Lacondon Indians and One Hunaphu in Guatemala.

**Huyubkaan**  The left of the three stars in the belt of Orion. The third of the three kings bestowing a gift at the birth of this creation.

**Itz**  The dew of divine energy, which has its correspondence in the human body. The ancient Maya called it the 'dew of the sky'. Today's shamans call it 'lightning in blood'. For a Maya to be struck by lightning meant that he was in a state of radical alteration.

**Itzam Yeh**  The Celestial Bird – the Big Dipper star group.

**Itzamna**  God of childbirth, sorcery and medicine. Sometimes referred to as 'God D'.

**Ixchel**  Goddess of childbirth and rainbows.

**Ixim**  Corn.

**Ix-Ma-Ux**  Goddess of the moon.

**Ix-May-Ek**  Goddess of stars and sky.

**Ix-Mukane**  Ancient and wise grandmother.

**Ix-Zac-Ek**  First Mother of the Milky Way.

**Ix-Zuhuy-Ha**  Water priestess.

**Ix-Zuhuy-Kaak**  Fire priestess.

**K'ak**  Fire.

**K'an**  Yellow.

**K'an che**  Bench or seat of the supernaturals.

**K'in**  The Sun. One day in time. Used as a mantric word.

**K'inan**  Spirit.

**K'ul Ahau (Ch'ul Ahaw)**  Holy or divine lord.

**Kak Uleu**  Red earth. A reference to Atlantis.

**Kinich Ahau**  Lord of the Sun. The realized solar mind.

**Ku-kuul-kaan** (Maya)  The Feathered Serpent.

**Kunil**  A bewitching place.

**Lam**  Eternal – a mantra.

**Land of the Sun**  The whole of the Americas.

**Li**  To arise. Stand up.

**Lil**  Vibration.

**Mishule**  Star brothers/sisters.

**Mu**  Ancient Motherland.

**Muchuchumil**  Another word for the Pleiades.

**Nagual** (a term borrowed from Nahuatl)  One of our two souls or a spirit guide.

**Och Bih**  'He entered the road'.

**Ol**  Portal to the other worlds.

**Palapa**  Maya home constructed from wood and palm thatch.

**Pibna**  Underground house. A *pib* is also an underground oven.

**Pom**  Resin from the copal tree. Used as incense.

**Pop**  First month in Haab. A ceremonial mat upon which elders would sit in council.

**Popol**  The council.

***Popul Vuh***  Sacred book of the Kiché Maya nation.

**Quetzalcoatl** (Aztec/Mexican)  The Feathered Serpent.

**Sac Bé**  Straight white or sacred road. Many examples in Yucatan. Also the Milky Way.

**Sak-a' che' t'an**  'Clear water tree speech'.

**Sastun** (Yucatec)  A stone of light, usually of quartz and for a healing purpose.

**Stele (pl. Stelae)**  Carved monuments of stone, often showing detailed and complex information.

**Stucco**  Plaster with natural resin or fibre added that was used to make sculptural reliefs.

**T**  Tree. Shape known as '*Ik*', the wind or spirit; it also signifies the sacred twins.

**T'Zama**  Old name for the Maya city of Tulum.

**Tepeu**  The right-hand star of three in the belt of Orion. First of the three kings bestowing a gift at the birth of this creation.

**Te-tun**  'Tree stone' – a stele.

**Tulix**  Double cross and name of the dragonfly, a living symbol of Ku-Kuul-Kaan, the Feathered Serpent.

**Tunben K'ak**  New fire ceremony celebrated every 52 years.

**Tzek'eb**  Pleiades star group. Our sun makes up the eighth major star in the group.

**Tzitze seeds**  Red seeds used for divination.

**T'zolk'in**  260-day sacred calendar.

**Tzut**  Headcloth or scarf worn by Highland Maya women.

**Uich Hunab K'u**  Eye of the Absolute Being.

**Uxlab** (pronounced 'oosh lahb')  One of our two souls – the 'breath' soul.

**Votan**  Snake/Serpent Lord.

**Wakah Chan**  'Raised-up sky' – the Milky Way.

**Way (pl. Wayob)**  Animal companion spirit.

**Waybil**  Lineage shrine.

**Winclil**  Human body (from '*winic*','vessel', '*lil*', 'vibration').

**Witz**  Personified or sacred mountain.

**Xaman**  Maya shaman. The north.

**Xibalba** (pronounced 'shibalba')  The Underworld. The 'awesome place'. Land of the dead.

**Xmukane**  First Mother, creator Goddess.

**Xuc** Transformation of the mind.

**Yax** Blue green.

**Yaxche** The sacred ceiba tree. The World Tree at the centre of all things.

**Yaxk'in** Centre.

**Yemal K'uk Lakam Witz** 'Descending Quetzal Big Mountain'.

**Yum Balam** Father Guardian.

**Yumil Ka'ax** A jaguar, a young lord of the cornfields.

**Zak** White.

# Bibliography

Calleman, Carl Johan *The Maya Calendar* Garev Publishing Intl, 2001

Castañeda, Carlos *The Art of Dreaming* HarperCollins, USA, 1993

Hunbatz Men *Secrets of Maya Science/Religion* Bear & Co, 1990

Jenkins, John Major *Maya Cosmogenesis 2012* Bear & Co, 1998

Johnson, Kenneth *Jaguar Wisdom: Maya Calendar Magic* Llewellyn Publications, 1997

Meadows, Kenneth *Shamanic Experience* Element Books, 1991

Mercier, Patricia *Chakras: Balance Your Energy Flow for Health and Harmony* Godsfield Press, 2000

Mindell, Arnold *The Shaman's Body* HarperCollins, USA, 1993

Recinos, Adrian (trans.) *Popul Vuh: The Sacred Book of the Ancient Quiche Maya* University of Oklahoma Press, 1950

Rupflin-Alvarado, Walburga *El T'zolk'in es mas que un calendario* CEDIM, Iximelew, Guatemala, 1999

Rutherford, Leo *Principles of Shamanism* Thorsons, 1996

Sanchez, Victor *The Teachings of Don Carlos* Bear & Co, 1995

Sawyer-Laucanno, Christopher *The Destruction of the Jaguar: Poems from the Chilam Balam* City Lights Books, 1987

Schele, Freidel, Parker *Maya Cosmos* William Morrow, 1993

Schele, Linda & Freidel, David *A Forest of Kings* William Morrow, 1990

# Further Studies

For spiritual journeys and solar initiations in Mexico, spiritual journeys and traditional fire ceremonies in Guatemala, and shamanic groupwork with the author in Europe, contact The Sun and the Serpent Maya Mysteries School by email:

mikhailfrancis@hotmail.com

or visit:

www.mayasunserpent.com

# Index

Note: page numbers in *italics* refer to illustrations. *Plate* numbers are also given.